高校英语选修课系列教材

WESTERN LEARNING AND MODERNITY IN CHINA

西学东渐与中国现代化

纪康丽 著

清华大学出版社

北京

内 容 简 介

本书共分 14 章，以独特的视角，遵循知识分子思想演变的轨迹，围绕晚清士大夫如何应对西方文明而进行论述，具有系统完整的特点。通过本书的学习，学生不仅能运用英语表达具有中国地域特点的文化，更能通过课堂讨论、短文和论文写作来增强批判性思维能力。

本书适用于本科生和研究生的通识教育课程。

图书在版编目（CIP）数据

西学东渐与中国现代化：英文 / 纪康丽著. —北京：清华大学出版社，2021.9
高校英语选修课系列教材
ISBN 978-7-302-57446-0

Ⅰ.①西… Ⅱ.①纪… Ⅲ.①东西文化—文化交流—中国—高等学校—教材—英文 ②现代化—中国—近代—高等学校—教材—英文 Ⅳ.① G129 ② K250.7

中国版本图书馆 CIP 数据核字（2021）第 022468 号

责任编辑：刘细珍　白周兵
封面设计：子　一
责任校对：王凤芝
责任印制：沈　露

出版发行：清华大学出版社
网　址：http://www.tup.com.cn, http://www.wqbook.com
地　址：北京清华大学学研大厦 A 座　**邮　编：**100084
社 总 机：010-62770175　**邮　购：**010-62786544
投稿与读者服务：010-62776969, c-service@tup.tsinghua.edu.cn
质量反馈：010-62772015, zhiliang@tup.tsinghua.edu.cn
印 装 者：三河市龙大印装有限公司
经　销：全国新华书店
开　本：185mm×260mm　**印　张：**16.5　**字　数：**295 千字
版　次：2021 年 9 月第 1 版　**印　次：**2021 年 9 月第 1 次印刷
定　价：69.00 元

产品编号：083991-01

前　言

我国大学英语教学目标正从过去注重语言技能训练逐渐向培养具有国际交往能力的人才方向发展。所谓具有国际交往能力，是指学生应该对不同文化社团的历史、思想、哲学、文学有相当程度的了解与把握，同时具备本国的文化和历史知识。只有这样，才能在国际舞台上游刃有余，与世界各国顺利地进行交往，在建立世界命运共同体中起到应有的作用。要具备以上知识，仅仅依靠语法纠错、完形填空和恢复原文逻辑等常见的课堂语言练习是无法完成的，而是要靠高质量的、具有专业内涵的教材来完成。《西学东渐与中国现代化》正是基于这样的理念来设计、撰写的。本书的历史跨度为晚清 72 年（1840—1912）。在这 72 年里，中国发生了前所未有的剧变，使中国从过去封闭自满、睥睨天下的“天朝大国”，转变为国际大家庭中的一分子。其中经历的痛苦、踌躇与争斗展现出中华民族如何迈出走向现代文明的艰难一步。这种奋发图强与一些睁眼看世界的晚清士大夫紧密相连，他们是林则徐、魏源、徐继畬、曾国藩、徐寿、李善兰、华蘅芳、容闳、郭嵩焘、严复、王韬、张之洞、康有为、梁启超、詹天佑和梁诚。此外，中国的进步和发展与西方传教士和外交人员的翻译、办学、媒体以及联络也是息息相关的。本书涉及的晚清西方人士有丁韪良、赫德、蒲安臣、马礼逊、傅兰雅、林乐知、李提摩太等。本书探讨的中心议题是：面对西方文明的冲击，中国士大夫为什么用了半个世纪来回应？而我们的邻国日本仅仅花了 15 年时间，就开始了明治维新，并很快成为一个现代化国家。

本书共分 14 章。第 1 章是全书的背景介绍，讲解第一次鸦片战争前晚清的政治、经济和文化背景。具体涉及三个方面：闭关锁国政策、华夷之辨思想以及鸦片在中英两国的滥用。第 2 章讲解中国士大夫如何回应西方文明的冲击。主要围绕魏源的《海国图志》和徐继畬的《瀛寰志略》进行讨论，分析两部著作的重要段落和它们在中国和日本的接受状况。第 3 章讨论新建的国际事务管理部门——总理衙门的成立和《万国公法》的引入。第 4 章讨论同文馆的成立及其遇到的困惑与争论，特别

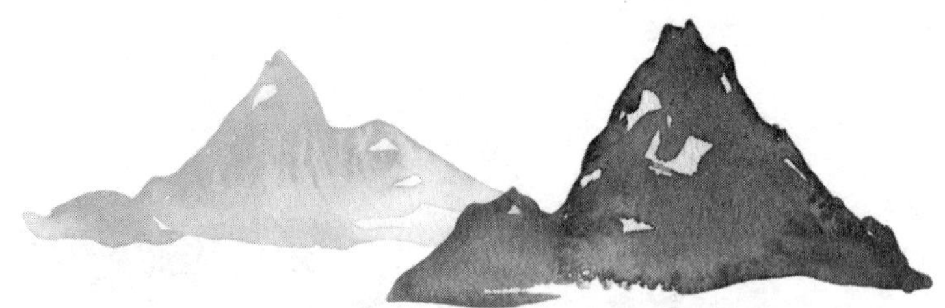

是奕䜣与倭仁有关增加天文算学馆的争论，反映了不同的价值取向。第 5 章讲解清政府的对外关系，涉及海关总税务司赫德以及外交官蒲安臣。第 6 章讨论洋务运动，具体讲解曾国藩、左宗棠和李鸿章对中国机器、轮船制造业与军事人才培养的计划与贡献。第 7 章讲解江南制造局翻译馆，涉及傅兰雅、徐寿、李善兰、华蘅芳等英汉翻译家。第 8 章讨论林乐知与中文报纸，具体讲解《教会新报》和《万国公报》的创办与发行。第 9 章讲解西式教育引入中国的情况，具体探讨普通教育和医学教育的引进。第 10 章是关于容闳及其留美幼童计划的产生与流产，以及美国耶鲁大学的教育内容与理念。第 11 章讨论中国启蒙思想家严复和他的译著。第 12 章讨论和比较张之洞的《劝学篇》与福泽谕吉的《劝学篇》。第 13 章讨论康有为与戊戌变法，具体分析《新学伪经考》和《孔子改制考》两部著作。第 14 章是关于梁启超在变法中的思考与行动，具体分析《新民说》和《开明专制论》两部著作。

目前，国内高校所开同类课程不多，教材也不多见。张星烺于 2000 年由商务印书馆出版的《欧化东渐史》，侧重西方传教士向中国引入物质及精神文化的过程，时间跨度大，从元代的马可·波罗、明代的利玛窦到清末的马礼逊、傅兰雅和林乐知等。但都是简单介绍，没有深入探讨，而且不够系统。全书是由发表于其他印刷品的文字集合而成。北京外国语大学张西平教授于 2010 年由生活·读书·新知三联书店出版的《东西流水终相逢》，收录的大都是为各图书、报纸撰写的前言、后记或议论性散文。内容涉及面较广，从欧洲汉学、传教士汉学到东方学等，可谓面面俱到。熊月之于 2011 年由中国人民大学出版社出版的《西学东渐与晚清社会》，与本书内容比较接近，但其重点放在西学的传播上。本书采取了不同视角，围绕着晚清士大夫如何应对西方文明而进行论述。通过分析一些重要文本，让学生了解当时左右士大夫思想的主要是什么，以及外界的思想是如何冲破牢笼而进入官僚体制的。只有具备了历史知识，我们的学生在国际舞台上才能施展才华，与各国人士平等对话，站在世界角度来讲好中国故事。

本书的创新之处在于视角的新颖，遵循知识分子思想演变的轨迹，具有系统完整的特点。最突出之处则在于本书用英文写就，在国内尚不多见。本书适用于本科生和研究生的通识教育课程。通过学习，学生不但能逐渐掌握如何用英语表达具有中国地域特点的文化，更能通过课堂讨论、短文和论文写作来增强批判性思维能力。

在本书的撰写过程中，我得到了同事和同行的热情帮助，在此一并致谢。首先，我要感谢外文系同事日语教师陈爱阳。每当我遇到日本学者的汉语名字时，就请陈老

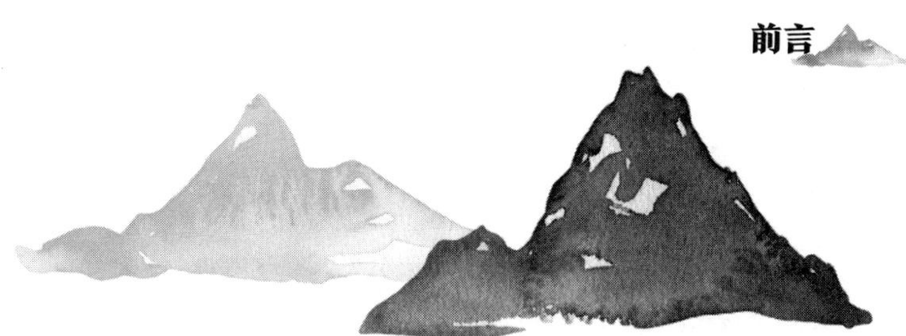

师帮我找出其对应的英文称呼，这占用了陈老师许多的宝贵时间。其次，我要感谢外文系的外教同事 John Olbrich，John 听说我在上“西学东渐”这门课，主动借给我一些相关书籍。最后，我要感谢同行 Donald S. Lopez Jr. 教授。在一次学术交流会上，我向 Lopez 教授请教本领域的相关文献，他回到母校密歇根大学亚洲语言与文化系后，给我发来相关文献的书单及几篇论文。

本书在撰写过程中参阅并引用了大量国内外文献，在此表示衷心的感谢。主要的参考文献已列于章节后，由于时间有限，难免挂一漏万，敬请相关作者海涵，并恳请广大师生批评指正。

纪康丽

2021 年 1 月

Contents

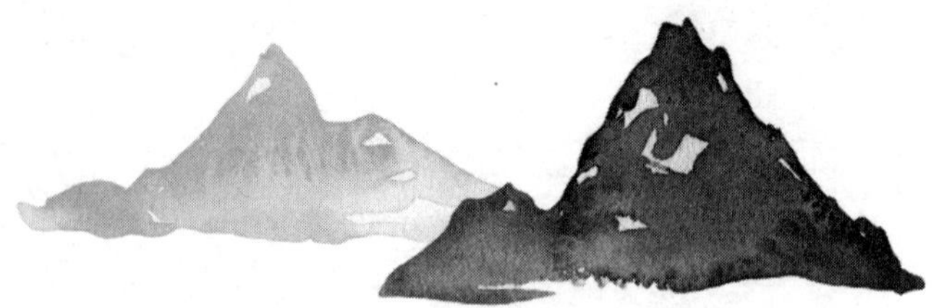

Chapter One

Historical Background
背景介绍

本章介绍第一次鸦片战争前晚清社会的政治、经济和文化背景，以便对晚清社会有一个总体概念。本章重点讨论三个方面：闭关锁国政策、华夷之辨思想和鸦片在中英两国的滥用及其后果。闭关锁国政策的实施使中国人对外界事物一无所知，故在战争中处于劣势。华夷之辨思想影响中国人看清世界趋势、奋起直追、改变落后状况。鸦片的滥用影响了中国人的世界形象。

Drastic changes had taken place between the First Opium War and the end of the Qing Dynasty (1840–1912). The signing of many unequal treaties between China and the foreign countries awoke the Chinese to the serious situation faced by the country. The agonizing moments forced some elites or the scholar officials to open their eyes to the world and began to engage themselves in a series of reforms, such as the Self-Strengthening Movement (洋务运动), the One Hundred Days Reform and the Constitutional Movement. Whether those endeavors were successful or not, China at least took the first hard step toward modernity. People began to peacefully or impartially acknowledge the fact that China was far left behind the other nations and it needed to make a tremendous effort to catch up and join the world-wide competition so as to become a member of the international community. The consensus was that seclusion should be abandoned and integration into the world was the only way out.

When the gate of both China and Japan was pushed open by Western civilizations, the attitudes of the two nations were entirely different. For China, the products of science and technology were something that made the Western countries superior so China urgently needed to learn those things. Accordingly, the Chinese began to invite foreign experts to build up arsenals and manufacture weapons. The Qing government also sent young people to study science and technology abroad. But the progress was still slow and the Self-Strengthening Movement proved to be a failure. However, the Japanese quickly realized that the most important thing to learn was not science and technology but the ideas behind them. So they sent students abroad to study law and politics who came back to change their institutions. The question we ask is: Why does it take China more than 50 years (1840–1895) to respond to Western civilization while it only takes Japan 15 years (1853–1868) before the Meiji Restoration of 1868? And this is also the focus of the whole book. In order to have a better understanding of what had happened, we will provide some background information regarding the social, economic and political situation prior to the Opium War of 1840. This chapter covers three issues: the Seclusion Policy, the Chinese-barbarians distinction, and the opium abuse in the late Qing Dynasty and the 19th century Britain.

1.1 The Seclusion Policy 闭关锁国政策

The Seclusion Policy refers to the policy China adopted since the Ming Dynasty (1368–1644) in order to avoid contacts with other countries by closing the borders. As a matter of fact, China had maintained good relations with its neighboring countries in ancient times. During the Jin and Southern-Northern dynasties (两晋南北朝, AD 222–589), China was trading with some island states in Western Asia and the commodities were basically luxuries, such as wood, spice, coral (珊瑚), incense (香), dye (染料), gem (宝石), opaque glass (不透明玻璃), turmeric (姜黄), styrax (苏合香), and medicine. Due to the introduction of Buddhism to China in the Southern Liang Dynasty (南朝梁代, AD 502–556), the traded commodities with other nations included more products, such as ivory (象牙), sandalwood (檀香), and statues of the Budda (Leonard, 1984: 37). People in the Tang Dynasty (618–907) were tolerant with different religions. Believers of Nestorianism (景教), Judaism, Islam, and Manichaeism (摩尼教) were allowed to enter China, were received by the emperor and stayed in Chang'an, the capital of the Tang Dynasty. Marco Polo (马可·波罗) and his relatives traveled around China during the Yuan Dynasty (1271–1368) and the emperor received Marco Polo (苏慧廉, 2007).

Kublai Khan (忽必烈), Emperor of the Yuan Dynasty, was the first Chinese emperor who began to adopt a closed-door policy. Since he invaded Japan and was twice defeated by the Japanese, Kublai Khan decided not to have any contact with them and ordered a ban on maritime trade. But this seclusion situation was worsened in the Ming Dynasty because Emperor Zhu Yuanzhang (朱元璋) was facing two threats coming from the sea. The first threat was from the remnants of Zhang Shicheng (张士诚) and Fang Guozhen (方国珍) along the Coast of Fujian. During the late Yuan Dynasty, both Zhu Yuanzhang and the above mentioned groups were rebels and intended to overthrow the Yuan Dynasty. Yet the two parties were not united and became enemies. Thus, Zhu Yuanzhang was frequently assaulted by Zhang Shicheng's and Fang Guozhen's armies after he took the throne. The second threat was from the Japanese pirates. Fearing that the maritime trade would facilitate the collaboration between the people living along the coast and the Japanese pirates, Zhu Yuanzhang issued a series of orders not to allow the Chinese to trade with people coming from the sea. The second but decisive ban was issued in 1374, the seventh year of Hongwu (洪武七年), four years after the first ban, and this time three ports were closed. They were Quanzhou in Fujian (福建泉州), Mingzhou in Zhejiang (浙江明州) and Guangzhou in Guangdong (广东广州), which had existed for more than 800 years since the Tang Dynasty. The following four orders of banning the maritime trade were increasingly stricter and were issued respectively in 1381, 1390, 1394 and 1397. Finally, no single boat could be seen from the sea (佚名, 2017). The bans of maritime trade were not effective in deterring piracy and smuggling. On the contrary, it had forced ordinary people who made a living by fishing and trade before became penniless under the bans and turned into pirates and smugglers themselves. In addition, the ban on trade prevented the Chinese from knowing the outside world and made the Chinese lose the chance of developing science and technology too, because the 15th century was an age of discovery. When the Westerners traveled around the world making explorations and seeking treasures, they made great inventions and discoveries in terms of surveying and mapping, seamanship and art of navigation, which promoted the development of science and technology. It was a pity that by banning the trade China lost precious opportunities to communicate with people of different cultures and to make progress in science and technology. Someone might say that China had Zheng He (郑和) who for seven times traveled around the West Pacific Ocean and the Indian Ocean which showed that China had already enjoyed high marine technology. The sad truth was that those valuable navigation materials had all been burnt by the ignorant official Liu Daxia (刘大夏) (李西堂, 2016).

The seclusion in the Qing Dynasty had become even worse. According to Li Xitang (李西堂, 2016), in the early period, Emperor Shunzhi (顺治) issued several maritime bans in 1647, 1655, and 1656 due to Zheng Chenggong's (郑成功) conspiracy. Zheng Chenggong followed his father's steps in rebelling against the Manchu power because they were loyal to the Ming court. Zheng Chenggong led his army to attack the border along the southern coast, which annoyed Shunzhi a great deal. The maritime ban had come to its climax in 1661 and 1662 when both Shunzhi and Kangxi (康熙) ordered the people living near the coast to move 30–50 *li* toward the inner land. This edict destroyed the living habitat of the local people and made them destitute and homeless. Many of the people affected had to depart from their families tramping and begging and some even died of hunger and disease. The relocation edict greatly disturbed the social order and economic life of the local people, leaving the once prosperous land a wasteland. It showed that the Qing rulers lacked creativity in administration. Instead of finding ways to deal with the rebels, they made hundreds and thousands of farmers victims of the migration. The Seclusion Policy did nothing to deter the piracy and smuggling, but caused tremendous troubles and pains to the local people. So we can say that the policy was directed to the Chinese people instead of the pirates and rebels (曾燕, 涂楠, 2012). When historians lauded highly the achievement made by the so-called Kang-Qian Flourishing Age (康乾盛世), they needed to take into consideration the failure of the policy and the sufferings inflicted on ordinary people. The long-period of stagnation was interrupted by the strong warships and cannons of the Westerners.

The conflict between China and Britain originated from the bilateral trade. Beginning from 1716, tea became one of the important products that Britain bought from China, in addition to other commodities like raw silk, silks and satins (绸缎), homespun (土布) and porcelain (仲伟民, 2010). However, the demand for tea in Britain had surged after 1784 when the Commutation Act (《抵代税条例》) was issued and the British merchants felt it increasingly inconvenient to trade with China under the Canton System[1] and they needed to have a place to put their goods in. The Commutation Act was a counter measure to deter other European countries, such as France, the Netherlands, Sweden and Denmark from selling smuggled tea to Britain and it successfully dispelled those countries from tea smuggling. In this way, Britain was able to occupy the large share of the tea market in China.

The Canton System was a trade system initiated by Emperor Qianlong (乾隆) in 1757 and continued until 1842. In order to control the Western trade, it regulated that all foreign merchants trading with China needed to contact the Hongs (行商), the Chinese merchants, instead of local officials because they were considered lower in position than the latter. In this way, the merchants instead of real officials functioned as the external liaison intermediary between the Qing Dynasty and foreign countries (Anon, 2016).

Against such background, Lord Macartney (马戛尔尼), British Envoy, was sent to China in 1792 on a mission to negotiate with the Chinese government for more freedom and space for storing their commodities. The whole journey for Macartney China Mission

---

1 the Canton System 指广州十三行制度，其中 Canton 是广州的威妥玛式拼法，因为是专有名词，后文连用时仍然保持原有拼写，但单独指广州时则使用汉语拼音。其他类似的词也递循这一原则。

lasted two years from 1792 to 1794. In order to gain a favorable impression, they came under the name of celebrating Emperor Qianlong's 83rd birthday and Macartney had brought with him the most recent products of science and technology and presented them to the emperor as gifts. Things like telescopes, clocks, barometers, airguns and a hot-air balloon were on the list and they hoped that the emperor would like those things (Lovell, 2011). However to Macartney's great surprise, the Chinese officials showed little interest in those modern products, but paid more attention to how Macartney should follow the rituals for the audience (觐见), i.e. whether he should perform the three rapping ceremony (三叩九拜仪式) and what kinds of gifts the British monarch had brought to the emperor. Although Macartney did have an audience with Qianlong, he was not given any chance to discuss the issues expected. Eventually, the emperor wrote a letter to King George Ⅲ and let Macartney bring it back home.

Fig. 1-1 乾隆接见马戛尔尼[1]

Having spent ten months on the sea and suffered the pains from his rheumatism, Macartney did not fulfill the mission required of him. Instead, the China Mission group were shown around Re He (热河)[2] where the emperor celebrated his birthday and the Old Summer Palace (圆明园). Finally, their ship moved to Guangdong via Tianjin and

1 本书部分图片为作者自拍，也有一部分图片选自“百度图片”和“360 图片”，在此对相关作者和网站表示衷心的感谢。

2 热河的威妥玛式拼法为 Jehol，常见于西人所著作品中。热河在今河北承德。康熙四十二年（1703）建避暑山庄，乾隆七年（1742）改名为承德府。威妥玛式拼法普遍用于晚清时期的中国地名和人名的注音。

Zhoushan Islands (舟山群岛) and went back home. Macartney seized the opportunity of traveling around China making observations and believed that this country had little hope of moving forward and one day it would be defeated by some powerful states. Macartney's mission simply included some requests from the Qing government:

> The first is to request to allow the English merchants to trade to Cheusan (舟山)[1], Limpo (宁波)[2], and Tiensing (天津)[3].
>
> Second, to allow them to have a warehouse at Pekin (北京)[4] for the sale of their goods, as the Russians had formerly[5].
>
> Third, to allow them some small, detached, unfortified island in the neighborhood of Cheusan as a magazine (仓库) for their unsold goods, and as a residence (住宅) for their people to take care of them.
>
> Fourth, to allow them a similar privilege near Canton, and some other trifling indulgences.
>
> Fifth, to abolish the transit duties (过境税) between Macao and Canton, or at least to reduce them to the standard of 1782.
>
> Sixth, to prohibit the exaction (勒索) of any duties from English merchants, over and above those settled by the Emperor's diploma (公文), a copy of which is requested to be given to them, as they have never yet been able to see it for their unequivocal (明确的) direction. (Robins, 2010: 333)

No matter how anxious and painful Macartney was, he had never found a formal occasion for the negotiation. The local officials were perfunctory and avoided talking directly about the business. A mission of almost a hundred people were wasting their time doing something unrelated to their mission. In addition, Macartney was suffering from rheumatism and the long journey made things worse. But sometimes he had to go through the formalities in spite of the pain. In the letter to King George Ⅲ, Qianlong boasted that China did not need to buy anything from Britain because the tributary states came with abundant goods that satisfied China. But paradoxically in the royal palace, Qianlong kept a great variety of British objects that were worthy of two millions sterling. They were various toys, jewelry, glass, musical automatons, and other figures, instruments of different kinds, clocks, watches, etc. (Robins, 2010). When Qianlong criticized the Western products as

1-4 这几个地名的拼写皆沿用了威妥玛式拼法。

5 Russia had good relation with the Qing government and was given a place for storing their commodities.

clever tricks and wicked craft, he did not really mean it. What it suggested was that the emperor felt so ashamed of his own country that he had to play down Western goods in order to save face or to hide his jealousy. The assumption was that Qianlong might have felt a certain threat from the Westerners but he did not want to acknowledge it. Therefore, he had to find some excuse like what he had written in the letter to evade the shyness. But the refusal to trade with Western countries was the least wanted measure because it would prevent China from advancement.

By visiting different places in China, Macartney found that the development of science was very slow. Take printing for instance. Printing in China was quite backward compared with that of the West because the Chinese were still using block printing (雕版印刷) though the art of printing was said to be invented in China and it was not known in Europe a hundred and fifty years after Marco Polo's return from China. It showed that the dissemination of knowledge was extremely slow in China. Compared with the four-wheeled open carriage, the Chinese two-wheeled carriage without springs appeared less convenient and less comfortable. Perhaps the Qing ministers had already noticed it and were surprised at seeing Macartney using phosphorus to light a fire and carry it in his pocket. They very much admired Macartney's description of how to save the drowning person and how to treat glaucoma. When the parts of the telescope were put together in the Old Summer Palace, the Chinese ministers were attracted to it and even asked Mr Barrow to make another one on the spot (Robins, 2010).

But many Chinese showed little interest in the British products of newly developed science and technology. For instance, when Macartney introduced the hot-air balloon, the latest achievement in Britain, it drew no one's attention. It made Macartney wonder why Kangxi's interest in science was not passed down to the following generations. He found that the Chinese did have great interest in smallwares (小商品), such as dressing tables (梳妆台), dressing table mirrors (梳妆台镜), pocket instruments (袖珍仪表), and collapsible knives (可折叠刀), which made him think that those petty commodities might have market in China. Seeing the Chinese using their hands or chopsticks when eating, Macartney did not think it hygienic and wanted to introduce British cutlery like knives and forks to China. Yet what Macartney did not expect was that tableware was a kind of custom or tradition that could hardly be changed. So cutlery found no market in China and neither did the woolen cloths because it was pretty warm in Guangdong Province.

Qianlong's foreign policy was modeled after by the following Qing emperors. In 1816, twenty-three years after Lord Macartney's visit, the British government sent another China

Mission led by Lord Amherst (阿美士德勋爵) and this time it was under the reign of Emperor Jiaqing (嘉庆). The main reason for this mission was to ask the Qing government to loosen the restraints imposed on the British merchants caused by the Canton System. Specifically, the following two requests were made:

1. To replace the current Hongs with the ones that the Commission Agent thinks proper;

2. To establish a direct connection with Beijing by sending British envoys to China. (埃利斯, 2013: 32, 37)

Lord Amherst was not optimistic about this mission due to the shadow of the previous one. But still together with 70 members, he set off to China. After a five-month journey, Amherst China Mission arrived in Tianjin. Yet the thorny issue of kowtow rites was raised for the second time. Lord Amherst discussed with his assistant George Staunton Junior but the latter was firmly against following the Chinese kowtow rituals. Eventually, Lord Amherst did not have an audience with Emperor Jiaqing and the Mission had to follow the same route of Macartney to go back to Britain via Guangzhou.

The above two failures of the China Mission did not stop the British from having trade with China and trying for a third time. Eighteen years after the second mission, Lord Napier (律劳卑勋爵) was sent in 1834 to work as a trade superintendent in China when British East India Company was dismissed because of its monopoly. As an official, Lord Napier wanted to discuss issues directly with his counterpart in China. But under the Canton System, foreigners should talk with the Hongs instead of the ministers. Not following this rule, Lord Napier deliberately sent his letter to Guangzhou Governor Lu Kun (卢坤), asking to discuss business. When being rejected, Lord Napier began to criticize the Qing government by distributing leaflets. He even resorted to force. The situation was becoming more sensitive this time because it involved the drug opium. Eventually, Lord Napier had to withdraw to Macao where he died of malaria.

Following Lord Napier's death, William Jardine (威廉·渣甸) and James Matheson (詹姆士·马地臣), together with 64 British merchants, wrote a petition on December 9, 1834 to the King's cabinet. They requested sending three warships to China demanding from the Qing court the dismissal of Lu Kun and renewing the trade. They thought that Lord Napier had been maltreated by the Qing government and the British honor was harmed. Therefore, a war seemed to be the only way out (Anon, 2017). Six years later, in 1840 the war truly took place between Britain and China[1].

1.2 The Chinese-Barbarians Distinction 华夷之辨

The fact that the British failed three times in their attempt to open the gate of China was closely related to the Chinese arrogance and contempt for foreigners and this mentality was derived from the idea of the "Chinese-barbarians distinction". In ancient China, Zhongyuan or the Central Plains comprising the middle and lower reaches of the Yellow River (part of Henan, Shanxi, Hebei, Shandong, Anhui and Jiangsu), was deemed to be the best place and people living in this area were deemed to be civilized and cultural, while people living in the peripheral areas were thought to be barbarous and uncivilized. This was very much like the ancient Romans, who considered themselves cultural and civilized but other Europeans, such as Angles, Saxons, Goths, and Vandals as barbarians. Four terms were given to those uncivilized Chinese: Beidi (北狄), people living in the northern periphery, Xirong (西戎), people living in the western edge, Dongyi (东夷), people living in the eastern border, and Nanman (南蛮), people living in the southern periphery. These four terms Di (狄), Rong (戎), Yi (夷) and Man (蛮) all stood for barbarians. Initially in the Western Zhou Dynasty (西周, 1046–771 BC), this concept only had its geographical connotation. Yet when it came to the Spring and Autumn Period and the Warring States Period (770–221 BC), the geographical terms had gradually evolved into a cultural one entrenched in the mind of every Chinese (雷颐, 2017; 尹传政, 2016).

Once formed, this attitude of exclusion or anti-foreignism had become part of the Chinese national character. That explained why Qianlong refused to acknowledge the superiority of the British products. Although he fully understood those products were much more sophisticated and better in quality, Qianlong never wanted to admit it in public. On the contrary, he took a dismissive attitude to foreign products and openly claimed that China had no need for British goods.

Seeing the rapid development of the Western countries, Qianlong felt ashamed being the emperor of such a large and civilized country, especially when the Chinese always boasted about their own culture. Behind the superficial contempt, Qianlong in his heart had deep worries about it so that the emperor decided to close the country's door to the

1 Regarding the beginning of the First Opium War, Western scholarship has different views from the Chinese one. The former thinks that the war began in 1839 due to the fire opened between the two countries, while the Chinese scholarship has the opinion that the war began in 1840 because in that year the British government formerly declared war against China. (王建朗, 黄克武, 2016)

foreigners, isolating China from the outside world. The "a single port" (一口通商) policy began in the era of Qianlong and he closed the other three ports: Shanghai Customs (江海关), Ningbo Customs (浙海关), and Fuzhou Customs (闽海关), leaving only Guangzhou Customs (粤海关) open. The reason to keep just one port open was that the Royal Family needed a large amount of money and the bilateral trade between China and foreign countries could bring a lot of profits. From that we can see when Qianlong said that China did not have the need to buy products from Britain, he was not telling the truth.

The notion of the Chinese-barbarians distinction was turned into cultural values since the Spring and Autumn Period in which Confucius, the recognized sage, lived and proposed such an idea. In *The Analects* (《论语》) and *Spring and Autumn Annals* (《春秋》), Confucius pointed out that there was a huge gap between Huaxia Nationality (华夏民族) and the peripheral barbarians in terms of the evolution of civilization. The former possessed outstanding rites and music culture (礼乐文化) which helped keep the social order, while the latter came from a lower social order, which could hardly be distinguished from savages. In the "Baxiu" section of *The Analects* (《论语・八佾》), Confucius stated, "Even if the barbarians had a monarch it would not be matched to the Huaxia which had no monarch at all." (夷狄之有君，不如诸夏之亡也。) (毛子水, 2011: 33). Generally, what Confucius meant was that countries with low levels of civilization could hardly be compared with the one that enjoyed high levels of civilization. In the "Xianwen" section of *The Analects* (《论语・宪问》), Confucius also alluded to the barbarians' inferiority and lowliness. He highly praised Guan Zhong (管仲), the advisor to the king of Qi (齐王) for his cleaning up the world so that his people refrained from being reduced to the barbarians. In the name of "honoring the king and driving off the barbarians" (尊王攘夷), Guan Zhong aided the king of Qi in ensuring the culture of the Western Zhou Dynasty to last and laid the foundation for the grand unification.

In *Zuo Zhuan* (《左传》), *Gongyang Zhuan* (《公羊传》) and *Guliang Zhuan* (《穀梁传》), you can see the expression of Yi from time to time, which was in great contrast to the Huaxia civilization (华夏文明) (关嘉耀, 2011). For instance, in "The First Year of Duke Min" of *Zuo Zhuan* (《左传・闵公元年[1]》), Guan Zhong talked about Di and said, "Those barbarians from the peripheral areas are like jackals and wolves. They could never be satisfied. But the states within the Central Plains are like brothers and sisters. We should never give up our friendship." (戎狄豺狼，不可厌也；诸夏亲昵，不可弃也。) (孟

1 闵公元年指公元前 661 年。

子等, 2016: 704) As a result, the State of Qi sent the army to help the State of Xing (邢国). Another example in "The Fourth Year of Duke Cheng" of *Zuo Zhuan* (《左传·成公四年》) was a statement made about the State of Chu, "Those who were not my breed must be aliens." (非我族类，其心必异。) (孟子等, 2016: 704) Here it meant that the uncivilized people from the State of Chu did not have the same faith as them, so they needed to be on their guard. There were also such descriptions in the book *Mencius* (《孟子》), like "using Xia style to change Yi style" (以夏变夷), which meant the same thing as the "Chinese-barbarians distinction" put forward by Confucius. It was obvious that like Confucius, Mencius had the similar prejudice against the barbarians.

The above examples are all taken from the Confucian classics. When young people, who intended to pass the Imperial Civil Service Examination (科举考试), immersed themselves in reading and memorization, they were bound to be influenced by the discriminative ideology. And that would definitely make a negative impact on the society. It was the Imperial Civil Service Examination that had cultivated such arrogant and ignorant mentality, widely disseminated and gradually intensified the culture. That explained why Grand Secretariat (大学士) or scholars like Woren (倭仁)[1], Song Jin (宋晋) and Weng Tonghe (翁同龢) showed great contempt for Western science. Even when China was frequently defeated by their gunboats, those conservatives never gave up their prejudice against Western civilization. It made things worse when those diehards had many followers.

Not surprisingly, scholar officials like Lin Zexu (林则徐) and Wei Yuan (魏源) were also heavily influenced by such prejudice. In many of his official writings, Lin Zexu openly displayed his disdain for the British.

For instance, in his mind the British were very different from the Chinese because they could not walk properly due to the puttee they used in war:

> The barbarians can only win the war in the sea because they are good at sailing against the wind. Yet they could do nothing if we do not confront them in the sea. Once they get to the estuary where the water is shallow the British soldiers would get stuck...In addition, our enemies are only good at shooting their guns, but not fighting with bayonets because of their binding feet, which are not easy to stretch. Being ashore they become useless and we are likely to defeat them. Those barbarians are greedy and good at trade. They make profits by exchanging goods with Chinese. (蒋廷黻, 2014: 63)

1 倭仁的威妥玛式拼法为 Wojen。

夷兵船"只能取胜外洋，破浪乘风，是其长技，惟不与之在洋接仗，其技即无所施。至口内则运棹（zhao）不灵，一遇水浅沙胶，万难转动……且夷兵除枪炮之外，击刺步伐，俱非所娴。而其腿足缠束紧密，屈伸皆所不便。若至岸上更无能为，是其强非不能制也。该夷性奢而贪，不务本富，专以贸易求赢，而贸易全在中国畀（bi）以马头，乃得籍为牟利之薮"。（蒋廷黻，2014：63）

The above quote exhibited that Lin Zexu knew little about the outside world and truly thought the British were of an inferior race. He also thought their outward appearance disgusting. "Foreign dress looked undignified, even ghastly to him. Men wore short coats and tight trousers, which reminded him of the hare and fox costumes of the Chinese theater; women sported light garments on top and heavy skirts below, while shamelessly exposing their naked shoulders. The dark complexion of some, 'blacker than lacquer', appalled him, as did the profusion of men's facial hair. The curly beards and mustaches gave them a frightful look, which the Cantonese had aptly likened to that of 'the devil' (*guizi*)." (Kwong, 2008: 1494) The epithets Lin Zexu used to describe the foreigners were all negative such as "malefactors (奸宄)" "evil barbarians (奸夷)" "extravagant but wasteful (华糜)" "deceptive and haughty (虚骄)" "treacherous (诡谲)" (蒋廷黻, 2014: 61-63).

Wei Yuan's main purpose of writing *Haiguo Tuzhi* or *Illustrated Annals of Overseas Countries* was to utilize Western technology to defeat the Westerners so that China could still assume a superior position to the barbarian countries. Deep in his mind, Wei Yuan did not consider the Westerners as equal and still cherished the belief that China was the center of the world and superior to other countries due to the honor and pride enjoyed by China in ancient times.

It is natural that people from different cultures are suspicious of each other and humans tend to regard people of a different civilization as "other". However, when such misunderstanding and alienation are broken either by wars or by trade, it is extremely hard to understand that the less advantageous side still pretends not to see the reality. When the Westerners proved their superiority by using their gunboats, some Chinese conservatives still insisted that they were barbarians. The tenacity was either out of bravado (虚张声势 / 冒险) or inability to pocket their pride. The ups and downs of the late Qing society illustrated that it was the refusal to acknowledge their own inferiority and complacency about their own culture that made the Qing Dynasty move extremely slowly and be left far behind the developed countries.

The fact that Wei Yuan's *Haiguo Tuzhi* (1843) and Xu Jiyu's *Yinghuan Zhilue* (1848) received little response in China, but found a large readership in Japan revealed that the Chinese were still intoxicated in their own illusion and did nothing to strengthen the country after the defeat in the First Opium War. When *Haiguo Tuzhi* was brought to Japan through a trade vessel during 1851–1854, it immediately attracted the reformers' attention. For instance, Yoshida Shōin (吉田松阴), Saigo Takamori (西乡隆盛), Sakuma Shōzan (佐久间象山), Yasui Sokken (安井息轩), Yokoi Syounan (横井小楠) and Hashimoto Sanai (桥本左内) all rushed to read the book and were influenced by it (吴泽, 黄丽镛, 1963). It was *Haiguo Tuzhi* and *Yinghuan Zhilue* brought in later that made a great impact on the Japanese Meiji Restoration. It was also the two books that had enlightened the Japanese to learn from the more civilized Western countries and make a change to Japan. We are going to have a detailed discussion about this issue in the next chapter.

Regarding the concept of the Chinese-barbarians distinction, Liu He (刘禾), a professor of Tsinghua University, stated in her book *The Clash of Empires* (《帝国的话语政治》, 2014) that the Chinese character Yi used in the Treaty of Tianjin (《天津条约》)[1] did not necessarily refer to "barbarians". On the contrary, she thought it meant "foreign" "strange", etc. We cannot deny that in ancient China the character Yi did have the meanings as mentioned by Liu He (2014). However, in the context of the Treaty of Tianjin, it undoubtedly stood for "barbarians", because the British were much annoyed by its derogatory sense when being such addressed either orally or in the written form. The author of this book disagrees with what Liu He said and thinks that we should show respect for history, but not to distort the facts in order to fit the meaning into a certain theory (方维规, 2013).

1.3 The Opium Abuse in the Late Qing Dynasty and the 19th Century Britain 鸦片在晚清和 19 世纪英国的滥用

When discussing the opium trade, we need to trace back to its origin and make a comparison between the late Qing Dynasty and the 19th century Britain in terms of opium addiction, so that we could see clearly how much knowledge people living in that period of time had about opium's poisonous nature, and why one group of people were more likely to be attracted to it than the other community.

There is a whole chapter devoted to opium and China in Julia Lovell's (蓝诗玲) book *The Opium War: Drugs, Dreams, and the Making of Modern China* (2011). According to

1 《天津条约》的威妥玛式拼法为 the Treaty of Tientsin。

Lovell, opium was introduced to China in the 8th century for the first time and it was used as medicine curing diseases like diarrhea, arthritis, malaria, coughs, etc. by way of eating or drinking. But three hundred years later during the 11th century, its entertaining function was discovered and people began to take it as pastimes. One of the reasons that the Chinese enjoyed it is that opium helped men prolong their ejaculation time so as to bring more sexual pleasure. This has a lot to do with Daoism (道教), which links sex art with health maintenance. Aphrodisiacs (春药) made from opium was popular in the Ming Dynasty and eleven out of sixteen Ming emperors died before forty probably because of opium taking. Wanli (万历), the late Ming emperor, was found to have morphine in his dead body.

The reason for opium to become so popular in China was the new way of consuming it. In the early 18th century, people in Java found that tobacco would taste better when it was soaked in opium syrup (鸦片糖浆). This was introduced to the mainland of China via trade with the Taiwan region. Opium smoking would avoid the bitter taste and at the same time give pleasure to people. That explained why opium smoking had quickly spread around China (仲伟民, 2010). That the Chinese enjoyed smoking opium is out of three reasons. First, opium creates a kind of intoxicated, pleasurable feelings on people. Second, it promotes social communications. Third, opium smoking is a sign of wealth and power because only wealthy people could afford to smoke it without going bankrupt.

In the eyes of the Westerners, only those morally weak people got addicted to opium and it was a sign of degradation and abandonment. When British East India Company helped smuggle opium to China, the British were worried that this bad habit would be extended to themselves. The so-called Yellow Peril referred to this kind of mixed feelings: guilt and fear. Knowing the drug was poisonous, the merchants felt guilty when selling it to China. On the other hand, they were afraid that this bad habit would be transmitted to the British people one day. As humans share the similar disposition, any bad habit can be passed from one community to another and they can hardly avoid it.

When British East India Company was involved in opium dealings with China, what was the situation of opium use in Britain? Compared with China, opium addiction in Britain was limited to two groups of people: men of letters and the working class. Some of the 19th century British poets, writers or artists were addicted to opium because they thought they could find inspirations from it. Samuel Coleridge (柯勒律治), for instance, used opium first for treating his ailments and then became addicted to it. The well-known poem "Kublai Khan" was said to be written under the anesthetic effect because Coleridge admitted that he could not remember how he had written it. Similarly, the British essayist and critic De Quincey (德·昆西) ate opium first to treat his stomachache but later became addicted to it. He wrote a book confessing his opium addiction entitled *Confessions of an English Opium-Eater and Suspiria de Profundis* in 1851. Other poets or writers ate opium for the recreational purpose. John Keats (约翰·济慈) was a case in point.

In British literary works, we also see characters that are opium addicts. In *Silas Marner*, George Eliot described a woman called Molly who became addicted to and died of opium eating because she was abandoned by her partner and her 2-year-old daughter was adopted by the poor weaver Silas Marner. Mrs Gaskell also described in her novel *Mary Barton* the miserable situation which a textile worker was in due to his addiction to opium. John Barton, out of his failure in persuading the Parliament to improve the workers' living condition, took to opium to relieve his depression, leading to his doom in the end. There were other blows in his life, i.e. the death of his wife and his younger son, and his own loss of job. After taking opium, John's personality had a great change. He tended to burst into a rage and that frightened his only daughter Mary. The following interpretation provided by Mrs Gaskell was concerned with John Barton's self-destruction:

> It is true that much of their morbid power might be ascribed to the use of opium. But before you blame too harshly this use, or rather abuse, try a hopeless life, with daily cravings of the body for food. Try, not alone being without hope yourself, but seeing all around you reduced to the same despair, arising from the same circumstances; all around you telling (though they use no words or language), by their looks and feeble actions, that they are suffering and sinking under the pressure of want. Would you not be glad to forget life, and its burdens? And opium gives forgetfulness for a time. (Gaskell, 2006: 164)

The Moonstone (《月亮宝石》) written by Wilkie Collins, narrated a detective story in which the precious moonstone mysteriously disappeared and that led to the complicated procedures of cracking the criminal case. Eventually, it turned out to be none other than the wealthy young man called Franklin Blake who had unconsciously taken opium and stolen the precious stone.

While the British middle class poets or novelists were not blamed for taking opium, its working class people who took opium were criticized for their moral degradation. In the eyes of the critics, the fact that people of lower social status indulged themselves in opium meant they had abandoned themselves as opium was a luxurious product. Those who did not earn much deliberately caused their own doom, which was unsympathetic.

When the British mocked Chinese addicts, the thing they were afraid of did happen one hundred and seventy years later. Drug abuse became a more serious social problem in Britain and other Western countries than in China. The lesson we take from it is that we need to be very cautious when making negative comments on some indecent human behavior of a community because it is likely to spread to other communities as well. All humans share similar traits and weaknesses. Anything that happens to one community is likely to appear in other human groups, too.

To summarize, in this chapter we have reviewed the Chinese history prior to the First Opium War in terms of the Seclusion Policy, the concept of the Chinese-barbarians distinction, and opium addiction in both China and Britain.

◆ Topics for Discussion

1. The reason for Emperor Qianlong to adopt "a single port" policy.
2. The origin of the "Chinese-barbarians distinction" idea.
3. The opium abuse in Britain during the 19th century.
4. Explain why Qianlong refused to trade with Britain.
5. Was it true that China had no need to buy goods from foreign countries?
6. Your comment on the Canton System.
7. The reasons for the Opium Wars.

◆ Reading Assignments

1. Hsu, I. C. Y. 2000. Chapter 7 and 8 of *The Rise of Modern China*. Oxford: Oxford University Press.
2. 魏源. 1998.《海国图志 · 筹海篇》1–4 页. 长沙：岳麓书社.

◆ Bibliography

Anon. 2016. Canton System. 02–29. From Wikipedia website.

Anon. 2017. How It Evolved in History. 09–24. From China Mirror website.

Gaskell, E. 2006. *Mary Barton*. Oxford: Oxford University Press.

Kwong, L. S. K. 2008. Chinese Myth of Universal Kingship and Commissioner Lin Zexu's Anti-Opium Campaign. *The English Historical Review*, *123*(505): 1470-1503.

Leonard, J. K. 1984. *Wei Yuan and China's Rediscovery of the Maritime World*. Cambridge and London: Council on East Asian Studies.

Lovell, J. 2011. *The Opium War: Drugs, Dreams, and the Making of Modern China*. New York: The Overlook Press and Peter Mayer Publishers, Inc.

Robins, H. H. 2010. *Our First Ambassador to China: An Account of the Life of George, Earl of Macartney*. Cambridge: Cambridge University Press.

晁中辰. 2012. 明代海外贸易研究. 北京：故宫出版社.

戴逸. 1998. 中国近代史通鉴·鸦片战争. 北京：红旗出版社.

方维规. 2013. 一个有悖史实的生造“衍指符号”：就《帝国的话语政治》中“夷/barbarian”的解读与刘禾商榷. 文艺研究，(2)：138–145.

关嘉耀. 2011.“华夷之辨”与文化中心主义. 05–06. 新法家.

亨利·埃利斯. 2013. 阿美士德使团出使中国日志. 刘天路，刘甜甜，译. 刘海岩，审校. 北京：商务印书馆.

蒋廷黻. 2014. 近代中国外交史资料辑要：上卷. 北京：东方出版社.

柯林斯. 2011. 月亮宝石. 王青松，译. 北京：中央编译出版社.

雷颐. 2017.“民族”何以成为“主义”：牛津通识读本《民族主义》中文版序. 07–15. 爱思想.

李西堂. 2016. 长期闭关锁国. 03–09. 共识网.

刘禾. 2014. 帝国话语政治：从近代中西冲突看现代世界秩序的形成. 北京：生活·读书·新知三联书店.

毛子水. 2011. 论语今注今译. 重庆：重庆出版社.

孟子，等. 2016. 四书五经. 北京：中华书局.

乔治·艾利斯. 2016. 织工马南传. 马渔，译. 北京：北京时代华文书局.

乔治·马戛尔尼，约翰·巴罗. 2015. 马戛尔尼使团使华观感. 何高济，何毓宁，译.

北京：商务印书馆.

苏慧廉. 2007. 李提摩太在中国. 关志远，关志英，何玉，译. 桂林：广西师范大学出版社.

王建朗，黄克武. 2016. 两岸新编中国近代史·晚清卷：上. 北京：社会科学文献出版社.

吴泽，黄丽镛. 1963. 魏源《海国图志研究》. 历史研究，(4)：117–140.

佚名. 2017. 明朝海禁. 02–19. 百度百科.

尹传政. 2016. 近代“夷夏观”传统思想变迁. 01–25. 学习时报.

曾燕，涂楠. 2012. 撬动中国，向近代转型的坚实支点：徐继畬“大变局”认识与涉外实务研究. 成都：四川大学出版社.

仲伟民. 2010. 茶叶与鸦片：十九世纪经济全球化中的中国. 北京：生活·读书·新知三联书店.

Chapter Two

Chinese Scholar Officials' Response to the First Opium War

晚清士大夫对第一次鸦片战争的回应

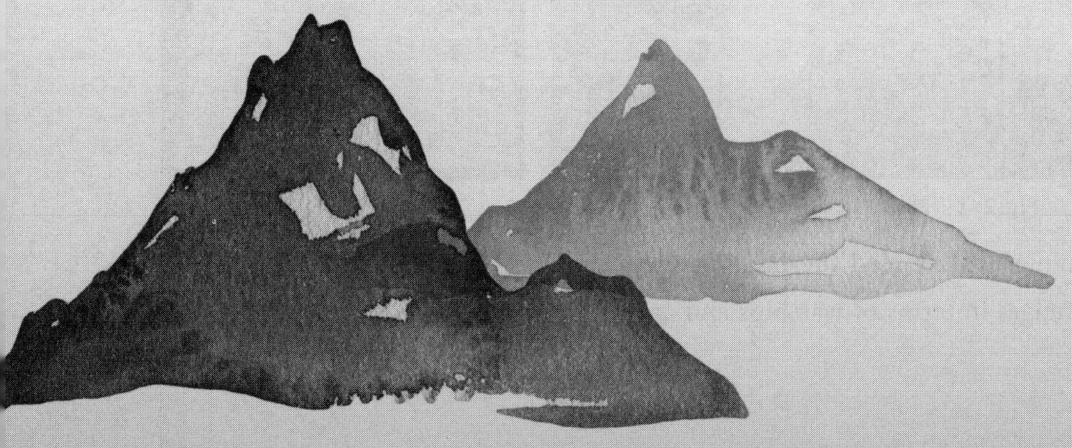

上一章介绍了鸦片战争前晚清社会在外交、文化和鸦片滥用等方面的情况，如闭关锁国政策、华夷之辨思想以及鸦片在中国和英国的滥用。本章探讨第一次鸦片战争在清朝士大夫中引起的反响，主要关注魏源的《海国图志》和徐继畬的《瀛寰志略》，介绍这两部著作的内容、外界的评价，以及在中国和日本引起的不同反响。

When comparing China with Japan in terms of the modernization process, Richard Smith pointed out that both countries needed to undergo four stages in response to the Western impact. First, they needed to recognize the superiority of the Western military. Second, they needed to recognize Western scientific technology as the basis of military superiority. Third, they needed to recognize the necessity to train native personnel in Western military technology. And finally they must understand that the military sphere needed to be combined with pure science and general learning of the West to take effect (Smith, 1976). While the majority of the Qing officials refused to recognize the superiority of the foreign invaders, Wei Yuan and Xu Jiyu did. The two scholar officials had the courage to admit that China was no match for the West in terms of the military and weaponry. It took China twenty years before they recognized the superiority of the Western military and began to put what Wei Yuan had suggested into practice. In the following, we will discuss in what way the Chinese began to learn about the West through the knowledge of geography.

2.1 Wei Yuan and His *Haiguo Tuzhi* 魏源与其《海国图志》

Fig. 2-1 魏源

Fig. 2-2 《海国图志》

Having experienced the First Opium War, Wei Yuan felt deeply about China's disadvantages in terms of warships and arms. He wanted to do something to help. Just coincidently, his friend Lin Zexu, demoted from the Viceroy (总督) due to China's failure in the First Opium War, saw him when passing through Zhenjiang, Jiangsu Province. There Lin Zexu urged Wei Yuan to write a geographical book based on the information he had collected including a book edited by him called *Sizhou Zhi* (《四洲志》) and some materials translated from *Chinese Repository* (《中国丛报》) and other sources. Both Lin Zexu and Wei Yuan realized how important the cultural knowledge of the foreign countries was and they were eager to let the Chinese understand the knowledge of geography, history, military, politics, and economy of different countries. At Lin Zexu's suggestion, Wei Yuan began to plan the outline of this book. In fact, the Chinese people were first enlightened via geographical knowledge of the world.

The book *Sizhou Zhi* or *The Geography of the Four Continents* was mainly based on *The Encyclopedia of Geography* by Hugh Murray. This was one of the major sources of *Haiguo Tuzhi* in addition to the translations from *Chinese Repository* and copies of histories and geographies written by Protestant missionaries (Leonard, 1984). The second source came from chronicles, memoirs of the previous dynasties, mainly concerning Southeast Asia. The third source of Wei Yuan's book was the maps and diagrams of ships and guns collected from other Western works (魏源, 1998; 吴泽, 黄丽镛, 1963). Yet Wei Yuan did not simply put all the sources together and turned them into a book. His purpose was to call upon the Chinese people to be open-minded and learn from the foreigners before effectively dealing with them. At the beginning of the book, Wei Yuan stated his purpose and the three reasons for writing this book:

> First, "to tackle foreigners with foreign things"; second, "to negotiate peace with the foreigners through the use of foreign methods"; third, "to learn foreign things to overcome the foreigners". (Geng, 2015: 37)
>
> 是书何以作？曰：为以夷攻夷而作，为以夷款夷而作，为师夷长技以制夷而作。（丁守和，1999：22）

Among the one hundred volumes of *Haiguo Tuzhi*, the first two volumes were commentary made by Wei Yuan himself which was named "The Blueprint of Maritime Defense" (《筹海篇》) and contained four essays, i.e. two in each volume. The first and second essays in Volume One discussed the importance of defense or garrisons. Essentially, Wei Yuan summarized the lessons the Chinese needed to learn from the First Opium War. The British Expedition launched the offensive at Zhoushan Islands, Zhejiang Province due to the location of the Grand Canal (大运河). It was said that the Qing Royal Family relied on the Grand Canal flowing between Beijing and Hangzhou to obtain their grains. Every year, grains produced in the southern provinces, such as Jiangsu and Zhejiang would be transported via the Grand Canal to Beijing. If the British controlled the canal, they would force the emperor to agree to let foreign consuls to reside in Beijing. That was why the British army first broke through Zhoushan Islands before moving southward to resolve the problem of the house arrest[1] of the foreign merchants.

Thus when Wei Yuan began his first essay on defense, he discussed Zhoushan Islands. In his opinion, the reason why Zhoushan was so easily broken into was that the Chinese military commander wrongly deployed the main force in Dinghai (定海), which was close to Zhoushan, rather than keeping guard over Ningbo (宁波), which was to the south of Zhoushan. In Wei Yuan's opinion, if the Chinese commander had deployed the troops in Ningbo and lured the enemy into Zhoushan first, the Chinese troops could have annihilated the enemy. Since Chinese weapons were not as good as those of the British, they needed to lure the enemy in deep before using fire to cut off the enemy's route of retreat.

> 乃宁波濒海连岸之南田山，垦成沃壤者，反禁不许开，而重兵以守孤悬之岛，使外夷得以挟制，此不得地利者一。然而如之何？曰：弃定海，移其兵民于南田，严守宁波，佯退镇海招宝山，以诱入之，而后于甬江下游狭港塞其去路，乘风火攻者，上策，专守镇海，不使入者，次之，分守定海者为下。（魏源，1998：4）

Similarly, Hong Kong was linked to Jianshazui (尖沙咀)[2] and Qundailu (裙带路), very much like Zhoushan. So Humen (虎门) was more important due to its position of trade with foreign countries. When getting hold of Humen, the Chinese would not worry about the enemy's attack.

> 香港与尖沙咀、裙带路三屿相连，周百余里，堪避风浪，而孤悬海面，亦粤之舟山耳。夷与我通商，则必入虎门方能贸易，不与通商，则夷虽孤处香港无益。其地距广州四百余里，距虎门二百余里，何预咽喉利害。次则沙角、大角炮台，远隔虎门之外，江面寥阔，大炮仅及中泓，不足遏夷艘，适足招夷炮，何必守？所宜守者，虎门之横档，三门与虎门内乌涌，再进曰猎得，曰大黄滘。（魏源，1998：4）

1 the house arrest 指林则徐为了迫使外国商人放弃鸦片贸易，将广州十三行中的350名外商围困其中，达六周以上。

2 尖沙咀的威妥玛式拼法为 Tsim Sha Tsui。

Having finished summarizing the advantages and disadvantages of the Chinese troop deployment in the First Opium War, Wei Yuan began to make comments on fighting battles with foreign troops, which was what the third essay was about. In this section, Wei Yuan pointed out the importance of information, i.e. knowing about our enemies. First of all, he discussed the three rival countries of Britain. They were Russia, France and America. In the meantime, Britain was also afraid of four other countries that were attached to China: Nepal, Burma, Thailand, and Vietnam. And this was where our edge lay.

> 筹夷事必知夷情，知夷情必知夷形，请先陈其形势；英夷所惮之仇国三：曰俄罗斯，曰佛兰西，曰弥利坚。惮我之属国四：曰廓尔喀[1]，曰缅甸，曰暹罗[2]，曰安南[3]……盖康熙中用荷兰以款俄罗斯，又联俄罗斯以逼准噶尔，故英夷之惧俄罗斯者，不在国都而在印度，此机之可乘者一……（魏源，1998：24）

Then, he talked about in what way China could gain knowledge about other countries. He criticized Chinese officials for knowing nothing about the outside world. That mainly brought about China's failure during the First Opium War. Then, he suggested that a translation house should be built to translate foreign works so that the Chinese could have a better understanding of what the British people were like and why their armory was so advanced, etc.

> 以通市二百年之国，竟莫知其方向，莫悉其离合，尚可谓留心边事者乎？汉用西域攻匈奴，唐用吐番攻印度，用回纥[4]攻吐番；圣祖用荷兰夹板船攻台湾，又联络俄罗斯以逼准葛尔。古之驭外夷者，惟防其协寇以谋我，不防其协我而攻寇也……然则欲制外夷者，必先悉夷情始；欲悉夷情者，必先立译馆翻夷书始；欲造就边才者，必先用留心边事之督抚始。（魏源，1998：26）

Wei Yuan made suggestions to the court but it was not actualized until twenty years later by Prince Gong (恭亲王).

Specifically, let us turn our attention to the commander-in-chief, Emperor Daoguang's (道光) knowledge about the invaders. According to Zeng Yan (曾燕) and Tu

1 廓尔喀指尼泊尔。
2 暹罗指泰国。
3 安南指越南。
4 回纥指维吾尔族。

Nan (涂楠), the emperor was totally ignorant of his enemy after being defeated by them. For instance, he did not know the geographical location of Britain in terms of its distance from China, the number of countries British invaders went past when they arrived in China. In addition, Daoguang had no idea of why Britain wanted to break into China from Zhejiang Province, and he wanted to know whether other countries which came to China like Bangladesh, Spain, the Philippines, and Austria were organized by Britain as well. Ironically, Daoguang was surprised to hear that those foreign invaders were not afraid of death. We can see that from what the emperor asked his courtiers: "It is said that England is over 35,000 kilometers away from the mainland. How many countries would it pass before arrival? How far away is it from Kashmir (克什米尔)? Is there a water route between the two countries and do they have any contacts? Why did England come from Zhejiang? What about Bangladesh, Spain, the Philippines, and Austria? Do they come together or are they led by England?"

> 英吉利距内地水程，据称有七万余里，其至内地所经过者几国？克食米尔[1]距该国若干路程？是否有水路可通，该国与英吉利有无往来？此次何以相从至浙？其余来浙之孟加利、大小吕宋[2]，双英（鹰）国[3]夷众，系带兵头目，私相号召，抑由该国王招之使来？……（曾燕、涂楠，2012：51）

Like the emperor, his officials were no better. According to Geng Yunzhi (耿云志), twenty years after the First Opium War Chinese officials and gentry still regarded the Westerners as beasts. For instance, Qiying (耆英), the Viceroy who together with Yilibu (伊里布) signed the unequal treaty, i.e. the Treaty of Nanjing (《南京条约》)[4] and later in 1843 he signed another treaty with Britain, i.e. the Treaty of Humen (《虎门条约》)[5]. In 1844, he signed two treaties again: the Treaty of Wangxia (《望厦条约》)[6] with America and the Treaty of Huangpu (《黄埔条约》)[7] with France. A person like him who had witnessed what the Westerners looked like said: "People speak of all barbarians, whether women or children, as 'foreign devils' and do not see them as worthy of being humans." (Geng, 2015: 30-31) It implied that Qiying himself had the similar opinion. Fang Dongshu (方东树), a scholar of Neo-Confucianism School (宋明理学派) and advisor to Deng

1 克食米尔指克什米尔。
2 大小吕宋指西班牙与菲律宾。
3 双英（鹰）国指奥地利。道光说出这些国家的名称，表明他对侵略者是谁毫无所知。
4《南京条约》的原始拼法为 the Treaty of Nanking。
5《虎门条约》的原始拼法为 the Treaty of the Bogue。
6《望厦条约》的原始拼法为 the Treaty of Wanghia。
7《黄埔条约》的原始拼法为 the Treaty of Whampoa。

Tingzhen (邓廷桢), also cherished the similar belief about foreigners as others. He said that the Westerners "cannot see into the distance and therefore cannot hit any mark with bow(s) and arrow(s), and have legs so weak they are unable to walk on land upon coming ashore" (Geng, 2015: 30-31). The Westerners were good at fighting at sea only but not on land. That reminds us of what Lin Zexu had said before. People at that time simply spread the rumor and took it as a fact.

More than two decades had passed since the First Opium War but the Chinese still had the wrong ideas about the Westerners and refused to admit they were our equals. The reason lay in the self-immurement (自我封闭) and habitual self-aggrandizement (自我膨胀). Matteo Ricci (利玛窦) had described in his book *The Chinese Extracts of Matteo Ricci* (《利玛窦中国札记》): "The Chinese don't know the size of the earth yet they are arrogant and think that only China deserves admiration. Regarding the state, politics and academics they consider people of other cultures as savages and irrational animals. In their eyes, no kings, dynasties or cultures in other places are worth praising. Thus the more arrogant they are due to their ignorance, the more self-contemptuous they feel once they found the truth. The Chinese regard all the foreigners as barbarians and they address them as such. They don't bother to learn anything from foreigners because they believe only they themselves possess true science and knowledge."[1] (何兆武, 柳卸林, 2011: 2-7)

Wei Yuan was the first person who admitted that the Westerners were superior in their military power. Thus, Wei Yuan urged China to learn from the Westerners and he stated that compared with Chinese military power, the Westerners were at the advantageous position in their warships, firearms and military training. He proposed that China should invite the Western craftsmen and military commanders to teach the Chinese how to manufacture warships and weapons, and train our soldiers according to the foreign method.

> 夷之长技三：一、战舰，二、火器，三、养兵、练兵之法……请于广东虎门外之沙角、大角二处置造船厂一，火器局一，行取佛兰西、弥利坚二国各来夷目一二人，分携西洋工匠至粤，司造船械，并延西洋柁师司教行船演炮之法，如钦天监夷官之例，而选闽、粤巧匠精兵以习之。工匠习其铸造，精兵习其驾驶、攻击。（魏源，1998：26–27）

Haiguo Tuzhi was published three times in 1843, 1847, and 1852. The first version had 50 volumes, the second 60 volumes and the third 100 volumes. Wei Yuan expanded

1 引号中的英文部分是根据中文引文翻译的。

his book in 1852 by drawing heavily on *Illustrated Geography* (《地球图说》) compiled by Richard Quarterman Way (袆理哲) in 1848. Way was an American missionary and came to Ningbo with his family in 1844. He wrote a brief introduction to world geography for Chinese readers in beautiful classical Chinese language. In addition, the information contained in this book was accurate and reliable. Wei Yuan borrowed 34 places from Way's book (徐春伟, 2018).

Since the British were China's major enemy, Wei Yuan devoted a large proportion of *Haiguo Tuzhi* to describing Britain's geographical location, British characters and customs, their superior skills, and their political institutions. "British people believe in God and they praise God and say prayers every day. On Sunday they would gather and sing hymns or make confessions in front of God. They only kneel down for God, not anybody else. A young British couple neither need a matchmaker nor seek permission from their parents when getting married. The Chinese and the British had exchanged goods since 1838, i.e. the 18th year of the Daoguang's reign. The Chinese bought things like trepang (海参), cubilose (燕窝), borneol (冰片), wax, glass, lead, iron, and tin from Britain and the latter bought tea, silk, lacquer, silverware, etc. from China." (魏源, 1998: 1406-1407) This was quite contradictory to Qianlong's statement that China needed to buy nothing from the Westerners. Wei Yuan described the British people as follows:

Having a deep and fierce temper, the British people are ingenious, good at making clocks, ships and cannons...They rose in national power, depending on their strong weapons, which worried other nations.

夷性沉鸷，多巧思，所制钟表仪器，中土所重，而船炮尤至精利……英吉利恃其船炮，渐横海上，识者每以为忧。（魏源，1998：1453–1454）

Wei Yuan also introduced British institutions, i.e. Parliament including the House of Lords and the House of Commons and how they were composed and what they did in dealing with national and international affairs. The Upper House[1] was composed of aristocrats and prelates while the Lower House[2] was made up of common people who were learned and intelligent. When deciding on an issue, the King would inform the Prime Minister, who convened a parliament, discussing the issue. The final was determined by the majority of people from the Lower House.

1 the Upper House, 即 the House of Lords，指英国上院。其成员由贵族及教士世袭而成。

2 the Lower House, 即 the House of Commons，指英国下院。其成员由选举产生。

> 内分两所：一曰爵房，一曰乡绅房。爵房者，有爵位贵人及耶稣教师处之；乡绅房者，由庶民推择有才识学术者处之。国有大事，王谕相，相告爵房，聚众公议，参以条例，决其可否；辗转告乡绅房，必乡绅大众允诺而后行，否则寝其事勿论。（魏源，1998：1446）

Wei Yuan's intention was clear: the more the Chinese knew about their enemies, the easier they dealt with them. The sad truth was that what Wei Yuan suggested had only been practiced twenty years later when Zeng Guofan (曾国藩) and Li Hongzhang (李鸿章) set up the Jiangnan Arsenal in Shanghai. Zuo Zongtang (左宗棠) and Shen Baozhen (沈葆桢) established the first dockyard in Fuzhou and trained students to build and drive warships.

2.2 Xu Jiyu and His *Yinghuan Zhilue* 徐继畬与其《瀛寰志略》

Like Wei Yuan, Xu Jiyu was the second scholar official who realized that China was not as powerful as Western countries and we needed to know about them so as to confront the challenging world. Yet compared with *Haiguo Tuzhi, Yinghuan Zhilue* written by Xu Jiyu is not as long and diversified. It is only an introduction to the world geography. Unlike Wei Yuan who expressed his opinions in the form of essays, Xu Jiyu only made remarks along with his passages. One thing that distinguishes Xu Jiyu from Wei Yuan lies in the tone of the work translated. It seems that Wei Yuan used the derogatory Chinese character Yi meaning barbarians all the way through, but you can rarely find this character in Xu Jiyu's book. The reason was said to be that Xu Jiyu had turned those irreverent characters into something neutral after the first version. Thus, when it was published in 1848, most of the character Yi were deleted and the tone of the book became objective and peaceful.

Fig. 2-3 徐继畬

Having worked as the Governor of Fujian (福建布政使), Xu Jiyu had the opportunity to get in touch with Western missionaries and doctors whom he often consulted about the geographical and political knowledge of the other countries. From those contacts, Xu Jiyu was aware that previously the Chinese people did not truly understand the Westerners and he was eager to let the Chinese know how the Westerners really looked like. So his main purpose of writing this work was to pass information to the Chinese people. But what

Wei Yuan intended to do was to bring those Westerners under control, which was of the Celestial Empire mentality. While Wei Yuan was highly vigilant against the Westerners' ambition of occupying Chinese territories, Xu Jiyu's worries were much on Chinese own military strength as shown in the following passage:

> The intractable barbarians depend on trade for their livelihood and regard profit as their sole goal. They did not want to attack (our) cities, steal land, and occupy territory. All they wanted (originally) was to secure some famous Chinese harbors in order to facilitate the trade of their goods. (But) now they see our officials and soldiers have been regularly defeated in these years, and they know China is weak and incapable (of defense). As (Britain's) desires increase, the more cunning are her plans. If we do not defeat their vanguard decisively there will be no end to it. (Drake, 1975: 26)

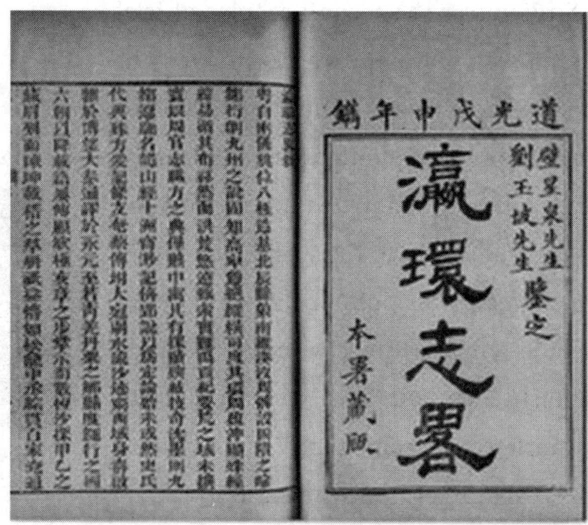
道光戊申年鐫
壁星泉先生
劉玉坡先生
鑒定
瀛環志畧
本署藏版

Fig. 2–4 《瀛寰志略》

The book *Yinghuan Zhilue* drew on many reliable sources of recent Western publications, such as printed books, periodicals, newspapers as well as manuscripts, and Xu Jiyu checked with his Western friends regarding the accuracy of the information collected. Those materials were provided by the Protestant missionaries, such as William Milne (米怜), Walter Henry Medhurst (麦都思), Karl Friedrich August Gutzlaff (郭实腊), and Elijah Coleman Bridgman (俾治文). The people he sought help from were mainly David Abeel (雅裨理), an interpreter of Britain's first consul in Amoy[1], Captain Henry

1 Amoy 是威妥玛式拼法，指厦门。广东、广西及福建地名拼法是根据客家语、粤语、闽语的发音而来的。

Gribble, George Tradescant Lay, a naturalist, Rutherford Alcock (阿礼国), the British consul, and two doctors: Dr Cumming and Dr James Curtis Hepburn (Drake, 1975). Revision based on the talk with the above mentioned people had ensured the quality of Xu Jiyu's book.

A look at some sections taken from *Yinghuan Zhilue* could give us some knowledge of Xu Jiyu's idea. First of all, Xu Jiyu corrected the wrong notion of the Chinese that China was at the center of the world.

> Asia extends north to the Arctic Ocean[1], east to the Great Ocean-Sea (Pacific), and south to the Indian Sea; it includes all of the Moslem areas in the west and extends to the Black Sea in the southwest. Of the four continents Asia is the largest. China is located in the southeastern portion (of Asia). (Drake, 1975: 63)
>
> 亚细亚者，北尽北冰海，东尽大洋海……西南抵黑海，在四土中为最大。中国在其东南。（徐继畬，2006：2）

As a matter of fact, when Matteo Ricci came to China in the late Ming Dynasty, he brought with him a world map and showed it to the scholar officials and gentry in the court. The knowledge of the world geography came to be known to the Chinese at that time. It was only because of the Seclusion Policy adopted especially by Yongzheng (雍正) and Qianlong in the Qing Dynasty that kept people in the dark. Now thanks to Xu Jiyu's efforts, the knowledge came to the Chinese again.

As we know, the Chinese began to dislike the Japanese from the Yuan Dynasty when Kublai Khan failed to subdue them. From then on, the Japanese pirates began to harass China along the coast. Therefore, the Chinese did not have a good impression on the Japanese. But when describing the Japanese people, Xu Jiyu did not seem to bear any grudge against them. Instead, he could take an objective tone and narrate them as they really were, which was not so easy at that time. Take a look at the following introduction to the Japanese people:

> Japan was known in ancient times as Wo-nu ("dwarf-slaves", a pejorative term dating from at least as early as the *Hou Han Shu*[2])...Laws are strictly enforced and the people seldom fight. Those who have broken the law go at once to (a) ravine[3] and

1 the Arctic Ocean 指北冰洋。

2 *Hou Han Shu* 指《后汉书》，作者是范晔。

3 ravine 指峡谷。

commit suicide. To summon a servant-boy one has only to clap and he will respond; a whole day may pass without hearing a person's voice. (Drake, 1975: 73)

日本古称倭奴……立法严，人少斗争，犯法者辄走山谷自杀。呼童仆鸣掌则应，竟日不闻人声。（徐继畬，2006：10）

You can see how impartial Xu Jiyu was when depicting his opponents. Perhaps Xu realized that no matter what discord the two nations had, he needed to write what was true about this nation. So he kept his tone calm and undisturbed.

(The Japanese) love Buddha and revere their ancestors. If they obtain fragrant flowers or good fruit, they must offer this (them) to Buddha or present it (them) to their ancestors' graves. It is the custom to esteem cleanliness; the streets are always swept. Men and women both (wear garments) with large collars and broad sleeves. (Drake, 1975: 73)

好佛，敬祖先，得鲜花佳果，必供佛，或走献祖坟。俗尚洁，街衢时时扫涤。男女皆大领阔袖……（徐继畬，2006：10）

The women all fix up their hair and wash it daily; for fragrance they wash it with cedar[1]...Both the men and women have handsome features and look similar to (the) Chinese. Truly the elegance of the East is gathered here. (Drake, 1975: 74)

女多美发，日洗涤，熏以楠沈……其男女眉目肌理，仿佛华土，信东方秀气之所钟也。（徐继畬，2006：10、12）

In describing the Europeans, Xu Jiyu was trying to take an objective tone as well though many of them had invaded China and signed unequal treaties with China. But facts were facts. Xu Jiyu did not want to be blinded by what they did in the past and tried to present them as they were. The Europeans were different from the Chinese in which they attended to details a great deal, which enabled them to be creative in producing something new. Look at the following passage:

The people are by disposition (inclined to work with) minute details. They are talented in dealing with ideas and making things. Their work in metal and wood is so ingenious that it is hard to believe. Their use of water and fire (for power) is especially marvelous. Firearms were first invented in China, but other lands copied these and improved on them to make them wonderfully excellent. (Drake, 1975: 115)

1 cedar 指雪松。

欧罗巴人“长于制器。金木之工，精巧不可思议。运用水火，尤为奇妙。火器创自中国，彼土仿而为之，益加精妙。铸造之工，施放之敏，殆所独擅”。（徐继畲，2006：117）

Their work in making castings[1] and the refinements[2] of their (cannon) are dared by them alone. Their vessels are especially marvelous; their sails, ropes, and tools are all finely made. In surveying the maritime routes they record depths in every place without missing by a foot or an inch. That they have come across 70,000 *li* to China is no accident. (Drake, 1975: 116)

造舟尤极奥妙，蓬索器具，无一不精。测量海道，处处志其浅深，不失尺寸。越七万里而通于中土，非偶然也。（徐继畲，2006：117）

As a Chinese official who received good education and possessed keen observation and vision, Xu Jiyu tried to present what it was about the Westerners to the Chinese people and didn't want to obscure their true personality. Then, Xu Jiyu went on to introduce the Portuguese. As we know, the Portuguese were the first nation that invaded and occupied the Chinese territory Macao, due to the Treaty of Tordesillas (《托德西勒斯条约》)[3] signed between Spain and Portugal in which Pope Alexander Ⅵ (教皇亚历山大六世) divided the hemisphere into two parts. The Western part was for the Spanish to explore and colonize while the Eastern part was for the Portuguese to explore. Thus, the Portuguese came to China and occupied Macao. Let's see how Xu Jiyu described the Portuguese:

The Portuguese were skilled in reckoning with mathematical and astronomical instruments, measuring the movement of the sun and the courses of stars. They used calculations to know directions and distances on water and land. In the early Ming period their king sent men who were good at managing boats to sail large war vessels to the south. (Drake, 1975: 125-126)

葡萄牙人精于算术，习天文，用仪器测量日出入并星缠度数，知水陆之方向远近。明初，其国王遣善操舟者，驾巨舰南行……（徐继畲，2006：239）

---

1 castings 指铸件。

2 refinements 指改进。

3 the Treaty of Tordesillas 是在西班牙与葡萄牙之间达成的开发殖民地协议。教皇亚历山大六世将地球在大西洋亚速尔群岛和佛得角群岛 100 里格（约为 550 千米）的地方，从北极到南极划一条分界线。线东部新开发的殖民地属于葡萄牙，线西部新开发的殖民地属于西班牙（吴彦鹏，2016）。具体原因参见第 3 章。

> They turned eastward from the western coast of Africa, passed the eastern coast and pressed on eastward to Malacca (马六甲)...The Portuguese then established a port at Macao; this was the first time that a European state had traded in Kwangtung. (Drake, 1975: 125-126)
>
> 由亚非利加之西境，转而东，历亚非利加之东境，抵五印度之西境。复转而东至麻剌甲，又从苏门答腊、葛罗巴之海峡遍历东南洋诸岛国。所至辄留葡人，营立埔头……葡萄牙人遂立埔头于澳门，是为欧罗巴诸国通市粤东之始。（徐继畬，2006：239）

When it came to Great Britain, Xu Jiyu continued to use an objective tone and went to great length to show to the Chinese what the British really looked like in order to understand what kind of people the Chinese were dealing with. As has been stated by Wei Yuan, you needed to know who your enemies were before you were able to confront them. The following quotes are taken from *Yinghuan Zhilue*:

> The British are tall and dazzling white; their hair and eyes are either black or yellowish-red. Their clever schemes are precise; in their actions they firmly endure, and their manner is brave and determined. Their resolution (has made Britain) foremost of the various European states. (Drake, 1975: 142)
>
> 英吉利之人，身材长大白皙，须发与睛或黑色，或黄赤色。心计精密，作事坚忍，气豪胆壮，为欧罗巴诸国之冠。（徐继畬，2006：262）
>
> The British custom when guest and host meet is to take off their hats (as a sign of) respect; each extends his right hand and they mutually grasp (hands) as a ritual. Outside of kneeling in worship to their god, they do not kowtow to their king...the men constantly obey the orders of their women, and this is true of the whole state. (Drake, 1975: 142)
>
> 英俗，宾主相见，以脱帽为恭，各伸右手相握为礼。除跪拜天帝救世主外，见君王亦无叩头之礼。尊卑杂坐，无上下左右之分。（徐继畬，2006：262–263）

Since China was extremely isolated from the outside world, few people knew Western culture and their customs before the First Opium War of 1840. If the cultural knowledge of the West was known to the Chinese people, the emperor might have had a second thought about the kowtow rituals when Lord Macartney came.

The figure Xu Jiyu paid great tribute to was George Washington, the first president of the United States. He admired Washington's generosity and refusal to continue to be in the office after seven years (1789–1796) of service as President of the United States (伍德, 2018). And he also expressed his admiration for such a good administration.

> When Washington had settled the country, he handed over his military authority and desired to return to his fields. The people were unwilling to part with him and chose him to be the state's ruler (*kuo-chu*). Washington then said to the people that it was selfish to take a state and pass it on to one's descendants; he said it was better to choose a person of virtue for the responsibility of governing people... (Drake, 1975: 164)
>
> 顿既定国，谢兵柄欲归田，众不肯舍，坚推立为国王。顿乃与众议曰："得国而传子孙，是私也。牧民之任，宜择有德者为之。"（徐继畬，2006：300）
>
> Washington was an extraordinary man. In raising a revolt, he was more courageous than (Ch'en) Sheng or (Wu) Guang. In carrying out an occupation, he was braver than Ts'ao (Ts'ao) or Liu (Pei). When he took up the three-foot, double-edged sword and opened up the boundaries for ten thousand *li*, he did not assume the throne and was unwilling to begin a line of succession. (Drake, 1975: 164)
>
> 华盛顿，异人也。起事勇于胜、广，割据雄于曹、刘。既已提三尺剑，开疆万里，乃不僭位号，不传子孙……（徐继畬，2006：301）

Xu Jiyu's book was motivated by China's loss in the First Opium War. As the Governor of Fujian, Xu Jiyu witnessed how the Chinese were defeated by the British and he felt intensely about this failure and decided to write a book to let the Chinese understand the outside world. *Yinghuan Zhilue* was finished in 1848, but not well received among officials. Even Zeng Guofan did not think it right for Xu Jiyu to praise the Westerners for their intelligence and institution (孙丽萍, 2008). The Case of Shenguang Temple (神光寺) which happened in 1851 in Fuzhou eventually led to his downfall (王龙, 2014). Emperor Xianfeng (咸丰) blamed Xu Jiyu for his belatedness in solving the problem that two Englishmen, one doctor and one missionary, rented a place there for six months. According to the Treaty of Nanjing, the Westerners were not allowed to reside inside the treaty port. But Xu Jiyu wanted to smoothly resolve the problem instead of abruptly forcing them to leave. Due to his inaction, Xu Jiyu was removed from office in 1852 and went back home in Shanxi Province. Xu Jiyu's dismissal was also related to his newly published book for thinking highly of the Western civilization. An enlightenment thinker like Xu Jiyu had such miserable experience, which was a great loss to China's advancement in technology and institution.

2.3 The Response Difference Between China and Japan 中国与日本的不同反应

Neither Wei Yuan's *Haiguo Tuzhi* nor Xu Jiyu's *Yinghuan Zhilue* were welcome in China after publication but both books were warmly received in Japan and had a great impact on the Japanese Meiji Restoration in 1868. Deng Tingnan (邓廷桢), Wei Yuan's colleague thought it impossible to contain the foreigners using their techniques. In the same manner, Zeng Guofan sneezed at *Yinghuan Zhilue* because Xu Jiyu highly lauded George Washington, the first president of the United States and commended the American institution. In Zeng Guofan's opinion, China should never learn the political system from the foreigners, but stick to the hierarchical system under the principle of benevolence (孙丽萍, 2008).

Ma Yong (马勇) summarized the reasons for *Haiguo Tuzhi* not to gain the respect it deserved. The Chinese rulers refused to make any progress because they were still intoxicated by the self-knitted myth of the "Flourishing Age" (盛世). Some Chinese elites showed no support for Wei Yuan due to their fear of offending the emperor. Others attributed the failure of the First Opium War to the poor technology compared with Britain and some treacherous officials who ruined Lin Zexu. They firmly believed that Lin Zexu would have the ability to defeat the British invaders (佚名, 2005). Although Wei Yuan suggested that the Chinese should face the challenges posed by the Westerners by developing our own industry, commerce, ship transportation, and financial industry, he also introduced the political system of Britain and America, their election system, judicial system of power separation. Wei Yuan urged the Chinese to broaden their horizons and open their mind instead of regarding Western civilization as great scourges (洪水猛兽) or dreadful monsters. However, Wei Yuan's efforts received no response because the Chinese during that period of time did not realize the inevitability of China's failure in the First Opium War, neither did they know the essential distinction between Western and Chinese civilizations (马勇, 2014).

However, both *Haiguo Tuzhi* and *Yinghuan Zhilue* attracted great attention when they were transported to Japan by Chinese merchants who wanted to find a market there during 1851–1856 (范凡, 2011). Having read the book, Sakuma Shōzan, a Confucian, very much agreed with what Wei Yuan had said, i.e. to contain the foreigners using their techniques because the distinction between the Chinese and barbarians advocated by Confucianism could no longer explain the situation faced by Japan and Sakuma Shōzan was shocked at China's defeat in the First Opium War. Similarly, what Yoshida Shōin had learned from *Haiguo Tuzhi* was that if you were not good at learning from the foreigners, you would certainly be beaten by them (王文勋，张文颖, 2014) and he put forward the political stance, i.e. "Honor the king and drive off the barbarians" (马国川, 2018).

According to Ma Guochuan, Yoshida Shōin established an old-style private school (私塾) and used *Haiguo Tuzhi* as the textbook. Among the talents trained from the Yoshida Shōin's school are the founders of the Japanese Meiji Restoration, i.e. Kido Takayoshi (木户孝允), Yamagata Aritomo (山县有朋), and Itō Hirobumi (伊藤博文) (马国川, 2018).

Huang Wenxiong (黄文雄), a Taiwan scholar, commented that the 200,000 new Chinese characters created by the Japanese reformers during the period between the late Shogunate (幕府末期) and the Japanese Meiji Restoration played an important role in transmitting information and new concepts in the areas of society, natural sciences and journalism to China and 85% of the legal characters used in China's constitution originated from the Japanese newly coined words via Chinese characters. The modern Chinese characters, such as right (权利), authority (权威), rights and interests (权益), -ism (主义), and revolution (革命) are all borrowed from the Japanese (徐瑾, 2016).

Having made little impact on China's reform, Wei Yuan and Xu Jiyu's ideas enlightened the Japanese people, who took the lesson from China's failure in the First Opium War and avoided confrontations with America. After Admiral Perry's (佩里将军) arrival, the Japanese realized Japan was left far behind those Western countries and decided to catch up by absorbing Western science and technology, and the ideas behind them. Within nearly thirty years (1868–1895), Japan rose to power and turned their role from a student to a teacher of China. But it took China more than half of a century (1842–1895) to realize the necessity of learning from the West and the important role played by their legal system and political institution in modernity.

◆ Topics for Discussion

1. Why did Emperor Daoguang know so little about the invaders?

2. Your comment on Wei Yuan's statement: "To beat foreigners by learning their advantages."

3. Why did the First Opium War have little impact on Chinese scholar officials?

4. Your comment on Xu Jiyu's attitude to foreigners.

5. The impact of *Haiguo Tuzhi* and *Yinghuan Zhilue* on Japan.

6. Your comment on the quick response of the Japanese to foreign invasions.

◆ Reading Assignments

1. Hsu, I. C. Y. 2000. Chapter 9 of *The Rise of Modern China*. Oxford: Oxford University Press.

2. Fairbank, J. K., and Goldman, M. 2006. *China: A New History.* Cambridge: The Belknap Press of Harvard University Press.

◆ Bibliography

Drake, F. W. 1975. *China Charts the World: Hsu Chi-yu and His Geography of 1848*. Cambridge: Harvard University Press.

Geng, Y. Z. 2015. *An Introductory Study on China's Cultural Transformation in Recent Times*. Beijing and Berlin: Foreign Language Teaching and Research Press and Springer-Verlag Berlin Heidelberg.

Leonard, J. K. 1984. *Wei Yuan and China's Rediscovery of the Maritime World*. Cambridge and London: Council on East Asian Studies.

Liu, J. P. 2006. The Evolution of Tianxia Cosmology and Its Philosophical Implications. In P. M. Mitchell (trans.), The Limits of Reformism: Wei Yuan's Reaction to Western Intrusion. *Modern Asian Studies*, *6*(2): 175-204.

Smith, R. J. 1976. Reflections on the Comparative Study of Modernization in China and Japan: Military Aspects. *Journal of the Hong Kong Branch of the Royal Asiatic Society*, *16*: 12-24.

Wakeman, F. J. 1975. *The Fall of Imperial China*. New York: The Free Press.

丁守和. 1999. 中国近代启蒙思潮：上卷. 北京：社会科学文献出版社.

范凡. 2011. 晚清中国“西学”对日本的影响：以《瀛寰志略》为例. 文学界，(12)：120–121.

戈登·伍德. 2018. 革命品格：建国者何以与众不同?. 周顺，译. 上海：上海人民出版社.

何兆武，柳卸林. 2011. 中国印象：外国名人论中国文化. 北京：中国人民大学出版社.

马国川. 2018. 国家的启蒙：日本帝国崛起之源. 北京：中信出版集团有限股份公司.

马勇. 2014.《海国图志》：一本启发了日本的中国新书. 07–31. 新京报.

孙丽萍. 2008. 徐继畬的开放思想与中国近代化进程. 晋阳学刊，(6)：35–39.

王龙. 2014. 徐继畬：“东方伽利略”的遭遇. 同舟共进，(3)：72–77.

王文勋，张文颖. 2014. 日本明治维新时期的舆论研究. 北京：中国传媒大学出版社.

魏源. 1998. 海国图志. 长沙：岳麓书社.

吴彦鹏. 2016. 教皇子午线. 06–21. 文明百科.

吴泽，黄丽镛. 1963. 魏源《海国图志》研究. 历史研究，(4)：117–140.

徐春伟. 2018. 一部晚清汉译地理名著，如何影响了近代日本的世界观?. 05–05. 澎湃新闻.

徐继畬. 2006. 瀛寰志略校注. 宋大川，校注. 北京：文物出版社.

徐瑾. 2016. 魏源在日本. 04–02. 中国经营报.

徐中约. 2012. 中国近代史. 北京：世界图书出版公司.

佚名. 2005.《海国图志》成明治维新催化剂，在日本洛阳纸贵. 05–26. 中国青年报.

佚名. 2019. 威妥玛式拼音法. 09–05. 百度百科.

约翰·海达德. 2013. 初闯中国：美国对华贸易、条约、鸦片和救赎的故事. 广东：花城出版社.

曾燕，涂楠. 2012. 撬动中国，向近代转型的坚实支点：徐继畬“大变局”认识与涉外实务研究. 成都：四川大学出版社.

Chapter Three

Aisin Gioro Yixin and Zongli Yamen

爱新觉罗 · 奕䜣与总理衙门

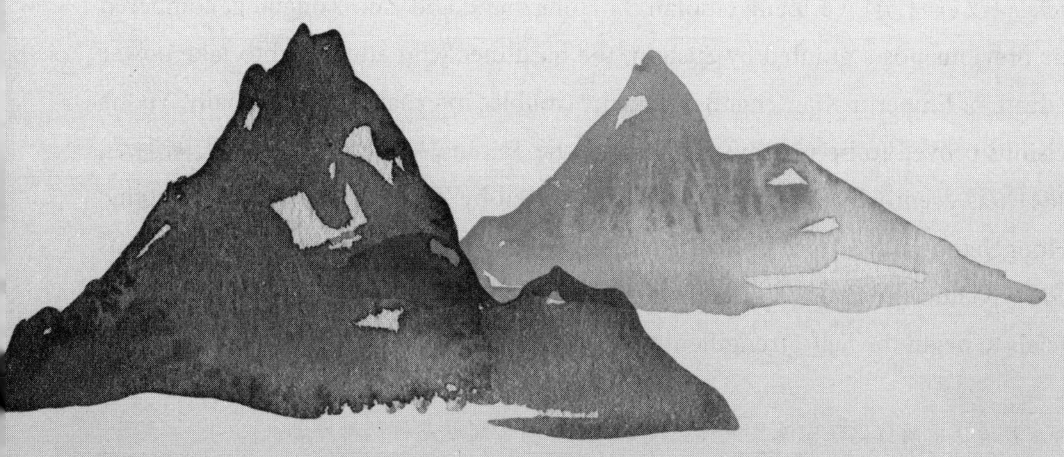

西方的坚船利炮不但打开了中国的大门，还迫使清政府用条约制度替换纳贡体制。在经过了阵痛之后，洋务派领袖爱新觉罗·奕䜣决定学习西方的“游戏”规则，以便在国际争端中有可供参照的条例。于是，《万国公法》进入了晚清政府官员的视野。美国传教士丁韪良和英国翻译赫德在将惠顿的《万国公法》译成汉语方面起到了举足轻重的作用。

3.1 Yixin 奕䜣

Emperor Xianfeng's runaway to Re He in September 1860 and the signing of the Treaty of Beijing put Yixin, Prince Gong, to the front desk. He was granted by the emperor to be responsible for foreign affairs in Beijing. In dealing with Western powers, Prince Gong took a different attitude from the hardliners[1], such as Xianfeng and Sushun (肃顺) who were extremely anti-foreign. Having suffered from humiliations and the agonizing moment, Yixin strongly felt the necessity to make concessions with the Westerners and the importance to abide by the clauses delineated in the treaties. Given the fact that the breach of the treaties caused tremendous losses for China, Yixin decided to gain knowledge from the international rules. And in the meantime, it was highly imperative for the Chinese to learn from the Westerners in terms of military weapons and manufacturing technology.

Fig. 3-1 恭亲王奕䜣

Being open-minded and far-sighted, Prince Gong endowed more power with the Han officials (汉族官员), i.e. Zeng Guofan, Li Hongzhang and Zuo Zongtang, compared with their previous posts granted by Sushun, the hardliner who attempted to take power after the death of Emperor Xianfeng. Beset by the troubles internally and externally, Yixin's bold decisions proved to be worthwhile because the Taiping Movement (太平天国运动, 1850–1864) was eventually suppressed by the army led by Zeng Guofan, Zuo Zongtang, and Li Hongzhang with a joint effort of the foreign-led troops, i.e. the Ever Victorious Army (常胜军) and the Ever Triumphant Army (常捷军). Yixin also relied on the three Han officials to begin the Self-Strengthening Movement.

1 hardliners 指清廷中的极端保守派，或称强硬派。咸丰与肃顺就是极端排外者。

Yixin's courage was also exhibited in the coup d'etat of Xinyou (辛酉政变) in 1861 conspired jointly with the two dowagers: Empress Cixi (慈禧) and Empress Ci'an (慈安). Seeing that Sushun and other princes plotted to take the emperor's place, Yixin, with the help of his confidants Wenxiang (文祥), Guiliang (桂良), Baojun (宝鋆), and Shengbao (胜保), was able to arrest and kill those rebels. But the decisive allies came from the British Minister or Envoy Frederick Bruce (卜鲁斯) and his secretary Thomas Wade (威妥玛). Compared with Sushun, the British preferred Yixin to be in power because of his open-mindedness and willingness to co-operate with the Westerners. According to Guo Tingyi (郭廷以, 2012b), it was under the encouragement from the British envoy that Yixin decided to seize power from Sushun et al. And the bargain he made with Cixi might be to become Prince Regent (议政王) (郭廷以, 2012b).

The lesson Yixin took from the late emperor's disregard of the treaty obligations was indeed profound. One of the provisions of the Treaty of Tianjin read that British representatives were allowed to reside in Beijing but Emperor Xianfeng was trying to defy it. First of all, the emperor offered to cancel the tariff levied on foreign goods if Britain agreed to undo the treaty. Seeing the impossibility, Xianfeng issued a decree to change the place of exchanging ratification from Beijing to Shanghai. The landing port had also been unilaterally changed from Dagu (大沽)[1] to Beitang (北塘)[2], where the Qing army led by Senggelinqin (僧格林沁), the Mongol General, ambushed the British troops. The breach of the treaty obligations reached its peak when Sir Harry Parkes (巴夏礼爵士), British Consul in Guangzhou and thirty-eight of his men including Henry Loch, Nal Singh and two French soldiers were detained in September 1858 and twenty-one of them were tortured to death. This incident extremely angered Lord Elgin (额尔金勋爵)[3], High Commissioner and Plenipotentiary in China (驻华高级专员兼全权代表) who ordered to burn the Old Summer Palace, i.e. Yuanmingyuan Garden to its ashes (邓, 2013).

Having witnessed all those confrontations and losses, Yixin decided to establish a foreign affairs office, which was called Zongli Yamen (总理衙门)[4], and introduced the international law to Chinese officials.

1 大沽的威妥玛式拼法为 Taku。

2 北塘的威妥玛式拼法为 Peitang。

3 额尔金勋爵是苏格兰贵族封号，1633 年 6 月确立并授予享有盛誉的布鲁斯家族。此处的额尔金名为 James Bruce，是额尔金第八伯爵（the eighth Earl of Elgin）。

4 总理衙门的威妥玛式拼法为 Tsungli Yamen。总理衙门为清政府办理洋务及外交事务、派出驻外国使节，并兼管通商、海防、关税、路矿、邮电、军工、同文馆、派遣留学生等事务而特设的中央机构。

3.2 Zongli Yamen 总理衙门

Fig. 3–2 总理衙门

The establishment of Zongli Yamen in 1861 indicated that the Qing government began to act according to the Treaty of Beijing and handle diplomacy with the Western powers on an equal footing. Unlike what was practiced previously, foreign relations to the Manchu court meant tributary relations (纳贡关系) and came under Beijing's Board of Rites (礼部), or Lifan Yuan (理藩院), managing affairs of Mongolians, Muslims, and Tibetan ethnic minorities, as well as foreign affairs concerning Russia (佚名, 2019c). European maritime trading powers were handled by high provincial officials, i.e. viceroy. Yixin, at this moment, needed to find certain principles mutually understood and shared by both sides in order to guide his actions. Twenty years ago, when Lin Zexu was trying to solve opium smuggling problems with the Westerners, he invited Peter Parker, an American doctor in Guangzhou to translate *International Law* written by Vattel (瓦泰尔), a Swiss law expert (林学忠, 2009). But Henry Wheaton's (惠顿) *Elements of International Law* (《万国公法》) was much more popular and widely used in solving diplomatic issues.

Here we need to introduce the American missionary William Alexander Parsons Martin (丁韪良), who was the first Westerner who had translated and later published Wheaton's *Elements of International Law* in 1865 for the use of the Qing government (林学忠, 2009). Martin was quick to learn new dialect when he came to Ningbo, China between 1850 and 1860 and was able to speak Ningbo dialect, in addition to the mandarin and Beijing dialect. When the Treaty of Tianjin was negotiated between China and America, Martin was hired in June 1858 as the interpreter for William Bradford Reed (列维廉),

the American Minister Plenipotentiary (美国全权公使) and his secretary Samuel Wells Williams (卫三畏). The negotiation did not go on smoothly and for three days the two sides spent seven hours on June 14, five hours on June 15, and another seven hours on June 17. The Qing government sent Guiliang and Huashana (花沙纳) to discuss the issues and Martin had witnessed the whole process. Perhaps it was because the Chinese knew little about the diplomatic rules adopted by the Westerners that Martin decided to translate Wheaton's book into Chinese in order to help them understand the principles followed by most Western countries.

In his autobiography *A Cycle of Cathay, or China, South and North* (《花甲忆记——一位美国传教士眼中的晚清帝国》[1], 1896), Martin clearly recorded some unhappy incidents which happened between the diplomats of Britain and America and the Qing government officials. Immediately after the signing of the Treaty of Tianjin between Britain and China on June 19, 1858, the Chinese envoy informed that their emperor firmly refused to accept some of the important items proposed by the British envoys. The emperor disagreed to allow the foreign envoys to reside in Beijing and rejected free trade across the country. A week later however, the British plenipotentiary Lord Elgin obtained the treaty with the signature of the Imperial Commissioner. On another occasion, the thorny issue of kowtow to the emperor became increasingly problematic and it took both sides two-week's time for discussion. Under the insistence on the part of the American envoy not to perform kowtow, the concession had been made by the Chinese side. But on the day of the audience, the message brought by the Daotai (道台)[2] was that the foreigners needed to follow all the rituals required of the Chinese tradition, i.e. kneeling down and performing kowtow in front of the emperor. When the Americans refused, the venue of exchanging rarified copies of their treaties was changed to some coastal city instead of Beijing.

Viewing all those frictions and collisions, Martin might have thought it extremely necessary to turn *Elements of International Law* into Chinese so that the Manchu government would have some ideas regarding diplomatic procedures followed by European countries. It was also because of this translated version that Anson Burlingame (安森·蒲安臣), the American Envoy (美国公使), introduced Martin to Yixin in case that this document could be of use to Chinese officials. During the following years, Prince Gong found Wheaton's *Elements of International Law* very useful in solving diplomatic problems.

1 后文简称为《花甲忆记》。

2 道台的威妥玛式拼法为 Tao-tai。

For instance, in 1864 the Prussian minister M. von Rehfues (普鲁士公使李福斯) accidentally captured three Danish vessels off the Chinese coast because the two countries were at war. But Prince Gong found it a serious problem if China failed to stop the war between the two foreign countries in China's coastal areas, and it would set a bad example for other countries. So Yixin immediately protested the Prussian wrongdoing and quoted Wheaton's principles on questions of jurisdiction (管辖权) within a nation's coastal waters. To his great surprise, without saying a word Rehfues backed off and released the Danish vessels. Such an incident taught Prince Gong a good lesson which was how useful Wheaton was in dealing with international conflicts (Haddad, 2013).

The second lesson learned was from the Lay-Osborne Flotilla. Chief Inspector Horatio Nelson Lay (李泰国) was sent by Zongli Yamen to purchase a flotilla of gunboats in Britain in order to confront the Taiping group. But Lay's secret intention was to have full control over the flotilla and use it to patrol the Yangtze River (长江) and crush piracy. He also appointed Sherard Osborne (阿思本) as Captain of the small fleet. Nobody noticed it because the document was ambiguously written. When it came back in 1863, Prince Gong discovered Lay's real motive and consulted Anson Burlingame, the American consular about the issue. The reason was that Prince Gong did not want to offend Britain and as a neutral state America could mediate between China and Britain. With the effort of Burlingame, the British minister Frederick Bruce agreed to arrange the flotilla to return to England. The Qing government dismissed Lay as Customs Inspector and replaced him with Robert Hart (罗伯特·赫德) who worked as Inspector General (总税务司) in Chinese Customs House for 45 years (1863–1908) (Haddad, 2013).

The third incident took place in 1885 during the Sino-French War when the French destroyed the Chinese fleet and seized their arsenal in Fuzhou, Fujian Province. Zongli Yamen consulted William Alexander Parsons Martin in terms of dealing with the enemy's non-combatants (敌方居民) according to the international law. Martin showed part of the international law translated by himself and soon China declared war against France and they issued a decree that the French residents would be guaranteed safety if they did not join the hostile act and sure enough the Qing government kept its promise and all of the French missionaries were protected and the issue was resolved (Martin, 2005).

Having experienced those incidents and seen the necessity of the knowledge of the international law, Yixin persuaded the emperor to publish Wheaton's *Elements of International Law* so that they had something to abide by when dealing with foreign affairs. The Qing government agreed in 1864 and sponsored 500 *taels* of silver to print it out in 1865.

From what has been discussed above, we can see that Yixin was a man with rationality and he could make sensible decisions by weighing advantages and disadvantages. The Sino-French War (1883–1885) was a case in point. Yixin disagreed to stage war against France given that they only wanted to open a route of trade in the Red River in Tongking, Vietnam[1] and they thought it a better route compared with the Mekong[2] to China's Yunnan Province. As such France signed a new treaty in 1874 with Vietnam which confirmed the French possession of Cochin China, i.e. the three eastern provinces of Annam. China had suffered losses in the Taiwan crisis and the Margary murder. But the Qingliu Group (清流党) represented by Zhang Zhidong and Zhang Peilun (张佩纶) were strongly for a war because they thought protecting a tributary state like Vietnam was the duty of the Qing government. Worse still, Cixi, the person at the top, was vacillating between keeping the honor of China and the power of the Western country and eventually spoiled the opportunity to win the battle. The price China paid was the failure of the self-strengthening efforts (Hsu, 2000).

3.3 *Elements of International Law* 《万国公法》

Fig. 3-3 丁韪良译《万国公法》

Lin Zexu, the Imperial Commissioner, was the first Chinese who used the international law to deal with the British opium smugglers during the First Opium War.

1 the Red River in Tongking, Vietnam 指越南铜陵红河。其中，Tongking 是威妥玛式拼法。

2 Mekong 指湄公河，是威妥玛式拼法。

Just before the war, Lin Zexu asked Dr Peter Parker (伯驾医生), the American medical missionary to translate three paragraphs of Vattel's *International Law* into Chinese, regarding war, counter measures (应对措施), blockades (封锁) and embargoes (禁运) (Hsu, 2000; 林学忠, 2009). However, the British thought their life and property were threatened because of the six-week siege. Therefore they initiated the First Opium War.

Modern international law could be traced back to the Dutch jurist Hugo Grotius (格劳秀斯), who wrote *The Freedom of the Seas* in 1608 to make the case that the Netherlands had the right to sail to the West Indies (西印度群岛) when obstructed by the Portuguese. During the 15th century, the Portuguese discovered and colonized some of African territories and tried to explore more, which won the praise of Pope Nicolas Ⅴ (教皇尼古拉斯五世) who in 1454 gave the ownership of the lands discovered or to be discovered to Portugal. However, when Christopher Columbus (哥伦布) in 1492 discovered the new continent in America, Pope Alexander Ⅵ authorized Spain to look after the lands discovered and yet to be discovered. This caused disputes between Portugal and Spain, leading to the decision of the Pope to draw a line from the North Pole to the South Pole along Cape Verde (佛得角) and the Azores Islands (亚速尔群岛) in the middle of the Atlantic Ocean. The areas to the west belonged to the Spaniards and the areas to the east belonged to the Portuguese. In 1494, the Treaty of Tordesillas was signed by both Spain and Portugal, which indicated Spain occupied most of the Americas while Portugal had Africa and Brazil in its control. That explains why people in Brazil speak Portuguese nowadays while people living in the rest of South America speak Spanish (吴彦鹏, 2016).

Dutch East India Company formed in 1602 attempted to trade with the East Indies but was obstructed by the Portuguese who claimed the Atlantic south of Morocco (摩洛哥) and the Indian Ocean. Thus the Dutch captured a Portuguese galleon. Upon this young Grotius was consulted and wrote his treatise on the law of the prize, which was published later under the title of *The Freedom of the Seas* when the Netherlands was dealing with the Spanish requirement for the right to trade in the East and West Indies (Grotius, 1916). Based on the natural law (自然法), Grotius argued that "every nation is free to travel to every other nation, and to trade with it" because the law we observed was derived from nature, "whose bounty falls on all, and whose sway extends over those who rule nations, and which is held most sacred by those who are most scrupulously just" (Grotius, 1916: 10). Just like personal belongings, no one would deny that every man is entitled to manage and dispose of his own property. In the like manner, all the rivers and public places should be accessible to all people because they do not belong to any particular person or state.

Here Grotius introduced the concept of sovereignty (主权) and argued that neither the Spaniards nor the Portuguese had the right to deny the travel of other people in the Indian Ocean or the Atlantic Ocean because neither of them possessed those places. Even if the Pope allowed them to control the areas, it was not justified.

Following Grotius's concept of the natural law, Henry Wheaton, the American jurist introduced some key concepts, such as sovereignty, equality, treaty, and mutual respect. When different nation states (民族国家) interact with each other and come across problems or disputes, they should follow the principles described by Wheaton in order to solve the problems and keep peace. Specifically, the major principles were summarized by He Qinhua (何勤华) (惠顿, 2003: 14-22) as follows:

1. Respect for each nation's sovereignty (尊重各国主权).
2. Equal exchanges among different nations (各国之间平等往来).
3. Compliance with international conventions and bilateral treaties (遵守国际公约和双边条约).

The word "sovereignty" in the first principle above refers to the nation right to protect and dispose of its territory, people and property, and the right to set up the independent legislation, administration, and judiciary. The second principle indicates that every country, no matter its size, should enjoy equal rights in exchanges. For instance, the countries take turns to preside over the international affairs and the use of language is determined by the consent of each country. In addition, the dispatch of diplomatic envoys is negotiated between countries concerned. Finally once the treaties are signed, both sides should strictly comply with the treaties in order to show sincerity.

The Treaty of Nanjing between Britain and China was criticized for its breach of the international law in terms of the extraterritoriality (治外法权) and fixation of tax by way of co-operation between Britain and China. Now let us take a look at these two items in the Treaty of Nanjing and make a close study of it.

Article Ⅰ

There shall henceforward be peace and friendship between Her Majesty the Queen of the United Kingdom of Great Britain and Ireland and His Majesty the Emperor of China, and between their respective subjects, who shall enjoy full security and protection for their persons and property within the dominions of the other. (Anon, 2019)

凡系大英国人，无论本国、属国军民等，今在中国所管辖各地方被禁者，大清大皇帝准即释放。（佚名，2019d）

Normally, a foreign merchant or a business person who breaks the law in another country should be tried and sentenced by the legal system of the target country. But the above rule indicates that foreigners would be tried by their own consuls. In this case, it means the British who stays in China will be tried when breaking the law by the British consuls rather than the Chinese one, i.e. the Chinese recognition of extraterritorial rights (治外法权) of Britain. But what is the reason for that? Why should the British residing in China be protected and secured for their persons and property by their own government, rather than the Chinese government? This has much to do with the British understanding of a civilized nation, which lives up to the standard of a Christian country. In the eyes of the Westerners, China was a non-Christian country, whose legal system was extremely cruel.

Hsu described in his work *The Rise of Modern China* (《中国近代史》) two cases where the suspects were executed without being tried. In the case of 1875, an English seaman was killed by a Chinese, who was immediately sentenced to death and executed. Similarly, in the Lady Hughes incident (“修斯夫人号”事件) which happened on November 24, 1784, two minor mandarins were accidentally killed by the salute cannon. Before the gunner was found out, the supercargo George Smith (乔治·史密斯) was held as a hostage. Smith was eventually released when the gunner was seized and quickly strangled (Hsu, 2000). According to the British law, the two criminals mentioned above did not deserve death. Because of the huge difference in legal systems between the Qing Dynasty and the rest of the Western countries, the British government decided to impose extraterritoriality in the Treaty of Nanjing. The following were the comments made by several foreigners concerning the Chinese legal system.

Lord Napier's failure in his diplomatic endeavor with Lu Kun left an impression on the British that “the emperor's man in Canton had menaced the life of the king's man in Canton; British life, liberty and property had been insulted and lost—insults that British hawks now insisted could only be avenged by an armed response” (Lovell, 2014: 8). This “unjust and oppressive” treatment of foreigners prevented them from trusting the Chinese law.

In a letter to the British Foreign Secretary Viscount Palmerston (巴麦尊子爵), Huyh Hamilton Lindsay (胡夏米), an India company's businessman and one of the leaders of the merchant lobby during the First Opium War expressed tremendous discontent with the Chinese legal system whose statutes concerning murderers went against humanity and reason and he did not think that a foreigner's life and property could be protected by such a law (王建朗, 黄克武, 2016; 林学忠, 2009).

Hosea Ballou Morse (马士), Customs Commissioner under Robert Hart and a historian of China also criticized the Chinese legal system in terms of its arbitration and corruption, which went against the European concept of equality and justice (林学忠, 2009). Chinese scholar officials, such as Guo Songtao (郭嵩焘) admitted what was stated by those foreigners and tried to make a change.

The Western legal system was based on procedural justice (程序正义) and allowed the parties involved to state their opinions and debate with each other before reaching the final decision. Acting as a counterbalance mechanism in the court, the judge, procurator, and lawyer represented three different positions. The lawyer took the position of his defendant. The procurator stood for the state, and the judge took an objective and impartial position to keep the arbitration authoritative. Justice was done in this way. In the Qing court, however, a judge did the job of both the procurator and the detective and completed the investigation of the case before the formal hearing. There was no pleader/defender (辩护人) whatsoever in the process and the whole trial was no more than an announcement of the judgment. Therefore, the legal system in the late Qing period went against that of the Christian countries which defended the values of equality, liberty, security, democracy, justice, and human rights (杨师群, 2012).

Henry Wheaton discussed in *Elements of International Law* the practice that Christian states followed in non-Christian states in terms of jurisdiction, i.e. the Christian powers exercised jurisdiction according to their own law. Look at the excerpt taken from the book:

> ...The resident consuls of the Christian powers in Turkey, the Barbary States[1], and other Mohammedan countries, exercise both civil and criminal jurisdiction over their countrymen, to the exclusion of the local magistrates and tribunals. (Wheaton, Boyd, 1880: 152)

In fact, France and Britain practiced extraterritoriality respectively in 1535 and 1583 in some countries, such as Turkey and the Barbary States (林学忠, 2009). The Westerners

1 the Barbary States 指巴巴里诸国（海盗帝国）。

in the 19th century followed suit in the case of China. Wheaton quoted the Treaty of Wangxia signed in 1844 between China and the United States as follows:

> ...it is stipulated, Art. 21, that "citizens of the United States, who may commit any crime in China, shall be subject to be tried and punished only by the consul, or other public functionary of the United States thereto authorized, according to the laws of the United States". Art. 25. "All questions in regard to rights, whether of property or of person, arising between citizens of the United States and in China, shall be subject to the jurisdiction, and regulated by the authorities, of their own government..." (Wheaton, Boyd, 1880: 152)

The purpose of quoting the Treaty of Wangxia by Wheaton is to justify the extraterritoriality under the principle of the international law. Given that the Chinese legal system in the late Qing Dynasty indeed had problems, it left room for the Qing officials to initiate the New Administration Movement (新政运动) to renovate and transform it. Only in this way could China enter the international community and be accepted as a civilized state.

Article Ⅹ of the Treaty of Nanjing regulated that the taxes paid on imports and exports by British merchants should be discussed and negotiated between China and Britain:

> His Majesty the Emperor of China agrees to establish at all the ports which are, by the 2nd Article of this Treaty, to be thrown open for the resort of British merchants, a fair and regular tariff of export and import customs and other dues (税), which tariff shall be publicly notified (通知) and promulgated (颁布) for general information...(Anon, 2019)
>
> 前第二条内言明开关俾英国商民居住通商之广州等五处，应纳进口、出口货税、饷费，均宜秉公议定则例，由部颁发晓示，以便英商按例交纳……（佚名，2019d）

The above item suggested that China was not treated as an independent country and its sovereignty was violated. Because China's tax system was not in line with that of the Western countries, the problems existing with the Canton System made the British decide to supervise China's Customs House by appointing a foreigner as an inspector. As described by Hall, "The farming of the revenue to the Superintendent of Customs and the bargain system of paying duties—with the unjust exaction, the inequality of treatment, the rapacity of underlings, and the Customs House squalor and corruption which resulted—were among the grievances which had culminated in the war of 1840." (Hall, 2015: 8) That explained why the British authorities insisted on appointing Consuls to dwell at the five treaty ports to function as intermediaries between the Chinese authorities and the merchants. The purpose was "to see that the just dues and duties of the Chinese Government...are duly discharged by her Britannic Majesty's subjects" (Hall, 2015: 8).

For instance, the *lijin* system (厘金制度) practiced from 1853 onwards to gather military power to fight against the Taiping Movement, was much abused by both the ruler and local officials and became an exploitive tool for the people in power. In the late Qing period, goods or commodities were not only charged once on *lijin*, but for many times. There were various checkpoints in different provinces or counties. When passing a checkpoint, the goods would be charged for tax. The times that the goods were charged depended on how many checkpoints they would go through. In the end, the tax one needed to pay was a lot more than expected. What was more, the amount of the *lijin* required increased from 1% in the reign of Emperor Tongzhi (同治) to 5% in the reign of Emperor Guangxu (光绪). And the tax rate could be varied from 5% to 10%. In Jiangsu Province, it even exceeded 10%. That left room for corruption (张浩栋, 2017).

Since the 1870s, some scholar officials had realized the problems in consular jurisdiction caused by the clause of the Treaty of Nanjing, i.e. extraterritoriality. Xue Fucheng (薛福成) noticed the existence of extraterritoriality breached China's judiciary independence. Guo Songtao sent a memorial in 1877 asking the court to compile a trade rule in dealing with disputes with foreigners so as to rectify the unfair trial for the Chinese. Zeng Jize (曾纪泽) in 1879 suggested that China should follow the example of Japan to withdraw the consular jurisdiction (林学忠, 2009).

However, if China wanted to modernize its own legal system and become a member of the international family, it had to make changes first. Song Yuren (宋育仁), the envoy to Britain in 1896 observed the Chinese administration of prison affairs after visiting one of the British prisons. In Britain, prisoners were treated politely. They were questioned about their name, age, dwelling, and education. Then, they were put in a room where furniture, beddings, and books were placed. No prisoners were beaten or tortured. Sentences for minor offences would take two or three days, at most seven days while grave crimes would take forty days to have the decision. However in China, it took a long time for a convict to get the judgment. Minor offences were decided by lower-ranking wardens while heavy felonies would wait for the trial by officials. No specific rules were observed when the final decision was made and the sentence was often made arbitrarily. Before the trial, prisoners were treated badly. They were either beaten or tortured and the warden was not informed. Prisoners were not treated as a human like in Britain.

> 中国之政弊，莫狱为甚。文告即繁，相遁以伪。大讼至系至数年不决，小讼则一听官吏以意为轻重。听断无时。不肖之吏，恃刑求狱，动加桎梏；捕役狱卒，皆籍敲剥为生，相倚为奸，而狱官不诘。民未定罪，先受非法刑求，及入狱门，又有狱卒之私刑拷掠。观于外域之狱政，益恍然其中国迁流之失，大远于先王明刑弼教之心。（郭嵩焘等，2012：334）

Given the malpractice, measures should be taken to change the situation in Chinese prisons before China could modernize itself. Similarly, the tax system should be also reformed and put on the normal track before those unequal clauses could be eradicated.

To summarize, in this chapter we traced back to the history of the application of the international law and discussed in what way Yixin, the head of Zongli Yamen, was willing to abide by the law and solved some international disputes. We have seen the causes that China was willing to enter the international community by learning and following the rules and principles delineated in the international law. Moreover, we have explored the reasons why the British imposed the two unequal clauses in the Treaty of Nanjing on the Chinese.

◆ Topics for Discussion

1. Explain the concept of "sovereignty".
2. Your comment on Yixin's attitude to Han officials.
3. Why is there no mention of "opium" in the Treaty of Nanjing?
4. In what way did extraterritoriality and joint formulation of tax breach the international law?
5. Why was Emperor Xianfeng afraid of foreign envoys who resided in Beijing?
6. Why did Chinese emperors consider rituals as the most important?

Reading Assignment

Hsu, I. C. Y. 2000. Chapter 11 of *The Rise of Modern China*. Oxford: Oxford University Press.

Bibliography

Anon. 2019. Treaty of Nanking. 09–01. From Docin website.

Grotius, H. 1916. *The Freedom of the Seas*. Oxford: Oxford University Press.

Haddad, J. R. 2013. *America's First Adventure in China*. Philadelphia: Temple University Press.

Hall, B. E. F. 2015. *The Chinese Maritime Customs: An International Service, 1854–1950*. Bristol: University of Bristol.

Hsu, I. C. Y. 2000. *The Rise of Modern China*. Oxford: Oxford University Press.

Lovell, J. 2014. *The Opium War*. New York: The Overlook Press and Peter Mayer Publishers, Inc.

Martin, W. A. P. 1896. *A Cycle of Cathay, or China, South and North*. New York: Fleming H. Revell Company.

Martin, W. A. P. 2005. *The Awakening of China*. The Project Gutenberg Ebook.

Smith, R. J., Fairbank, J. K., and Bruner, K. F. 1991. *Robert Hart and China's Early Modernization: His Journals, 1863–1866*. Cambridge: Council on East Asian Studies.

Wheaton, H., and Boyd, A. C. 1880. *Elements of International Law*. London: Stevens & Sons.

丁韪良. 2004. 花甲忆记—— 一位美国传教士眼中的晚清帝国. 沈弘，恽文捷，郝田虎，译. 桂林：广西师范大学出版社.

郭嵩焘，等. 2012. 郭嵩焘等使西记六种. 上海：中西书局.

郭廷以. 2012a. 近代中国的变局. 北京：九州出版社.

郭廷以. 2012b. 近代中国史纲. 上海：世纪出版集团.

惠顿. 2003. 万国公法. 丁韪良，译. 何勤华，点校. 北京：中国政法大学出版社.

林学忠. 2009. 从万国公法到公法外交：晚清国际法的传入、诠释与应用. 上海：上海古籍出版社.

托尼 · 邓. 2013. 外国人眼中的恭亲王. 王纪卿，译. 长沙：湖南人民出版社.

王建朗，黄克武. 2016. 两岸新编中国近代史·晚清卷：上下. 北京：社会科学文献出版社.

吴彦鹏. 2016. 教皇子午线. 06-21. 文明百科.

杨师群. 2012. 中国历史的教训. 杭州：浙江大学出版社.

佚名. 2019a. 巴夏礼. 02-12. 360 百科.

佚名. 2019b. 额尔金勋爵是谁?. 09-05. 百度知道.

佚名. 2019c. 理藩院. 09-05. 搜狗百科.

佚名. 2019d. 中英南京条约（全文）. 09-06. 孤独图书馆.

张浩栋. 2017. 2017 春季学期选修清华大学《西学东渐与中国现代化》本科课程论文. 北京：清华大学.

张志勇. 2012. 赫德与晚清中英外交. 上海：上海书店出版社.

Chapter Four

Tongwen Guan
同文馆

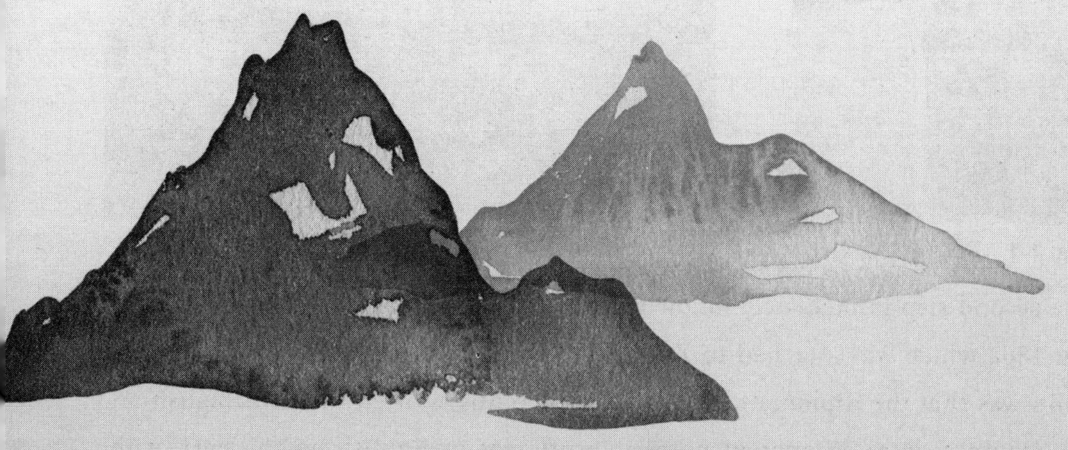

根据《天津条约》的要求，中英两国的文件暂时使用中英两种语言。但发生分歧时，则以英文为主。在《天津条约》中，法国也有同样的要求。故中国需要培养合格的英语、法语、俄语和德语人才，以便与他国进行交往。有鉴于此，1862 年，清朝政府决定成立同文馆。本章主要探讨同文馆成立的目的，办学宗旨以及办学过程中遇到的困难、挫折。此外，还重点介绍了美国长老会传教士丁韪良，因为他在同文馆的办学方针、课程设置和聘用人员方面起到了决定性作用。

4.1 The Establishment of Tongwen Guan 同文馆的建立

The establishment of Zongli Yamen in 1861 and the introduction of *International Law* could be regarded as the first step of China in moving toward modernity. It was also the first measure that the Chinese took in response to the pressure imposed by the Western powers because of the urgent need for a government department to deal with foreign affairs and obtain knowledge of the rules governing the international affairs. The way the Chinese behaved fit into the "impact and response" model proposed by John King Fairbank (费正清) (Wang, 1997: 1), meaning most of the measures taken by China in the late Qing period were galvanized by the external forces.

Fig. 4-1 京师同文馆

Fig. 4-2 老师与学生合影

The second step immediately following the first one was the opening of Tongwen Guan in 1862 which was attached to Zongli Yamen. The reason written in the Treaty of Tianjin was that the diplomatic documents currently written in both English and Chinese would require competent persons proficient in English on the part of the Chinese. Otherwise, if misunderstanding occurred, the English version would be used for authority. In fact, this clause objectively promoted Chinese modernization because nearly no knowledge of English did they possess while most of the British missionaries spoke Chinese fluently. Let's take a look at Article L of the Treaty of Tianjin between the Qing government and Britain:

> All official communications addressed by the Diplomatic and Consular Agents of Her Majesty the Queen to the Chinese Authorities shall, henceforth, be written in English. They will for the present be accompanied by a Chinese version, but, it is understood that, in the event of there being any difference of meaning between the English and Chinese text, the English Government will hold the sense as expressed in the English text to be the correct sense. (Anon, 2016a)

From what has been written above we can see it was imperative for China to produce quality personnel who could speak and write in English. Given that the revision took place ten years later, i.e. in 1868, it would be much better if China had competent interpreters to deal with the treaty negotiations by that time. The current situation was the consequence of the Qing government's long-term seclusion from the outside world and its people, especially the ruling class's arrogance and contempt for foreigners. The urgency could be further perceived because only six years was left for Zongli Yamen to train talents who were skilled at foreign languages and had the knowledge of the target nations. By the time Tongwen Guan was set up in 1862, it was only six years left for the treaty revision. Let us take a look at Article XXVII:

> It is agreed that either of the High Contracting Parties to this Treaty may demand a further revision of the Tariff and of the Commercial Articles of this Treaty at the end of ten years, but if no demand be made on either side within six months after the end of the first ten years, then the Tariff shall remain in force for ten years more, reckoned from the end of the preceding ten years; and so it shall be, at the end of each successive ten years. (Anon, 2016a)

In the eyes of the Westerners, it is quite natural for the two contracting countries to revise the treaty because things like tax and tariff would change after a certain period of time, say, ten years. Besides, this revision does not necessarily mean that one party intends to take advantage of the other one. But Emperor Xianfeng refused to recognize what had been written in the treaty. What's worse, he actually ordered his people to reject it in force, which caused heavy losses to China.

Article Ⅲ in the Treaty of Tianjin between the Qing government and France also stipulated that if disputes took place, they would rely on French for authority. Thus, the Qing government must cultivate competent interpreters as soon as possible.

> Official communication of consular and diplomatic agents of France with Chinese authorities will be written in French. But to help, they will be accompanied by a Chinese translation that is as exact as possible, until the moment when the Imperial Government of Beijing has interpreters who can handle French correctly, and then diplomatic correspondence will be in French for French diplomats and Chinese for Chinese officials. It is agreed that until then, disagreements in meaning between the French and Chinese texts, on the matter of clauses that have been laid out beforehand in conventions that are agreed on, the French text will be the one followed. This rule applies to this Treaty. (Anon, 2016b)

The British and French came to China for somewhat different purposes. Britain focused on developing trade with China while France intended to enhance its religious presence in China as the latter found it hard to compete with Britain in commerce. Gaining the upper hand in religious dissemination in China could equally demonstrate the French power among other Western countries. Both Britain and France imposed great pressure on China and China needed to satisfy the two powers by producing high quality interpreters and agreeing to revise the Treaty. Pressed by the situation, Prince Gong wrote a memorial in 1862 to Emperor Tongzhi, asking to have a school of interpreters built:

> ...to know the state of the several nations it is necessary first to understand their language and letters. This is the sole means to protect ourselves from becoming the victims of crafty imposition. (Martin, 1896: 296)
>
> ……臣等伏思欲悉各国情形，必先谙其言语文字，方不受人欺蒙。（蒋廷黻，2014：319）

This reminds us of what Wei Yuan stated in the essay "A Marine Blueprint for China" in *Haiguo Tuzhi*—building a house of translation was essential to China to deal with Western powers. The important reason that Prince Gong provided was to keep the Chinese informed so that the Qing court would not be cheated by foreign countries out of ignorance of their languages. That seemed a sound reason for the emperor. For a long time, the Qing government forbade foreigners to learn Chinese which was clearly written as "The Ten Regulations for Foreign Merchants" in Guangzhou during the early

1800s (Hsu, 2000). When the first British Protestant missionary Robert Morrison came to China in 1807, he had to secretly hire the local people to be his Chinese teacher. Once detected, the teacher would be strangled according to the law. It was not until the signing of the Treaty of Nanjing that the stipulation under the Canton System was abolished. The foreigners were keen to learn Chinese because they wanted to communicate with the local people either for business or for spreading Christianity. Prince Gong fully understood the dilemma faced by the court and was seeking permission from the court to hire foreigners to teach the Chinese their languages:

> Now these nations at large expense employ natives of China to teach them our literature, and yet China has not a man who possesses a ripe knowledge of foreign languages and letters—a state of things quite incompatible with a thorough knowledge of those countries.
>
> As therefore no native candidates were sent up from Canton and Shanghai, we have no resource but to seek among foreigners for suitable men. (Martin, 1896: 296)
>
> 各国均以重赀聘请中国人讲解文义，而中国迄无熟悉外国语言文字之人，恐无以悉其底蕴。广东、江苏既无咨送来京之人，不得不于外国中延访。（蒋廷黻，2014：319）

The emperor quickly permitted Yixin's request and Tongwen Guan opened in 1862. Initially, it was purely a language school where English, French, German and Russian were taught. The beginning stage was not smooth enough as few Chinese youths wanted to enter such a school although the stipend was provided. The obstacles mainly came from the Chinese prejudice and the Imperial Civil Service Examination which promised a bright future, i.e. an official position for the examinees. Once a person passed the exam, he would secure a place as the public servant and if lucky enough, the qualified person would be promoted in his career path. But Tongwen Guan did not promise anything to the would-be candidates, thus attracting few volunteers.

4.2 William Alexander Parsons Martin 丁韪良

One person closely connected to Tongwen Guan was William Alexander Parsons Martin, an American Presbyterian, and President of Tongwen Guan. As the first president of Tongwen Guan, Martin not only worked as the president there for 25 years (1869–1894) but also developed the school into a comprehensive college, i.e. Imperial University of

Peking (京师大学堂), the predecessor of Beijing University.

Fig. 4–3　丁韪良与他的学生

Although Christian missionaries like Martin contributed to the modernity of China, the reception of Martin in China was very mixed. One thing was that Martin, eloquent in Chinese, was invited to be an interpreter for the American consul during the negotiation of the Treaty of Tianjin. Martin helped America gain the rights for protecting the Christians residing in China. This was said to be an act of the imperialist accomplice (帝国主义的帮凶) (武海霞, 2003). Another thing was described in his narratives concerning the Siege of Beijing (围攻北京) during the Boxer Uprising (义和团事件). Two thousand Chinese Christians were in severe hunger and needed immediate help. Seeing this, Martin went to the grain shop taking a few tons of grain without payment and carried it to rescue them. This was said to be an act of robbery by Gu Changsheng (顾长声) (沈弘, 2009). But that was not true. Gu Changsheng's book *The Missionaries and Modern China* (《传教士与近代中国》, 1981) was full of ideological comments, leading to confusion for many readers. When human life was threatened by starvation, the priority for people to react would always be to get food for the dying people, no matter in what way. It was natural and understandable that Martin made efforts to gain benefits for the Christians. His belief made him act like that. Most of the Christians were Chinese converts. What's more, he left a note there saying the money of the grain would be returned afterwards. We would have a better understanding after reading what Martin had done for China and what attitude he held to China.

In the first ten years since he came to China in 1850, Martin stayed in Ningbo, one of the five treaty ports spreading Christianity. His language aptitude made him fluent not only in Ningbo dialect but also in the official language. Relying on this, Martin studied the Four Books and the Five Classics ("四书" 和 "五经"), established two old-style private schools, and taught the students by using the book (《天道溯原》) written by himself in Chinese. Martin's ambition was to build a modern school in China so that young people could be exposed to Western ideas. Yet it was not successful. Then he translated Henry Wheaton's *Elements of International Law* in 1862, hoping that it might be useful for the Chinese in power.

Fig. 4-4 英国使馆参赞威妥玛

Recommended by Anson Burlingame, the American Envoy and Thomas Wade, the English Counsellor (英国使馆参赞), Martin came to Tongwen Guan to teach in 1865. Yet the enrolment was not optimistic because teenagers were not allowed by their parents to study at Tongwen Guan. Only ten candidates remained among a pool of 90 applicants and few of them knew the English alphabet. Seeing this, Martin hesitated to take the job as he did not find any drive to teach those pupils and did not know what the future would be. Yet he remained anyway because Dong Xun (董恂), an official persuaded him by saying that someone from this class might become the emperor's tutor. Apart from teaching the students English, Martin also brought a telegraph machine at his own expense to the class and taught the students how to use it. He wanted to make the best use of the time at Tongwen Guan.

Two years later, he was appointed as professor of political economy and international law. So he went back to America and gained a law degree at Yale University. When he came back in 1869, Martin was appointed as Chief Provost (总教习) on the recommendation of Robert Hart. In addition, Hart promised to financially support the school using the tax gained from the Customs House. Naturally, it was permitted first by Zongli Yamen. Martin's appointment was made because "he brought the highest academic education attainments; a knowledge of the Chinese language, literature and history...much practical experience in dealing with the Chinese officials and non-officials alike...and enthusiastic belief that education in foreign languages, in world history, in western sciences, in international law, and in political science would do more for the advancement of China's welfare than perhaps any other agency; a high ideal of duty; very considerable literary skill; the gift of eloquence both in English and Chinese; a charming simplicity of manner combined with much natural dignity, and the complete confidence of his employers—the Tsungli Yamen" (Wright, 1950: 329).

Though it was a language school, Martin realized the close link between language and culture. Therefore, as Chief Provost, he organized a group of professors and advanced students to translate Western books of science and culture into Chinese. The areas covered international law, political economy, chemistry, natural philosophy, physical geography, history, French and English codes of law, anatomy, physiology, materia medica (药物学),

diplomatic and consular guides, etc. (Martin, 1896).

Living in the center of China, Martin had the opportunity to get a sense of the Chinese mentality at the initial stage of reform and made some valuable observations at Tongwen Guan. He found that the Chinese valued the past much more than the present and it was extremely hard for them to change the habit of thinking. In his first book *A Cycle of Cathay, or China, South and North*, Martin described three things in great detail.

Fig. 4–5 《花甲忆记》的封面

Fig. 4–6 《花甲忆记》的内文

The first thing was about building an observatory (天文台) to meet the need of teaching astronomy. The plea was made and agreed by the authority. Yet they found it very hard to secure a suitable place because the examined locations were not compatible with *fengshui* (风水), i.e. the geomantic omen which would exert influence on the fortune of people or bring bad luck if the goddess of Empyrean (九天玄女), who according to Daoism, was in charge of *fengshui* got offended. Consequently, it was not until the year 1888 that the observatory was finally set up, which took almost twenty years.

The second thing was related to the introduction of science to the Imperial Civil Service Examination. From the proposal to implementation, it took another twenty-two years. Martin noticed it because the officials came to Tongwen Guan to learn what science really could do. According to Guan Xiaohong (关晓虹, 2013), several officials made the proposal to include science in the Imperial Civil Service Examination in 1875. Xue Fucheng, Li Hongzhang and Shen Baozhen suggested to the court that the subjects examined should be expanded to include the subjects, such as electrics, mathematics, chemistry and artistry (技艺学) in order to cultivate talents for the state's modernization. It faced great challenges from the intellectual circle and Zongli Yamen simply left it on the shelf for seven years. Then other officials like Zheng Guanying (郑观应) and Zuo Zongtang raised the issue again and argued for its importance of making China powerful.

But the conservatives like Wang Bangxi (王邦玺) and Tang Chunsen (唐春森) listed how detrimental it would be to Chinese traditional culture. For the second time, this issue was put aside. In 1887, Chen Xiuying (陈琇莹) suggested to the court that those who passed the exam should be given another chance for a mathematics exam. But the result was unsatisfactory. In 1895, after the Sino-Japanese War, some scholar officials like Wen Tingshi (文廷式) and Pi Xirui (皮锡瑞) began to model after the Chinese Polytechnic Institute in Shanghai (上海格致书院) co-built in 1870 by John Fryer (傅兰雅) and Xu Shou (徐寿) to turn the academy of classical learning (书院) into a modern school in Jiangxi Province. In this way, subjects like geology, astronomy, mathematics, metrology (度量衡学), chemistry, and natural history (博物学) could be included. Gradually, other provinces such as Hubei, Guangdong, Guangxi, Yunnan began to build a similar type of modern schools. However, the problem was that there was a mismatch between what was learned and what was tested. Finally, Zongli Yamen in 1897 responded to the memorial of Li Duanfen (李端棻) and approved his suggestion of including science in the examination, which was eventually effective in 1898.

The third thing was related to a medical class opened under the administration of Martin (1896: 320). Dr Dudgeon (德贞大夫) of the London Mission was hired by Tongwen Guan to teach medicine. He was the most industrious and well received professor. When he proposed that the students should receive clinical instruction in the mission hospital, Zongli Yamen refused. One of the reasons was that they were afraid that Western medicine would one day become a threat to Chinese herbal medicine. And it took them ten years to obtain the permission. As a matter of fact, when Peter Parker came to China in 1834, his missionary work was replaced by his knowledge and skill as a medical doctor. Thousands of Chinese patients who had eye diseases were treated and cured by him. Eventually, Parker was remembered as a doctor rather than a missionary.

What Martin had experienced above showed that many Chinese especially intellectuals and scholar officials were bound by tradition and Confucianism. They were reluctant to make changes and give up obsolete knowledge. It was probably because of the huge benefits obtained through the examination provided by the institution. The success in the Imperial Civil Service Examination offered them opportunities to gain fame as well as social status, which satisfied their ambition to develop their careers and also rewarded them for their hard work of so many years. When they had the chance to update their knowledge with Western learning, they preferred to stick to the tradition and never let it go. In the final analysis, it was the fear of losing so many benefits that drove them to hang on the old institutions, which prevented them from recognizing the advantages of Western institutions. It could be further illustrated by the following section.

4.3 The Curriculum 课程设置

Tongwen Guan adopted a parallel system for education, i.e. an eight-year program and a five-year program. The former aimed for the younger students around fifteen years of age who could easily grasp foreign languages in addition to other subjects while the latter enrolled adults with a degree in classical Chinese who studied all subjects except foreign languages. Since the applicants were usually diverse and pretty poor in the educational background, quality candidates were also recommended for admission from Shanghai Tongwen Guan (上海广方言馆) set up in 1863 and Guangdong Tongwen Guan set up in 1864. Both language schools were proposed and established by Li Hongzhang who thought Shanghai and Guangzhou were better places for cultivating interpreters. Indeed, the two places offered more talented students proficient in language probably because these two ports were opened to the outside world much earlier and people living in those cities had broader horizons. In fact, the best graduates of Tongwen Guan were from the two treaty ports and some of them became Chinese envoys or diplomats residing in foreign countries, such as Wang Fengzao (王凤藻), Chinese Envoy in Japan, Qingchang (庆长), Chinese Envoy in France, Zhang Deyi (张德懿), Chinese Envoy in Britain, and Yinchang (廕昌), Chinese Envoy in Germany.

When Martin took charge of Tongwen Guan, he was responsible for supervising faculty members, designing the curriculum, and selecting and compiling teaching materials. When the science department was added in 1867, Martin in 1870 included more courses of different subjects into the curriculum, such as mathematics, mathematical physics (数学物理), astronomy, geography, mineralogy (矿物学), chemistry, physics, medicine (physiology), international law, political science, and world history, in addition to English, Russian, German, French and Japanese (邓, 2013). The following was the curriculum for the eight-year program students:

First three years: English, French, Russian or German due to their position of the first major treaties signatories.

Year 4: arithmetic, algebra (代数), translation of official dispatches;

Year 5: geometry (几何学), trigonometry (三角学), natural philosophy, translation of similar materials;

Year 6: theoretical and practical mechanics (理论与实践力学), differential and integral calculus (微积分), navigation and surveying (航海与测量);

Year 7: astronomy, chemistry, international law;

Year 8: astronomy, geology, mineralogy, political science. (Wright, 1950: 329-330)

Although the curriculum was compatible with that of the Western education system, the level of the education at Tongwen Guan was only between elementary and secondary studies because the students did not have any relevant knowledge before entering the school (熊月之, 2011).

Apart from available books and the faculty-compiled handouts, the third source of materials was translated ones from foreign languages into Chinese, a joint effort between the teaching staff and the students. Through such activities, translation had dual functions: the subject and the source of textbooks. The translated works covered three areas: the world knowledge such as *International Law* and *A History of the World*, science knowledge such as *An Introduction to Science, Chemistry, Manual of Political Economy* and dictionaries such as *Chinese-French Vocabulary* and *English Grammar*. Among those textbooks were Martin's Chinese version of *Elements of International Law* and his own works like *International Law in Ancient China* and *Natural Philosophy* (熊月之, 2011).

Robert Hart was mainly responsible for hiring faculty members from abroad as he was providing money for Tongwen Guan. The first cohort was five, but unfortunately only one of them managed to stay for a long time, i.e. Anatole Billequin (毕力干), a French chemistry professor. Having no knowledge of Chinese when employed by Tongwen Guan in 1866, Billequin spent about five years to learn Chinese before teaching the course. Once he began to teach chemistry in 1871, Billequin devoted wholeheartedly to his teaching. He began from chemical elements (化学元素), division of nonmetal (非金属) and metal, and moved to acid (酸), alkali (碱), chemical combination (化合), and decomposition (分解), etc. The level of learning was equivalent to that of the junior high school. Apart from teaching, Billequin also compiled a textbook *Chemistry for Beginners* (《化学指南》), and translated a series of books, such as *The Principle of Chemistry* (《化学阐原》). He was the pioneer to introduce chemistry and modern science from the West to China. In 1880, Billequin also translated books in other areas into Chinese, i.e. *French Civil Code* (《法国

民法典》)[1], the first foreign civil code translated under the permission of the Qing court (张功臣, 2018).

Among the Chinese faculty, apart from those who taught Chinese, Li Shanlan (李善兰), recommended by Guo Songtao, taught mathematics. Li Shanlan began to be interested in science at fifteen years old, found a copy of the first six chapters of Euclid's (欧几里得) *Elements* (《几何原本》) which was translated by Matteo Ricci and Xu Guangqi (徐光启) in the late Ming Dynasty and became familiar with geometry. After growing up, Li Shanlan published science books, such as *Fangyuan Chanyou* (《方圆阐幽》), *Hushi Qimi* (《弧矢启密》) and *Duishu Tanyuan* (《对数探源》). In 1852, in order to learn more about modern science, Li Shanlan traveled from Zhejiang Province, his hometown to Shanghai. There he got acquainted with Alexander Wylie (伟烈亚力), a professor in the Mohai Shuguan (墨海书馆). Then, Li Shanlan began to co-operate with Wylie and translated a large number of science books from English into Chinese. The proper nouns, such as calculus, formula (方程式), botany (植物学), algebra, cell (细胞) were first used by Li Shanlan and are still being used in modern China (张功臣, 2018).

4.4 The Dispute Concerning the Curriculum 课程争议

Tongwen Guan mainly taught foreign languages, which was far from enough to turn China into a modern country. Prince Gong planned to expand the college of interpreters into a more comprehensive one, that is, to add a department of mathematics and astronomy. So he submitted a memorial on December 11, 1866 to the throne and said:

> The machinery of the West, its steamers, firearms, and its military tactics, all have their source in mathematical science. Now at Shanghai and elsewhere the building of steamers has been commenced; but we fear that if we are content with a superficial knowledge, and do not go to the root of the matter, such efforts will not issue in solid success.
>
> Your Majesty's servants have accordingly to propose, after mature deliberation, that an additional department shall be established, into which none shall be admitted but those who are over twenty years of age, having previously gained a degree in Chinese learning. For we are convinced that if we are able to master the mysteries of mathematical calculation, physical investigation, astronomical observation, the

1 *French Civil Code* 指《法国民法典》，毕力干称之为《法国律例》。

construction of engines, the engineering of watercourses, this, and only this, will assure that (the) steady growth of the power of the empire. (Martin, 1896: 302)

因思洋人制造机器火器等件，以及行船行军，无一不自天文算学中来。现在上海（浙江等处）讲求轮船各项，若不从根本上用着实功夫，即习学皮毛，仍无裨于实用。臣等公同商酌，现拟添设一馆，招收满汉举人及恩拔岁副优贡，汉文业已通顺，年在二十以外者……举凡推算格致之理，制器尚象之法，钩河摘洛之方，倘能专精务实，尽得其妙，则中国自强之道在此矣。（丁韪良，2004：204）

Prince Gong's proposal met with no objection from the court. However, it was severely criticized by the conservative group. Zhang Shengzao (张盛藻), a censor (御史), was the first to attack it. In his memorial of March 1867, Zhang Shengzao expressed his disdain for Western learning and called it tricks or crafts, which could not be compared with Chinese learning which aimed to cultivate people's morality.

臣愚以为，朝廷命官，必用科甲征途者[1]，为其读孔孟之书，学尧舜之道，明体达用，规模宏远也，何必令其习为机巧专用制造轮船枪炮之理乎。（邓，2013：111）

Following Zhang Shengzao, Woren, President of Hanlin Academy (翰林院), went to great length defaming the act. Woren shared the similar idea with Zhang Shengzao and he thought that it was the etiquette rather than tricks that made a country powerful. Besides, Woren had three more points to make. First, the foreigners were not to be trusted because it was them who defeated China and made us extremely weak. If they wanted to help us, why on earth did they take advantage of us previously? Even if they agreed to teach Chinese youths their occult or computational arts (数术), they might not be committed to it as the Chinese and the Westerners were enemies. Second, given that the foreigners were honestly willing to teach it and the youths really wanted to learn it, it would amount to nothing. Because in history we had never seen any countries grow stronger relying on the so-called computational arts. Finally, if we really needed to learn those tricks, we didn't have to ask them. China was such a vast country and was never short of people who were good at it.

窃闻立国之道，尚礼仪不尚权谋，根本之图，在人心不在技艺。今求一艺之末，而又奉夷人为师，无论夷人诡谲，未必传其精巧，即使教者诚教，学者

1 科甲征途者指通过了科举考试的学者。

诚学，所成就者不过数术之士，古今来未闻有恃数术而能起衰振弱者也。天下之大，不患无才，如以天文算学必须讲习，博采旁求，必有精其术者，何必夷人？何必师事夷人？（邓，2013：111）

From what Woren had memorialized, we can see that Chinese intellectuals were extremely obstinate and they firmly believed that Chinese culture was superior to Western culture. People sharing similar opinions with Woren were not in a minority. Perhaps, this negative attitude to foreigners derived from the fear of being transformed by the barbarians' way. Though having realized the strength of Western learning, the scholar officials were not willing to be reconciled and refused to admit defeat. It might be because they had never doubted the truthfulness of Confucianism which had directed their thinking and behavior for thousands of years. But the question was why some intellectuals chose to be honest with themselves and tried to rise up through learning from the West. The majority of Chinese intellectuals remained stubborn about the entrenched idea that foreigners were always inferior. As stated earlier, it could be because of the long-term seclusion from the outside world and ignorance of how fast the world was developing. In the meantime, it also reflected how narrow-minded Woren was. He measured others' intention by his own template.

Compared with our neighbor Japan, things were entirely different. Seeing the failure of the Qing government in the First Opium War, the Japanese quickly realized that it was futile to confront such a powerful country like Britain and the best thing to do was to avoid possible detriment and take a co-operative attitude. After the Black Ship Incident (黑船事件)[1] in 1853, the Japanese decided to avoid confrontations and reluctantly opened its gate to the Americans. Unlike the intellectuals and scholar officials who detested learning from their enemies, the Japanese would not mind learning from someone who was more advanced and superior in many aspects. In 1871, the Meiji government dispatched the Iwakura Mission (岩仓使团) to the United States and other eleven European countries for investigation. Kido Takayoshi found the underlying cause of the Japanese backwardness lay in the difference of education. The Westerners studied the industry-related science while the Japanese studied the unpractical Confucian classics. If Japan wanted to catch up with the developed countries, it must cultivate a large number of practical talents. To do this, it must make fundamental reform of the old education system and the teaching

1 the Black Ship Incident 指黑船来航事件。1853 年 7 月 8 日，美国东印度舰队佩里准将率领四艘战舰驶入日本江户湾前，用武力威胁日本幕府停止“闭关锁国”政策。次年，日本结束了锁国政策，实现了开国。（佚名，2019）

content. Kido Takayoshi believed that there was no difference between the Japanese and the Europeans and the only thing that made the difference was whether they wanted to learn or not (马国川, 2018). That explained why China spent much longer time in the process of modernization. If the elites of a society were mostly opposed to advancement, the consequence would be that the whole society was likely to remain static and make little development.

To sum up, as the first modern school in China, Tongwen Guan introduced a new education system including the faculty with modern ideas, curricula based on the Western model and a cohort of competent interpreters who fulfilled the diplomatic tasks required of them. Yet generally speaking, Tongwen Guan was not successful. First, the obstacle came from the enrolment because few people wanted to study there. Second, most of the literati were against such a school because they still cherished Chinese traditional culture and Confucianism. Nothing could be compared with Chinese culture and the Westerners were not suitable to be the teachers of the Chinese as they were inferior in every aspect of their culture. Although the self-strengtheners like Yixin, Wenxiang, and Guiliang wanted to make a change, they were unable to challenge the literati as a whole. The foreign faculty really deserved respect because they were doing something that was not so rewarding. But one piece of observation made by Martin needed attention, that was, Chinese intellectuals were not curious about the achievements of modern science. They were still immersed in Confucian culture and regarded the Western learning as something incomparable. We could not help but ask why did the majority of Chinese intellectuals refuse to admit the advancement made by the West? The answer might lie in mistrust and victim mentality because since 1840, the Chinese were always bullied and defeated by Western powers. It was extremely hard to expect that the once sufferers could have benefited from the previous bullies. It was the mentality that dragged Chinese backward and made them refuse to move forward. It was a tragedy of China, indeed.

◆ Topics for Discussion

1. Your comment on Chinese traditional culture which did not include knowledge of natural sciences.
2. Why did Woren say mathematics originated from China?

3. Why did most of the Qing elites reject learning from the West?

4. What do you think of William Martin's approach to teaching at Tongwen Guan?

◆ Reading Assignment

Hsu, I. C. Y. 2000. Chapter 12 of *The Rise of Modern China*. Oxford: Oxford University Press.

◆ Bibliography

Anon. 2016a. Treaty of Tianjin 1858, Britain. 03–12. From Chinaforeignrelations website.

Anon. 2016b. Treaty of Tianjin 1858, France. 03–12. From Chinaforeignrelations website.

Hsu, I. C. Y. 2000. *The Rise of Modern China*. Oxford: Oxford University Press.

Martin, W. A. P. 1896. *A Cycle of Cathay, or China, South and North*. New York: Fleming H. Revell Company.

Smith, R. J., Fairbank, J. K., and Bruner, K. F. 1991. *Robert Hart and China's Early Modernization: His Journals, 1863–1866*. Cambridge: Council on East Asian Studies.

Wang, X. 1997. Approaches to the Study of Modern Chinese History: External Versus Internal Causations. In F. Wakeman Jr., and X. Wang (eds.), *China's Quest for Modernization: A Historical Perspective* (pp.1-21). Berkeley: The Regents of the University of California.

Wright, S. F. 1950. *Hart and the Chinese Customs* (I). Belfast: W. M. Mullan & Son (Publishers), Ltd.

丁韪良. 2004. 花甲忆记—— 一位美国传教士眼中的晚清帝国. 沈弘，恽文捷，郝田虎，译. 桂林：广西师范大学出版社.

丁韪良. 2010. 汉学菁华：中国人的精神世界及其影响力. 沈弘，译. 北京：世界图书出版公司.

关晓红. 2013. 科举停废与近代中国社会. 北京：社会科学文献出版社.

蒋廷黻. 2014. 近代中国外交史资料辑要：上卷. 北京：东方出版社.

马国川. 2018. 国家的启蒙：日本帝国崛起之源. 北京：中信出版集团股份有限公司.

沈弘. 2009. 丁韪良的三种面孔. 01-23. 中华读书报.

托尼 · 邓. 2013. 恭亲王奕䜣传. 王纪卿，译. 长沙：湖南人民出版社.

万齐州. 2011. 丁韪良与《万国公法》中译本. 02-10. 光明日报.

武海霞. 2003. 强盗？阴谋家？教育先驱？文化大使?. 04-10. 中华读书报.

熊月之. 2011. 西学东渐与晚清社会. 北京：中国人民大学出版社.

佚名. 2019. 日本黑船开国事件. 09-07. 历史上的今天.

张功臣. 2018. 洋人旧事. 02-04. 和讯读书.

Chapter Five

The Sino-Foreign Relations
中国对外关系

当中国国门打开之际，有两个西方人在中外交往中起到了至关重要的作用：一个是英国人罗伯特·赫德；另一个是美国人安森·蒲安臣。两人皆通过在清政府任职而做出努力。赫德以清朝海关总税务司的身份为中国的财政做出了贡献，在调节中外关系、解决中外矛盾方面也起到了不可或缺的作用。蒲安臣被任命为中国对外特使后，在中美关系的改善以及为中国争取平等权益方面做出了贡献。

With the opening to the outside world, China urgently needed someone who fully understood both Chinese culture and Western culture. Robert Hart and Anson Burlingame perfectly fit into the position. Employed as a Chinese civil servant, Hart served as Inspector General of China's Imperial Maritime Customs Service (IMCS, 中国海关总税务司) for 48 years (1863–1911). Not only did he reform the administration of China's Customs Service (中国海关总署), but he also managed to repay the huge amount of debts to the powers during the wars, and supported the building of Tongwen Guan, Beiyang Fleet (北洋水师), and many other services. Although in a shorter time Burlingame served as Chinese Ambassador, he succeeded in signing the Burlingame Treaty (《蒲安臣条约》)[1] between China and the United States whose equity nature actualized the Chinese Educational Mission (留美幼童计划) in 1872–1881. In this chapter, the two figures will be discussed.

5.1 Robert Hart 罗伯特·赫德

Robert Hart was renowned for his management of China's Imperial Customs House during the late Qing Dynasty. As corruption was rampant, Hart's disciplined and rigorous administration became all the more conspicuous. To fully understand how such things could take place, we need to turn our eyes to Hart's education background, personal belief, values and attitude to the Qing government.

First of all, we need to trace the origin of China's Customs Service and find out the

1 《蒲安臣条约》指1868年7月28日中美之间签订的平等条约。条约承认中国的平等地位，反对一切割让中国领土的要求。规定："大清国与大美国切念人民互相来往，或游历，或贸易，或久居，得以自由，方有利益。"美国在条约中声明不干涉中国内政，中国何时开通电报、修筑铁路，何时进行改革，完全由他们自己来决定。美国则通过这一条约得到廉价的华工，解决了南北战争后和修建太平洋铁路劳动力紧缺的问题。（佚名，2016）

Fig. 5–1 赫德

reason why a Chinese institution had to be run by foreigners. In 1853, an early period of the Taiping Movement, some unemployed sailors from Guangdong Province and Fujian Province formed a group called Small Swords Society (小刀会) in Shanghai and ransacked the local government on September 7, 1853. Wu Jianzhang (吴健彰), the Daotai, gave up his job of levying tariffs from the foreign merchants and ran away. Then, there was chaos in the treaty port Shanghai. Merchants from various countries took the advantage and sold their commodities without paying tariffs. Seeing this, Rutherford Alcock, British Consul, discussing with the consuls of France and America, decided to form a temporary Customs House in the legation (公使馆) because he thought that "the inability of the one Government to enforce its rights owing to calamities which beset it, so far from being a reason why the other should take advantage of the circumstances to ignore its rights, forms in truth the strongest argument for their honest recognition" (Hall, 2015: 10). Yet the Provisional System did not exist long as it only regulated the concerned countries while other states would not be bound by it. In addition, smuggling became uncontrollable.

Once again, Alcock proposed that a foreign Inspector of Customs should be jointly appointed by the Daotai and the consular officers of the Treaty Powers. The Inspector should be responsible for inspecting and checking all documents and duty receipts besides all Chinese records and registers and he should report to both the consuls and the Daotai. Although unwillingly the Daotai accepted the proposal and together with the three Consuls of Britain, America and France on June 29, 1854, they designed a blueprint and laid down regulations for the Customs House, which became the beginning of the modern Chinese Customs Service in the late Qing period (Hall, 2015).

1854 was the year when Hart came to Ningbo to work as an interpreter at British Consulate, and at the same time he also needed to study and perfect his Chinese. He was chosen as a civil servant by the British Foreign Affairs Office due to his excellent achievement records in Queen's College, Ireland, where he was equipped with classical knowledge or antiquity and influenced by liberalism. His parents were ardent Methodists (卫理公会派教徒) and emphasized discipline, industry, and integrity. Both his education and his family background enabled Hart to sympathize with Chinese people and determine to help them.

Hart was lucky enough to have a Chinese teacher who taught him Confucian classics required of those civil service examinees. Thus, the Four Books [*The Great Learning* (《大学》), *The Doctrine of the Mean* (《中庸》), *The Analects*, and *Mencius*] and the Five Classics (*The Book of Songs* (《诗经》), *The Book of History* (《尚书》), *The Book of Changes* (《易经》), *The Book of Rites* (《礼记》) and *Spring and Autumn Annals*], in addition to *A Dream in Red Mansions* (《红楼梦》) and *Emperor Kangxi's Imperial Edict* (《康熙皇帝圣谕》) became the teaching materials (方德万, 2017). In this way, Hart had a solid foundation for Chinese and Chinese culture, which ensured him to advance in his career path. Hart and Martin became friends in Ningbo, Zhejiang Province. In 1858, Hart worked as the interpreter of the Allied (Anglo-French) Commissioners (行政长官) in Guangzhou for Sir Harry Parkes and Sir Rutherford Alcock. He became Deputy Commissioner of Maritime Customs in Guangzhou (广东海关副税务司) between 1859 and 1861. When Horatio Nelson Lay, Inspector General of China's Imperial Customs Service, Shanghai (上海代理海关总税务司) went back to Britain for holidays during 1861–1863, Hart took his place. In 1863, Hart was chosen to be Inspector General of China's Imperial Maritime Customs Service (Smith, Fairbank, Bruner, 1991).

When working at different posts, Hart made keen observations on the Chinese management and administration and frankly critiqued some of the weak points in his memorial to Zongli Yamen on November 6, 1865, which was entitled "*A* Bystander's View" (《局外旁观论》). His comments covered many aspects of the administration, including domestic, military, civil, fiscal, as well as external problems. As we know, Hart had helped set up Tongwen Guan in Beijing, and hired foreign employees for both the Customs House and Tongwen Guan. He was eager to contribute to turning China into a modern country. When Hart was in charge of China's Customs Service, he was determined to make a change for the benefit of the Chinese government and people.

5.2 Introduction of the British Civil Service System 引进英国文官制度

In order to reform nepotism (裙带关系) and corruption existing in Chinese civil service, Robert Hart took the internationalization, education background, character and ability to use Chinese into consideration when hiring new staff. Since the Customs House offered service to people from various countries, the diversity of staff needed to be given a thought to. It could avoid envy between nations or partisan conflicts of different countries. The first published name list of the internal staff had people from Britain (57), France (14),

Germany (11), America (6) and Norway (1 or 2) and Switzerland (1 or 2) (方德万, 2017).

The candidates should have received good secondary education. It means that French candidates should have a bachelor degree. German candidates should have studied in preparatory schools for higher education. British candidates should at least finish schooling in first-class public schools, if not having received a bachelor degree, or a certificate of Oxford or Cambridge University.

Besides, the employees' characters, such as trustworthiness, punctuation, uprightness, conscientiousness, masculinity, and justice were much valued and used as the criteria for employment. Concerning irregularities, the China's Customs House Regulation (1869) stipulated the following: indolence, unpunctuality, negligence, incompetence, contentiousness, disobedience, unexcused absence, leaking official secrets, involved in civil or criminal prosecution, misconduct, embezzlement, bribe-taking, fraud, engagement in trade, intemperance, demoralization. People with the above mentioned flaws were not considered for employment (方德万, 2017).

What's more, the staff working at China's Customs House must speak Chinese fluently. If a person could not master Chinese within a limited time of training at Tongwen Guan, he must leave immediately.

You may wonder in what way Robert Hart gained his management skills and why he was so efficient in planning and organization. His experience at British Consulate in Ningbo, his interpretation experience with Parkes and Alcock, and his work experience with Lay all made contributions to his ability in management. In addition, the Protestant work ethics described by Max Webber (韦伯) also equipped Hart with qualities like discipline, rationality, problem-solving ability, etc. which enabled him to become a good manager. The staff under him all came from Western countries where enlightenment thinking had been entrenched in people's mind. As civil servants, they fully understood their obligations to obey rules and recognize Hart as authority.

The auditing system implemented at the Customs House not only put an end to embezzlement and corruption, but also introduced a new method of calculation, i.e. statistics. In 1873, by merging the Publishing House and Census and Statistics Department into the Statistical Department, Hart ensured uniformity of all the forms used at the Customs House. The Statistical Department mainly collected data produced by the Customs House, compiled them into annual trade statistics (贸易统计) and published it in the form of tables. In this way, the economic information or the official statistics had for the first time been turned into a public resource. Thus, the new knowledge in terms of statistics and the new idea in terms of the sharing mode were introduced from the West to China. In addition, James Duncan Campbell (金登干), Inspector General in the newly created Audited Accounts Tax Division (稽核账目税务司), had previous experience of working in the Treasury and Audit Department in the British government (英国政府的财政部和审计处) (方德万, 2017). Those experienced staff made valuable asset to the Customs House and helped transmit the Western learning to China. The introduction of the new accounting system ensured the separation of two accounts: one belonged to the Customs House, and the other the private account.

As a British citizen employed by the Qing government, some people had doubts about Hart's position between Chinese and British interests. In order to prove his attitude to the Qing government, we need to use some evidence both from what he wrote in his journals and what he did as Inspector General. When reading his journal on July 10, 1865, we can find evidence showing that he was loyal to his employer:

> The highly sentimental view of the position and duties of a foreigner in the employ of, or in official relations with, the Chinese Govt. is that, in addition to the performance of his own paid-for duties, he shall look upon the country as rotten to the core, and shall so act as though its salvation and regeneration depended on his exertions alone. I myself, in my most helpful moments, have been for holding this obviously sentimental view; I now commence—wearied and frustrated—to lay it aside, and content myself with, in the first place, trying to do, to the best of my ability, the work I am paid for, and, secondly, outside the work, to originate or assist in carrying out any plan that may seem to be of a useful kind, and for the working of which the time seems ripe and circumstances favorable. (Smith, Fairbank, Bruner, 1991: 301)

The above journal was written just after Robert Hart had taken the job of Inspector General for about one or two years. Obviously, he was facing the problem of to whom he should show loyalty. Having pondered over the issue, he seemed to be convinced that he should serve the employer, i.e. the Qing government because he was paid for doing the job. The phrase "paid for" repeated twice illustrated his determination of taking the side with the Qing government. Besides, he had something more important to fulfill, i.e. he regarded his job as a calling in terms of saving and regenerating the country which was heavily corrupted and extremely weak. Although doing secular work, Hart always kept in mind the mission, that was, to follow God's instruction and lead a meaningful life by helping China enter the modern age. Martin Luther's concept of "calling" exhibited power in Hart. Though with no religious mission, Hart wanted to honor God or gain grace from God by visible achievements in his work. This Protestant belief served as a drive for him to keep his dream alive. His lobbying between the British government and the Qing government with regard to extraterritoriality could be evidence.

When Hart made the decision to "be on the Chinese side and I will help them to the best of my abilities" (Smith, Fairbank, Bruner, 1991: 181), he would certainly have conflicts with the British interest, especially in solving foreign lawsuits. Two incidents recorded by Hans van de Ven (方德万) (2017) could illustrate the point. C. Kleczkowsky, a customs commissioner at Zhenjiang Customs House, committed suicide because of falsification of the accounting book. But his wife intended to prosecute Hart to the French Consulate Court. Hart talked to Anson Burlingame, American Envoy, and said it was an issue of internal discipline and should report to the Chinese government if need be. Foreign consulates should not interfere in this matter. Otherwise, they would lose their independence. When Burlingame passed the message to French Consulate, they gave it up.

On another occasion, one of the faculty members Johannes von Gumpach (方根拔) at Tongwen Guan applied for funds from the Customs House in order to build an astronomical library (天文图书馆) and an observatory. It was also this person who asked for a pay rise. Yet, he was rejected by Hart. Hart was prosecuted to the British High Court of Justice in Shanghai (上海大英按察使署). Edmond Hornby, the Chief Justice, supported Gumpach. Hart lodged an appeal to the Privy Council of London (伦敦枢密院). The case was dismissed because the charge was not grounded and more importantly, as Inspector General of China's Customs House, Hart should not be held accountable by the English court.

Hart could win the case because the British changed attitude to the clause of extraterritoriality stipulated in the Treaty of Nanjing. The British found it a heavy burden to attend to the lawsuits incurred by foreign merchants. So they helped establish China's Customs House where a foreigner, i.e. a British took the post of Inspector General, functioning as a bridge between the Qing government and the British government. When British merchants broke the trade law in the Chinese territory, they needed to rely on the Qing government to solve the problem, according to the British Foreign Secretary

Clarendon (克拉伦登). Britain would no longer deprive the Chinese of exercising the right of self-defense once they decided to unload the responsibility of levying tax by following the American agreement. Hart also thought it was right for China to exercise its sovereignty in its own territory, especially when those rights and powers were not claimed to be given up (方德万, 2017). The changed attitude of the British government to extraterritoriality deserves our attention.

Fig. 5-2 大清邮政

Fig. 5-3 北京什刹海

During the forty-eight years, Robert Hart remained conscientious and responsible at his post as Inspector General. The Customs House under his management contributed a great deal to China's modernity. It improved harbors' facilities, such as lightships, buoys, beacons, and other aids. It organized twenty-eight international exhibitions. It also organized and administered the National Post Office of China (Hall, 2015). Naturally, Hart did not forget to gain benefits for his own country. For instance, when China needed advanced warships, Hart helped contact the British company Armstrong and bought quite a few warships. However, those warships were not strong enough during the war. That explained why Li Hongzhang turned to Germany for the ironclads. Hart wasn't perfect, but we should not forget that it was under his leadership that the Customs House managed to repay the indemnities incurred in the wars with the Western powers. It was also under his suggestion that in 1866 the Qing government sent the first batch of officials to travel around Europe and brought back some narratives that broadened Chinese horizons.

5.3 Anson Burlingame 安森·蒲安臣

If Robert Hart contributed to China's modernity in terms of his service in the Customs House which included acting as a mediator between the Qing government and foreigners, Anson Burlingame's field of work was mainly in diplomacy between the Qing government and the treaty powers. Burlingame's contribution to China's modernity included implementing the Co-operative Policy (合作政策) on the part of America and establishing friendly rapport with America, Britain, Russia and France for China. As American Envoy during 1861–1868, Burlingame showed great sympathy for the Chinese people. He was a hero of anti-slavery movement and as a citizen from a new-born country, he witnessed and experienced the hardships and frustrations caused by the American Civil War and the supporter of the South, i.e. Britain. He fully understood how important it was to give a hand to the weaker country. Using his expertise in law, Burlingame recommended Henry Wheaton's *Elements of International Law* to Wenxiang and introduced Martin to Wenxiang because the former had translated Wheaton's book into Chinese. He also helped Prince Gong to refuse the flotilla bought by Horatio Nelson Lay who wanted to grab the controlling power. Taking the job as Chinese Envoy to the treaty powers, Burlingame spared no effort to gain trust and friendship from America and signed the Burlingame Treaty in 1868 there. He also tried hard to gain agreement from Britain to protect Chinese interests. Burlingame failed to persuade France to reach the agreement. He died in Russia due to overwork and anxieties.

Fig. 5-4 蒲安臣

The Co-operative Policy was dispatched by Secretary of State (国务卿) William H. Seward (西华德) to Burlingame and it was dated March 6, 1862. Take a look at the following:

> The interests of this country in China, so far as I understand them, are identical with those of the two other nations I have mentioned. There is no reason to doubt that the British and French ministers are acting in such a manner as will best promote the interests of all the western nations. You are therefore instructed to consult and co-operate with them, unless in special cases, there shall be very satisfactory reasons for separating from them. (Kim, 1971: 342)

Here, Seward thought that America, Britain and France had similar interests in China, i.e. trade and economy and the situation in China was getting better in that the treaty clauses were implemented and foreigners were allowed to reside in China as consuls. Thus, the gunboat policy was no longer suitable and should be replaced by "consult and co-operate" policy, meaning if any requirements were made by the treaty powers, the negotiation with the Qing government would be the number one choice. The "special cases" which referred to something unexpected on the part of China happened as before and then America needed to change their policy.

1862 was one year after a successful coup d'etat in the Qing court took place by which Prince Gong and Cixi jointly seized the power from the princes and Su Shun when Emperor Xianfeng died on August 22, 1861. Zongli Yamen, a foreign affairs office was established and Chinese officials could use this office to communicate with foreign consuls. During the peaceful time, together with Han officials like Zeng Guofan, Zuo Zongtang and Li Hongzhang, Yixin initiated the Self-Strengthening Movement. The Qing government was willing to co-operate with the treaty powers by acting according to what was written in the treaties. Against such background, the Co-operative Policy was likely to be implemented. Burlingame detailed the policy as follows:

> ...to consult and co-operate in China upon all material questions; to defend the treaty ports so far as shall be necessary to maintain our treaty rights; to support the foreign customs service in a pure administration, and upon a cosmopolitan basis; to encourage the Chinese government in its efforts to maintain order; to neither ask for nor take concessions of territory in the treaty ports, nor in any manner interfere with the jurisdiction of the Chinese government over its own people, nor even menace the territorial integrity of the Chinese empire. I call your attention to this policy, that you may know the commitments of our government and ourselves with the other treaty powers. (Kim, 1971: 352)

As an experienced statesman who helped Abraham Lincoln in his presidential campaign and jointly organized the Republican Party in America, Anson Burlingame actively proposed the Co-operative Policy to the other three countries. Sir Frederick Bruce coincided with Burlingame in the idea of co-operating with China because like America, Britain had similar interests in China, i.e. trade. France and Russia both agreed to it, too.

The policy treated China on an equal footing and showed respect for China's sovereignty. It also claimed to defend the treaty ports as long as their rights were fulfilled. A case in point was what had happened in 1863 when Li Hongzhang was trying to suppress the Taiping group. He first recruited the Guns team (洋枪队), an American mercenary army, led by Frederick Townsend Ward (华尔) and then co-operated with Charles George Gordon (戈登) as the general of the Ever Victorious Army. In the meantime, Zuo Zongtang allied with another foreign troop called the Ever Triumphant Army to fight the group. Eventually, the battle against the Taiping group was won with the help of the foreign mercenary armies.

Fig. 5–5 蒲安臣率领的中国使团（中间站立者为蒲安臣）

Burlingame was also the first person who introduced *Yinghuan Zhilue* written by Xu Jiyu to the US (徐国琦, 2017). In this book, Xu Jiyu highly praised the first American president George Washington who did not pass his presidency to his son and refused to take the second term after seven years of presidency. The generosity was something that the Chinese lacked and Xu Jiyu had good reason to admire him.

> ...He was very different from (the rulers) of other states. I have seen his portrait. His bearing is imposing and excellent. Ah! Can he not be called a hero?...Of all the famous Westerners of ancient and modern times, can Washington be placed in any position but first? (Drake, 1975: 164-165)
>
> ……其治国崇让善俗，不尚武功，亦迥与诸国异。余偿见其画像，气貌雄毅绝伦。呜呼！可不谓人杰矣哉。（徐继畲，2006：301）

As such Xu Jiyu's name was engraved in the monument of the founding father George Washington. The story in the Qing court was not optimistic because what the Americans did about Xu Jiyu's name was reported to the emperor and he was dismissed from his officialdom and the printing plate of his book was destroyed.

5.4 The Burlingame Mission 蒲安臣使团

When Burlingame finished his mission as American Envoy and planned to go back to America, he was swiftly employed by the Qing government to be the first Chinese Envoy visiting America and three European countries, i.e. Britain, France and Russia. Nobody was better suited to this post than Burlingame as China's long seclusion from the outside world produced few people who were familiar with Western countries, let alone fulfill the mission of negotiating with them.

Burlingame led a Chinese delegation of thirty members and spent almost two years (1868–1870) abroad and died on his post. The first country Burlingame visited was America and the team was warmly welcome. During his stay in America, he made quite a few public speeches publicizing for China's sovereignty and on July 28, 1868, he signed the treaty with the US, supplementing the Treaty of Tianjin on June 18, 1858. The treaty was also called the Burlingame Treaty (Anon, 2018). There were eight articles in the treaty and the main purpose was to relax restrictions on Chinese immigrants to America and make sure the Chinese immigrants in the US would enjoy the same treatment and rights as other immigrants. In the meantime, the treaty offered an opportunity for America to bring in cheap labor from China to build the Pacific railway (修建太平洋铁路) and solved the problem of labor shortage after the American Civil War (佚名, 2016b).

Articles Ⅰ, Ⅱ and Ⅷ recognized China's sovereignty over its own territory. Article Ⅵ ensured that the citizens of China and the US enjoy all the privileges of the most favored nation in travel and residence. Article Ⅶ stipulated that citizens of both countries would enjoy all the privileges of the government-controlled schools, which made it possible for China to send altogether 120 teenagers within four years to be educated in the US. Unfortunately, the Chinese Educational Mission during 1872–1881 was short-lived and failed to live up to its original plan of a 15-year program. Article Ⅴ stated that citizens from both countries had the right of travel and residence in each other's country. This article made it possible for Chinese citizens to work in the US and at the same time reminded the Qing government to attend to their own citizens abroad. When the Treaty of Tianjin between China and the US was signed, Dupont, the American representative, hoped that China could send consuls to America so as to look after the Chinese residing in America. But Tan Qixiang (谭其骧), Viceroy of Zhili (直隶)[1] dismissed it by saying that China had never dispatched officials to other countries because the emperor had so many

1 直隶为中国旧省名，特指今河北省。

people at home to attend to and had no time to care about the tiny group of undisciplined ones (佚名, 2016a). After signing of the Burlingame Treaty, China began to establish consulates in foreign countries.

Due to the treaty, China began to enter the international family by sending consuls abroad. Besides, China for the first time understood its responsibility to protect its citizens residing in other countries from discrimination, harm and absence of rights.

5.5 The Chinese Exclusion Act 排华法案

Jean Pfaelzer (琼·菲尔泽) stated in her book *Driven Out: The Forgotten War Against Chinese Americans* that Chinese immigrants in America had suffered from hostility and exclusion from the local whites for about half a century (1850–1906), and sometimes they lost their lives. With the discovery of gold in 1848 in California, the Chinese people from Guangdong Province and Fujian Province joined the gold rush. In the meantime, immigrants from other European countries, such as Ireland, France, Austria, Hungary, Italy and Germany also dreamed to make money and rushed to California. Thus, the presence of the Chinese gave rise to envy and hostility and then the driving out movement began (菲尔泽, 2016). In addition, the depletion of gold mining and the following dire economy in the 1860s led to the unemployment of those soldiers who had fought in the American Civil War, African Americans and Irish immigrants. However, the Chinese were more likely to be employed because they were good at mining with water, building railroads and intensive cultivation (菲尔泽, 2016). Even in the hardest times, they managed to survive by selling vegetables, doing the laundry, cooking for white women, babysitting and gardening, which caused jealousy and hatred. So the unemployed whites got organized to harass, threaten and even murder the Chinese who were eventually driven out of the place. The signing of the Burlingame Treaty could not do anything in the 1870s. A group of angry whites made a list of their enemies which included people:

1. who dismisses Whites or African Americans, but hires Asians instead;
2. who employs Asians to be their baby-sitters;
3. who bails Asians;
4. who testifies in court for Asians;
5. who hires Asians in bars, cafes, cigar stores and restaurants;
6. who imparts craft, or the art of White civilization to Asians;

7. who rents his house to Asians;

8. who encourages the Mongols to reside in America. (菲尔泽, 2016: 81)

From the above, we can see it was not the Chinese personality, living habit or custom that alienated American whites, but the Chinese industry, resilience and hard work that made the Chinese more competitive in job markets. Many of the jobs that the Chinese people did were disdained and unaccepted by the whites, who were choosy and lazy. Thus, the Exclusion Act in 1882 was the result of prejudice, fear and envy as shown in the following: "Much talk is made of the bad morals of the China 'coolie'," John Murray Forbes wrote, "The real trouble is he is such a good, thorough, and steady worker that the shiftless Irish or Yankee or Californian", who "look on him as a dangerous competitor", tried to "scare" the "innocents with predictions of being swamped by the millions from China" (Haddad, 2013: 230).

In 1882, the Exclusion Act was signed into law and it was underpinned by the scientific theory of ethnology (梁展, 2016). In the 18th century, the Swedish botanist Carl von Linné (卡尔·冯·林奈) published his book *Systeema Naturae* (《自然系统》) in which he not only created a classification system for plants, but also for human races. Thomas Jefferson made use of Linné's theory to justify for the enslavement of the blacks. Then, the French naturalist Georges-Louis de Buffon (乔治–路易斯·德·布封) produced a system of six human races: the Caucasian, the Mongolian, the American, the Malay, the African and the Australian. Johann Friedrich Blumenbach (约翰·弗里德里希·布鲁门巴赫) further elaborated the categories: the Caucasian referred to the white race; The Mongolian stood for the yellow race, including all East Asians and some Central Asians; The Malayan or brown race included Southeast Asians and Pacific Islanders; The Ethiopian or black races referred to sub-Saharan Africans; The American or red race stood for American Indians (Anon, 2017).

In America, Samuel George Morton (塞缪尔·乔治·莫顿), a natural scientist, claimed in his publication that there existed racial distinction between the two races "Caucasoid" and "Negroid", by analyzing numerous human skulls, i.e. the so-called craniology. His conclusion was that "the ruling elite of ancient Egypt had been 'Caucasian', while the subservient class had been 'Negroid'" (Renschler, Monge, 2017: 34). Morton's finding fueled the heated debates between the two schools, i.e. the monogenist school (人类同源论) which advocated all people today were descended from the original biblical pair, Adam and Eve, and the polygenist school (人类多源论) which believed all the various major human racial stocks were originally created in the areas where they are now predominantly located. Josiah Clark Nott (约西亚·克拉克·诺特), Morton's student, published a research paper in 1843 to argue about the impossibility of intermarriage between the whites and the blacks and justified for the white population who enjoyed the special privileges in the American South before the Civil War (Brace, 1974). Anthropology as a scientific area was the direct result of such debates.

When the Californian jurist, Judge Sawyer (索耶法官) was against the naturalization of the Chinese in 1878, he said that the white person referred to someone of the Caucasian race, and then turned for guidance to the racial typologies developed by European naturalists Johann Friedrich Blumenbach, Georges-Louis de Buffon, Carl von Linné, and Georges Cuvier (乔治·居维叶), observing that all grouped Caucasians were separately from Mongolians (Bindon, 2015).

According to Liang Zhan (梁展), the Exclusion Act in 1882 was based on the findings of both Morton and Nott in which the size of the Chinese human skull was ranked behind the British, American, German, and Celts. Since the Chinese race had been proved inferior to the whites, it was reasonable for them to be driven out of America. We would not feel surprised if we learned that Thomas Jefferson, one of the founding fathers of the US and the major draftsman of *Declaration of Independence*, promoted the institution of slavery in *Notes on the State of Virginia 1786*. Jefferson considered the black slaves were inferior to the whites because he believed in Linné's idea that black and native Americans were inferior races (Maree, 2010). Besides, Jefferson was trying to send the blacks back to Africa to avoid conflicts between the whites and the blacks.

> Comparing them by their faculties of memory, reason, and imagination, it appears to me that in memory they are equal to the whites; in reason much inferior, as I think one could scarcely be found capable of tracing and comprehending the investigations of Euclid: and that in imagination they are dull, tasteless, and anomalous.
>
> ...that though for a century and a half we have had under our eyes the races of black and of red men, they have never yet been viewed by us as subjects of natural history. I advance it, therefore, as a suspicion only, that the blacks, whether originally a distinct race, or made distinct by time and circumstances, are inferior to the whites in the endowments both of body and mind. (Franklin, 2010: 119-120, 122)

As one of the founding fathers of the United States, Thomas Jefferson could not avoid being prejudiced against the blacks and based his ideas on modern science, i.e. anthropology and biology. From this, we can learn that during the process of human civilization, it is quite natural for man to have misconceptions and they will be corrected as human society develops and our knowledge of human society deepens.

In this chapter, we discussed two distinguished Western figures Robert Hart and Anson Burlingame and the contributions they made to China's modernity. Hart strove to manage the Customs House according to the Western system of civil servants and achieved a great deal in eradicating corruption, introducing new equipment and paying off the debts that China owed to the powers. Burlingame tried hard to implement the Co-operative Policy, signed the equal treaty on behalf of the Qing government with the US and built rapport for the Qing government with Britain and Germany.

◆ Topics for Discussion

1. Your comment on Robert Hart's work ethics.
2. How to avoid nepotism and corruption?
3. The function of statistics introduced from the West.
4. Your comment on Hart's "A Bystander's View".
5. The Co-operative Policy and the Burlingame Treaty.
6. Your comment on the Exclusion Act in 1882.
7. Your comment on the impact of Carl von Linné's classification system on ethnology.

◆ Reading Assignment

Hsu, I. C. Y. 2000. Chapter 10 of *The Rise of Modern China*. Oxford: Oxford University Press.

◆ Bibliography

Anon. 2017. Blumenbach, Johann Friedrich. 03–11. From Wikipedia website.

Anon. 2018. Peace, Amity, and Commerce: Burlingame-Seward Treaty of 1868. 02–19. From Wikipedia website.

Bindon, J. 2015. Darwin's Borrowed Allegory and the Apocryphal Six Races of Buffon. 02–17. From Bama Anthro Blog Network website.

Brace, C. L. 1974. The "Ethnology" of Josiah Clark Nott. Presented as Part of a Symposium on Josiah Clark Nott, M. D., and 19th Century Medicine in the Southern United States: pp.509-528.

Drake, F. W. 1975. *China Charts the World: Hsu Chi-yu and His Geography of 1848*. Cambridge: Harvard University Press.

Franklin, W. 2010. *The Selected Writings of Thomas Jefferson*. New York: W. W. Norton & Company, Inc.

Haddad, J. R. 2013. *America's First Adventure in China*. Philadelphia: Temple University Press.

Hall, F. B. E. 2015. *The Chinese Maritime Customs: An International Service, 1854–1950*. Bristol: The University of Bristol.

Kim, S. S. 1971. Burlingame and the Inauguration of the Co-operative Policy. *Modern Asian Studies*, *5*(4): 337-354.

Maree, R. D. 2010. From Linneaus to Lewis: A Brief Examination of Racial Theory. 09–13. From Safe Haven website.

Renschler, E. S., and Monge, J. 2017. Historical Significance and New Research. The Samuel George Morton Collection. Volume 50. Number 3 expedition. 03–10. From Penn Museum website.

Smith, R. J., Fairbank, J. K., and Bruner, K. F. 1991. *Robert Hart and China's Early Modernization: His Journals, 1863–1866*. Cambridge: Council on East Asian Studies.

Wright, S. F. 1950. *Hart and the Chinese Customs*. Belfast: W. M. Mullan & Son (Publishers), Ltd.

方德万. 2017. 潮来潮去：海关与中国现代性的全球起源. 姚永超，蔡维屏，译. 太原：山西出版传媒集团 · 山西人民出版社.

梁展. 2016. 文明，理性与种族改良：一个大同世界的构想. 刘禾. 世界秩序与文明等级. 北京：生活 · 读书 · 新知三联书店.

琼·菲尔泽. 2016. 放逐：被遗忘的美国排华战争. 何道宽，译. 广州：花城出版社.

徐国琦. 2017. 中美“共有历史”中的蒲安臣. 03-30. 爱思想.

徐继畬. 2006. 瀛寰志略校注. 宋大川，校注. 北京：文物出版社.

佚名. 2016a. 论 1868 年中美《蒲安臣条约》的历史意义. 01-23. 蜀之飘梧.

佚名. 2016b. 蒲安臣. 01-23. 百度百科.

周大伟. 2011. 谁是中国第一位赴欧美的全权特使?. 11-16. 爱思想.

Chapter Six

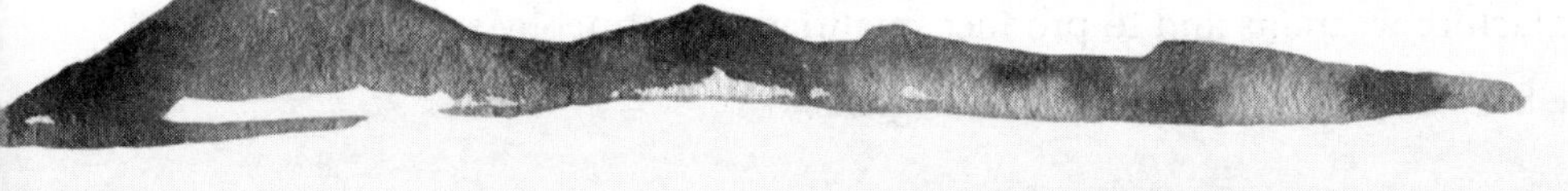

The Self-Strengthening Movement
洋务运动

中国的大门被英国的坚船利炮打开之后，曾国藩、左宗棠和李鸿章等士大夫认为，如果想不再受西方人的欺负，中国必须发展制造工业，要拥有自己的轮船和枪炮，军队也要请西方军事专家指导和训练。但洋务运动以失败而告终。本章主要探讨洋务运动失败的原因。

Having experienced failures in the two Opium Wars, the Chinese eventually realized that it was imperative to develop military industry in order not to be bullied by foreign invaders. The Manchu government ratified the motions made by Han officials to co-operate with foreign mercenary army in subduing the Taiping Movement, to build arsenals to manufacture weapons and to produce qualified personnel by setting up a navy school. Thus, the Self-Strengthening Movement began.

6.1 Military Training 军事训练

When analyzing the causes of failure for the Chinese military in the First Opium War, Wei Yuan stated in the first two volumes of *Haiguo Tuzhi* the importance of learning from the West in terms of conscription, training and deployment of soldiers, as well as the importance of armories (魏源, 1998). However it took Chinese scholar officials two decades to actualize what Wei Yuan had discussed in 1843.

The 1850s and 1860s witnessed the rise of the Taiping Movement and the Manchu government felt it urgent to seek help from the foreign mercenary army because of its advanced weapons and strategy and tactics. But the government did it reluctantly because they feared that equipping the Han soldiers with foreign army and weapons could undermine the Manchu force. Viceroy Zeng Guofan wrote a memorial to the Qing government asking the permission of using foreign troops. Facing the serious situation in Shanghai, Zeng Guofan stated in the memorial that the Taiping group colluded with some foreigners to fight against the government. He asked Zongli Yamen to discuss the issue with British and French envoys.

1862 年 4 月 22 日协办大学士两江总督曾国藩奏（发）（见《曾文正公奏稿》卷十八页四十三至四十七）：……上海被匪窥伺，势不能不借洋人之力，协同守御，曾国藩亦曾奏及……近复据英、法两国驻京公使声称，贼匪与洋人构衅，此时在沪洋人情愿帮助官军剿贼，并派师船驶往长江协同防剿等语……仍请饬下总理衙门照会英法公使，目前若进攻金陵、苏、常，臣处尚无会剿之师，庶几定议于前，不致贻讥于后人。（蒋廷黻，2014：306–307）

In the meantime, the British authority was facing the decision of whether it would keep its neutrality policy or simply support either the Taiping group or the Qing government. During this time, Lord Elgin wrote to his brother Frederick Bruce persuading the latter not to compromise with the Qing government because the British army suffered a great deal from its breach of the Treaty of Tianjin when Senggelinqin ambushed the British army, and detained the diplomatic team headed by Sir Harry Parkes, and its Emperor Xianfeng refused to give an audience to the foreign envoys in Beijing (Gregory, 1959).

But as the First Minister Plenipotentiary to China, Frederick Bruce did not share his brother's opinion. Instead under the instruction of the British Foreign Secretary, Malmesbury Ⅲ (马尔默斯伯里三世), Bruce planned to negotiate with the Manchu officials about providing military aid to them. Since the government he was dealing with was thought to be "unstable and untrustworthy", Bruce sent his secretary Thomas Wade to "convince Kung[1] of the essentially reasonable and peaceful attitude of the British government towards the existing dynasty, so long as the new treaty settlement was honestly observed" (Gregory, 1959: 13).

The change of the British policy from a neutral stand to a limited aid to the Manchu government took place in early 1862 because Bruce believed that Hong Xiuquan (洪秀全) and his men could never take the responsibility of governing China after some contacts with the Taiping group while "the Manchus, especially after the death of the Xianfeng emperor and the palace coup d'etat of October 1861, seemed to hold out some promise of reformation..." (Gregory, 1959: 19) In fact, the British consideration of helping the Qing government was for their own trade and economic interest. But this support enabled the corrupt and weak government to remain longer (Gregory, 1959).

An important figure need to be introduced here, who helped with the Qing military army in fighting against the Taiping group. His name is Frederick Townsend Ward, an American citizen who came to China to seek adventures and fortunes. Not much was known regarding Ward's education. Born in Massachusetts in 1831, Ward was educated

1 Kung 指 Gong，是恭亲王的威妥玛式拼法。

in a private college and gained some military knowledge. But he did not finish his college education. Instead, he became a ship officer sailing around the world including several trading voyages to China. When he came to China in the 1860s as a mercenary, it was during the peak of the Taiping Movement against the Qing government. According to Stevens (1998/1999), Ward was first employed by the Shanghai local government, fighting with the group. Later, he was hired by the central government in military service and engaged in the battles against the similar groups.

Initially, the force Ward gathered was several hundred Western mercenaries, including Filipinos, discharged soldiers and sailors or the Anglo-French expedition deserters. Their duty was to protect Shanghai from being attacked by the groups. Yet this force proved to be ineffective. Thus, Ward organized another force composed purely of Chinese soldiers, but commanded by foreigners. This army was highly competent and disciplined and the eventual number of the army force reached 8,000. Because of his bravery, leadership, and military tactics, Ward gained several important victories over his enemies and his army was given the name by the Manchu government the Ever Victorious Army and Ward became the de facto general. He even married the daughter of Yang Fang (杨芳), the Shanghai Chinese merchant-patron of Ward. Unfortunately during the battle in Ningbo, Ward was fatally injured and died in September 1862 at the age of 31 (Stevens, 1998/1999).

Fig. 6–1 华尔

Ironically, the Manchu government was obsessed with the fear of using Ward at the very beginning because of his unruly personality. And they were eager to know whether Ward showed admiration for Chinese customs. But the impression that Ward left on Chinese officials was nothing but arrogant and unmanageable. Prince Gong regarded Ward as "proud, boastful, and overly independent" (Smith, 1975: 126). And the throne showed grave concern over "Ward's failure to shave his head and change to Chinese clothing" because "when Ward failed to conform to the dictates of propriety, his actions cast doubt on his sincerity, and perhaps more importantly, on the efficacy of traditional restraints" (Smith, 1975: 126). But when he died in action, Chinese officials immediately changed their attitude and buried Ward on his drill-field in the city of Songjiang (松江). An inscription on a tablet went like this:

> An illustrious man from beyond the seas, he came 6000 *li* to accomplish great deeds and acquire immortal fame by shedding his noble blood. Because of him

Sungkiang[1] will be a happy land for a thousand autumns. (Stevens, 1998/1999: 287)

Whenever employing a foreigner in Chinese military service, the Qing government would require him to register as the Chinese subject or change to Chinese ways. This embarrassed or repulsed many of them. Like the successor of Ward, Henry Burgevine (白奇文) became the commander of the Ever Victorious Army. Yet he disliked the Chinese customs so much that he gave up his post and joined the Taiping group (Smith, 1975). So when Gordon, the British officer, assumed the commander of the army, he was not requested to do the same as before, but would be tightly controlled by Li Hongzhang, his sponsor. According to Smith (1975), the Manchu government was very good at reining foreign military officers by high salary, flattery, honor, and official titles. Although Gordon was notorious for his un-submissiveness or non-servility, he was in good terms with Li Hongzhang except for one occasion. During the battle against the Taiping group, eight heads from the enemy camp voluntarily surrendered to Li Hongzhang with Gordon as the witness. Li Hongzhang went against his promise of not killing them after eradicating the group and all the eight heads were killed. This angered Gordon who wanted to have a duel with Li Hongzhang. Eventually, the problem was resolved by the government and the relation of the two became normal again.

The recapture of Nanjing from the Taiping group in 1864 by the joint effort made the Manchu authorities see advantages in adopting Western military methods and technology and Li Hongzhang began a foreign training program in Fenghuang Mountain (凤凰山), Shanghai in 1863 using the remnant of the Ever Victorious Army. In the meantime, Britain and France expressed willingness to aid the Qing government in terms of military programs. Li Hongzhang's proposal of disbanding the Ever Victorious Army was rejected by Frederick Bruce, the British minister, under the excuse of protecting Shanghai in case of invasions. Yet this ten-year training program (1864–1874), according to Smith (1976) turned out to be unsuccessful because there was no uniform authority and each program had its own regulations. Things like discipline, drills, command were greatly different in various training spots. Obviously, the non-uniform approach in military training was the bane of the battlefield, which could be illustrated in the Sino-Japanese War in the years to come.

According to Smith (1976), the fact that the military training program was not coordinated by the government was not because the Qing officials failed to realize the importance of uniformity in training the officers and soldiers in terms of methods

1 Sungkiang 指 Songjiang，是松江的威妥玛式拼法。

and weapons, but because the authorities were afraid of losing control if they agreed to coordinate among the training programs in different areas.

6.2 Setting up Arsenals 建立兵工厂

6.2.1 Jiangnan Arsenal 江南制造局

Accompanied with the military training program in Fenghuang Mountain was the blueprint of establishing Jiangnan Arsenal and the chief designer was Zeng Guofan, the Viceroy of Liang Jiang, i.e. Jiangsu and Jiangxi. Twenty years after the publication of *Haiguo Tuzhi*, Zeng Guofan realized the importance of learning from the West and now he was determined to practice it. Zeng Guofan was a respected high-ranking official, deeply trusted by the Manchu rulers because of his firm belief in Neo-Confucianism. Zeng Guofan was a person who held a high moral standard and cherished talent. When he knew Yung Wing (容闳), a Yale graduate, had the knowledge of Western learning, Zeng Guofan decided to send Yung Wing to buy machines for the arsenal. But before that he needed to obtain permission from Zongli Yamen. He wrote a memorial and stated the importance of importing foreign-made warships and cannons and he used the example of the recent battle with the Taiping group in which those imported arms displayed its strength and advantages. Therefore, it was high time for China to possess an arsenal of the same kind.

1863 年 1 月 31 日协办大学士两江总督曾国藩奏（发）（见《曾文正公奏稿》卷二十一页十五至十七）窃臣等承准议政王军机大臣密寄，同治元年九月二十九日（十一月二十）奉上谕：总理各国事务衙门奏购买外国船炮，明春可到。请饬预派将弁水勇，以备演习；并请妥筹配派各折片。购买外国船炮，近以剿办发逆，远以巡哨重洋，实为长驾远驭第一要务。（蒋廷黻，2014：320）

Fig. 6-2　江南制造局

In 1864, a manufacturer producing military supplies, such as warships, and munitions (军需品) was established in Shanghai, i.e. Shanghai Arsenal, which became the predecessor of Jiangnan Shipyard (江南造船厂) nowadays. Then, Fuzhou Shipyard immediately afterwards was also built to produce warships. Following that, modern equipment, such as lathes (车床), boring machines (镗床), planing machines (刨床), and military machines (制造武器机床) driven by steam engines was entering China, which indicated that modern machinery industry came into being in China (Zhang, 1997: 236).

Yung Wing was sent to Washington in 1863 with 60,000 *taels* of silver to purchase machines because he had studied at Yale University and had some contacts there. In his autobiography, Yung Wing recorded his meeting with Zeng Guofan:

> ...I repeated in substance what I had said to my friends previously in regard to establishing a mother machine shop (机械母厂), capable of reproducing other machine shops of like character...I would recommend was not one adapted for making the rifles, but adapted to turn out specific machinery for the making of rifles, cannons, cartridges (子弹), or anything else. (Anon, 2014: 137)

Yung Wing came back to China in 1854 once he finished his college study at Yale University. He had many plans in his mind to build China into a strong country and one of them was to send Chinese teenagers to study in America and come back to serve the country. This plan was based on his personal experience and he saw many benefits of it. But he had no chance of actualizing the plan. When he was introduced to Zeng Guofan by his friends Xu Shou and Li Shanlan, he had no courage to mention the plan because he was afraid of being refused. This mission of buying machines in the US was a good opportunity to be known to the high-ranking officials and he was trying to do it well.

> ...the matter of the character of the machine shop was to be left entirely to my discretion and judgment, after consulting a professional mechanical engineer...the Viceroy, after having seen all the four men, had decided to empower me to go abroad and make purchases of such machinery as in the opinion of a professional engineer would be the best and the right machinery for China to adopt. It was also left entirely to me to decide where the machinery should be purchased,—either in England, France or the United States of America. The shop was Jiangnan Arsenal in Shanghai. (Anon, 2014: 137)

Having got to know Zeng Guofan gave Yung Wing the opportunity to present his idea of sending young Chinese to study abroad to the viceroy. But he had to wait for another few years before he had the courage to express his plan. Next, we will discuss Zeng Guofan and his scholarly background.

6.2.2 Zeng Guofan as a Neo-Confucianist 理学学者曾国藩

As a Chinese intellectual, Zeng Guofan was sure to have his own scholarly belief which made what he was. Although Confucianism was the mainstream scholarship, it had different schools. During Zeng Guofan's lifetime, there were four different Confucian schools, i.e. the Neo-Confucianism of the Cheng-Zhu School (宋明理学 / 程朱理学)[1], the Tong-Cheng School (桐城学派)[2], the Statecraft School (经世派), and the New Text School (今文学派). The last school advocated institutional reform while the other three did not. The New Text School was upheld by Wei Yuan, Gong Zizhen (龚自珍), Kang Youwei (康有为), and Liang Qichao (梁启超).

Fig. 6-3 曾国藩

We have discussed Wei Yuan's *Haiguo Tuzhi* in which Wei Yuan called upon the government to reform the military system by learning from the West. Kang Youwei will be discussed in Chapter Fourteen.

According to Shen Han-Yin Chen (1967), Zeng Guofan was essentially a Neo-Confucianist because he firmly believed that an emperor with a high moral standard could turn the weak and disadvantageous China into a strong one and he put emphasis on self-cultivation and self-reflection according to the doctrine *li* (理). The two ancient Chinese emperors Yao (尧) and Shun (舜) were the role models for the generations to come. In his letters to his family members, Zeng Guofan always lent advice to his brothers to cultivate their morals and become an upright and conscientious person. In the meantime, Zeng Guofan did not reject the other three schools. Instead, he very much agreed with the ideas stipulated in them. For instance, the Statecraft School put emphasis on practical values instead of abstract theories and by following the idea Zeng Guofan initiated the Self-Strengthening Movement. He suggested to the throne that people's welfare be the most important thing to care about and what he did was to promote people's economic gains, though the Neo-Confucianism made distinction between righteousness (义) and profit and emphasized morals instead of interests. Here we see the flexibility and inclusiveness of Zeng Guofan.

1 Cheng-Zhu School 的威妥玛式拼法为 Ch'eng-Chu School。其中，符号“'”为换气符。

2 Tong-Cheng School 的威妥玛式拼法为 T'ung-Ch'eng School。

When the First Opium War broke out, Zeng Guofan was studying in Hanlin Academy. He did not pay much attention to the foreign intrusions because he only mentioned in passing the British invaders (英夷) but was not aware of its impact (Shen, 1967). This seemed to suggest that too much focus on individual moral self-cultivation prevented Zeng Guofan from concerning the state security issue. When it came to political and administrative problems existing in the Qing government, Zeng Guofan took pains to point out its serious problems. Regarding administration, the reason why local officials refused to assume their responsibilities was the lack of communication between the emperor and his ministers. He suggested that the emperor should read all the memorials in person and coordinate and communicate with the local officials (Shen, 1967). Only in this way could local officials fulfill their obligations. The implication was that some emperors did not fulfill their obligations in running the country. Emperor Xianfeng, for instance, asked his concubine Cixi to read the memorials for him while he himself led a licentious life. Similarly in the Ming Dynasty, Emperor Wanli refused to convene meetings with his ministers for years, but endorsed eunuchs to govern the country, leading to tremendous chaos in China.

With regard to the military problems of pay and rations of the non-existent personnel, Zeng Guofan strongly recommended a cut in expenditure by reducing or disbanding the Green Standard Forces (绿营军), the soldiers of Han nationality whose system was different from the Manchurian Eight Banners (满洲八旗军) and whose army flag was in green. The detailed suggestion was written in the memorial of April 10, 1850:

> The method of weeding out superfluous (troops) may lie in leaving the strategically important and frontier areas alone but disbanding more troops in the interior; in combining the battalions where the rolls are not full; and in abolishing the outposts that are too scattered and then consolidating them. All these depend on the thorough investigation of the Board of War and the careful study of governors-general and governors. They should not be executed rashly. (Shen, 1967: 77)

Although Zeng Guofan did not suggest a fundamental reform in moral and political structure, he did hope to improve the paralyzed administration and this could be done only when the emperor agreed to pay attention to his own conduct. As a matter of fact, the suggestions made by Zeng Guofan were highly similar to what Robert Hart described in his memorial of 1865 entitled as "A Bystander's View". Hart frankly pointed out the problems in Qing's administration, finance, military, etc. but received no response.

Holding a firm belief in the Neo-Confucianism, Zeng Guofan showed no doubt whatsoever in its creed in spite of the great losses and defeats that China had suffered. On the contrary, the more frustrations he witnessed, the firmer he held the belief that the Chinese culture was superior to that of the West. Li Hongzhang shared the similar opinion. This seemed hard to explain. The fact that the late Qing intellectuals refused to confront the defects and weaknesses might have something to do with their political stance or the bullies from the West. Both Zeng Guofan and Li Hongzhang regarded "Everything in China's civil and military systems...morally superior to the West" (Swisher, 1958: 35). Zeng Guofan also expressed the similar idea that "China should acquire the West's superiority in arms and machinery, but retain China's superiority in Confucian virtue so that China could defeat the Taipings in the short-haul but still have the capacity to control the barbarians in the long-run" (Swisher, 1958: 35). The fact showed that when the backbone of the society, i.e. the 19th century Chinese intellectuals refused to change their scholarly belief, one could hardly see any social progress for the whole China. That might be partial explanation to China's problems in slow response to the Western civilization.

6.2.3 Fuzhou Shipyard and Its Navy School 福州船政局和福州船政学堂

Strategically speaking, the three ports along the Chinese eastern coastline took important position in self-defense and attacking enemies, i.e. Tianjin, Shanghai, and Fujian. Immediately after the establishment of Jiangnan Arsenal, Zuo Zongtang, the Governor General of Shaanxi and Gansu (陕甘总督, 1866–1878), proposed in his memorial to establish a dockyard and an academy in Fuzhou and quickly obtained the permission. In September 1866, together with two French navy officers, Prosper Giquel (日意格) and Paul d'Aiguebelle (德克碑), Zuo Zongtang made a five-year plan (1868–1873) to build sixteen gunboats, and to train the Chinese in shipbuilding, ship steering, ocean engineering, navigation and command of the small warships.

Fig. 6-4 福州船政学堂学生

The two Frenchmen were coordinated with Zuo Zongtang in repressing the Taiping group in Zhejiang in 1863 and the army led by them was called the Ever Triumphant Army, who fulfilled the similar tasks with that of the Ever Victorious Army led by Frederick Townsend Ward and Major Gordon in Jiangsu. Impressed by the advantageous methods exhibited in foreign steamers, Zuo Zongtang was determined to construct a Chinese navy modeling after the West. In this way, Zuo Zongtang sought assistance from Giquel and d'Aiguebelle and the two agreed to help. Yet the problem was that the two French navy officers had little knowledge of engineering. When making a budget for building the dockyard, they could offer little help. That preluded the subsequent debate concerning whether the dockyard should be stopped or not because of the excessive and unexpected expenditure. Anyway the experience Zuo Zongtang gained from this activity included not only making financial plans, selecting suitable locations, but also contract making because the two Frenchmen helped with hiring employees from European countries.

In 1866, Prosper Giquel was employed as the European director of the project, consultant, purchasing agent, and co-director of the European Educational Mission of 1877. Paul d'Aiguebelle was hired as the co-director, consultant, and purchasing agent. Giquel and d'Aiguebelle bought equipment of shipbuilding from France to China, which was sent on several steamers, and they employed 12 French ship builders, one doctor, two supervisors and one sailing teacher. As the chief supervisor (总监督), Giquel's salary was 1,000 *taels* per month and as the deputy chief supervisor (副总监督), d'Aiguebelle received similar payment.

Fig. 6-5 日意格

According to Shen Yan (2009), a clearly written contract was signed between the two parties in terms of employees' rights and obligations. Take a look at the following agreement:

1. Rights of foreign supervisors. Under its provisions, "the Chinese government authorized foreign experts to supervise and manufacture naval equipment. Foreign supervisors are responsible for subordinate supervisors, fellow workers and their jobs thereby".

2. Term. It is for five years from the starting of the iron factory. "If no more issues occur after five-year's term, foreign experts and their subordinate workers will thereby be dismissed and employed by the Chinese government no more."

3. Obligations and disciplines. Under its provision, within five years, "we should build 16 ships with an estimation of 3 million *liang* of silver in

value...supervisors, deputy supervisors and skilled workers that amount to thirty-eight employees and salary 8,978 *liang* of silver each month". All staff should "be serious and responsible... not neglect one's duty, not leave one's post without permission or take unauthorized personal jobs, not interfere with their supervisors or call on Chinese officials without rightful reasons". "If there are any supervisors, deputy supervisors, or workers who do not take orders from their superiors, follow laws and regulations, do their jobs rightfully, work efficiently, curse or beat Chinese officials, they will be sent back to where he (they) came from."

4. Rights. If no more issues come up after five-year's term, "Chinese staff could make out ships out of draft, be captains of the ship, and manufacture iron-products from imitation,(;) Chinese ministers will be rewarded additional silver of sixty thousand *liang*". "If any staff gets sick and dies because of job or disabled from job injuries, he will get six months' salary as compensation and silver of three hundred and seventy-eight *liang* as home traveling expenses." (Shen, 2009: 21-22)

The above contract was drafted by Zuo Zongtang first before gaining the agreement with the two French supervisors. Here we see that Chinese literati officials were quick to learn especially when it concerned the self-strengthening program. Unfortunately, Zuo Zongtang did not see the project to be actualized because he was assigned other responsibilities in 1866, the same year when he was designing the shipyard and the school. But he did not respond to the mission from the court until two years later when he successfully repressed the Nian Rebellion (捻军)[1]. Before leaving, Zuo Zongtang persuaded Shen Baozhen, the son-in-law of Lin Zexu, to be the successor and implementer of his plan. In fact, it was Shen Baozhen, the imperial commissioner (船政大臣), who supervised the shipyard and the school project. Through co-operation with the two French supervisors and other engineers, Shen Baozhen reached his final goal delineated in the contract. By the year 1873, the end of the fifth year, the shipyard was constructed and ships manufactured. In the meantime, a team of qualified Chinese engineers who could build ships and a crew who could steer ships were cultivated and trained. It was due to Zuo Zongtang's vision of constructing a shipyard and a school at the same time that China had the first modern technical school built. Zuo Zongtang fully understood that the school was crucial to cultivating competent talents for future use.

1 Nian Rebellion 的威妥玛式拼法为 Nien Rebellion。

6.2.4 Fuzhou Navy School 福州船政学堂

Fig. 6-6 福州船政学堂

Under the leadership of Shen Baozhen, Fuzhou Navy School was established, whose purpose was to educate technicians in Western sciences. The school was divided into the School of Navy Construction (造船学校), namely the French School because of French as the instruction medium and the Navy School (驾船学校), namely the English School due to English as the instruction medium. The French School was also called the school in front (前堂) due to its location in front of the Government Office and the English School was also called the school at the back (后堂) due to its rear position. Both the French and English Schools contained three branches respectively (Shen, 2009).

The three branches of the French School were the Shipbuilding, the Design and the Apprentice and the three English branches were the Naval, the Practical Sailing and the Engineer. The courses for the French School were arithmetic, geometry, analytic geometry (解析几何), physics, trigonometry, calculus, machine mapping, mechanics hull design and building, and French (Shen, 2009).

The courses for the English School covered arithmetic, geometry, algebra, trigonometry, physics, chemistry, higher mathematics, astronomy, geography, navigation mathematics, English and geographic navigation, in addition to mechanics, machine mapping, machine construction, the manipulation of machine and instrument (Shen, 2009).

The length of learning at Fuzhou Navy School was five years including three years of classroom study and two years of practice. After graduation, the students would go to

France and Britain for further education. And this was proposed by the chief supervisor Prosper Giquel who fully realized that the knowledge obtained by the students at Fuzhou Navy School was far from enough and if the Qing government wanted to be informed of the latest advancements in the area, it needed to send the students abroad for further studies. Here is what Giquel stated:

> A qualified engineer should be able to make machines of different types and know how to establish workshops. To acquire these abilities, students are supposed to study on the comparison of workshops and machines of different types and to draft as many different types as possible before they are guided to make machines of various sizes and types in their experiments. But unfortunately, in our school education, we can neither afford the time nor the ways to help our students to that far. (Shen, 2009: 171)

Since Fuzhou Navy School was only a technical school where students were exposed to the brand new knowledge of science and technology which had never been taught before, the level of teaching only amounted to the junior high school and if the goal set by Zuo Zongtang and Shen Baozhen was reached, there was much to be learned. Thus, Giquel was being honest when he wanted to make it clear that due to the constraints of academic environment what the tutors had taught was only a small part of the engineering knowledge.

> Only by sending them to Europe to study for at least four years, are they able to pick up experience from their study on engineering projects of different kinds...
>
> Chinese government should consider the question of whether to take immediate advantage of what students have acquired in the school and let them work in the workshop of the shipyard upon graduation, or to encourage students to study further to become engineers who are able to not only take charge of construction matters but also to provide, according to the latest development in industry, new blueprints and machine(s) that building of a new enterprise needs. (Shen, 2009: 171)

Following Giquel's advice, Shen Baozhen sent a memorial to the court asking permission of sending students abroad and got reply in 1874 (Shen, 2009), but sending overseas students was interrupted by the Sino-French War and picked up again in 1877.

During 1877–1896, four batches of Chinese students from the Navy School were sent to France, Britain to study shipbuilding and steering. Among them, Wei Han (魏瀚), Chen Zhao'ao, Zheng Qinglian, and Lin Yiyou studied at Sharp National College, France. Guo Ruigui, Liu Maoshun, and Qiu Guo'an studied at Baihaishideng National College, while Liu Buchan (刘步蟾), Lin Taizeng (林泰增), Yan Congguang, Jiang Chaoying, Fang Boqian (方伯谦), and Sa Zhenbing (萨镇冰) entered the Greenwich School (Shen, 2009). Those students coming back from European countries became the backbones of the early China navy and shipbuilding. The principal admirals of the Beiyang Fleet graduated from Fuzhou Navy School and studied in European countries. Liu Buchan and Lin Taizeng were Vice Admirals (左右翼总兵) and became Captains of the two ironclads Dingyuan ("定远"舰) and Zhenyuan ("镇远" 舰). They were commanding the warships during the Yellow Sea battle and committed suicide for the country in Weihaiwei (威海卫) naval warfare (王晓秋, 2014). During the Sino-Japanese War in 1894, sixteen admirals among the fifty war participants who graduated from Fuzhou Navy School died, among whom were Deng Shichang (邓世昌), Lv Han (吕瀚), Xu Shoushan (许寿山), Chen Ying (陈英), Lin Senlin (林森林), Ye Chen (叶琛), Lin Yongsheng (林永生), Liu Buchan, Lin Taizeng, and Lin Lv (林履). Their heroic spirits were admired by both the Chinese people and the foreign invaders (陈成沛, 2014).

To summarize, in this chapter, we discussed the Self-Strengthening Movement and its related projects, such as the military training program in Fenghuang Mountain, establishment of two arsenals and one technical school, i.e. Jiangnan Arsenal, Fuzhou Shipyard, and Fuzhou Navy School. Then, we focused on the role played by the two French officers Prosper Giquel and Paul d'Aiguebelle, who helped with hiring teaching staff abroad and supervising the workers in the arsenals. China's modern industry began to emerge due to the two arsenals. Ever since the 1860s, China started to integrate with the international trend of modern industry and management and it was Jiangnan Arsenal that lay the foundation for the modern shipbuilding company, i.e. Jiangnan Shipyard.

◆ Topics for Discussion

1. Was it possible for Zeng Guofan to initiate a deeper reform in China?

2. Your comment on Li Hongzhang's idea of containing the barbarians by means of the barbarians (以夷制夷).

3. The role played by Prosper Giquel and Paul d'Aiguebelle in training Chinese students.

4. Compared with private education in China, what are the advantages and disadvantages of Western education?

5. The relationship between science, technology and democratic ideas underneath.

◆ Reading Assignments

1. Shen, H.-Y. C. 1967. Tseng Kuo-Fan in Peking, 1840–1852: His Ideas on Statecraft and Reform. *The Journal of Asian Studies, 27*(1): 61-80.

2. Elman, B. A. 2004. Naval Warfare and the Refraction of China's Self-Strengthening Reforms into Scientific and Technological Failure, 1865–1895. *Modern Asian Studies, 38*(2): 283-326.

◆ Bibliography

Anon. 2014. The Search for Modern China: A Documentary Collection. New York: W. W. Norton & Company, Inc.

Anon. 2016. Zuo Zongtang. 01–28.

Gregory, J. S. 1959. British Intervention Against the Taiping "Rebellion". *The Journal of Asian Studies, 19*(1): 11-24.

Shen, H.-Y. C. 1967. Tseng Kuo-Fan in Peking, 1840–1852: His Ideas on Statecraft and Reform. *The Journal of Asian Studies, 27*(1): 61-80.

Shen Y. 2009. Chuan Zheng School. Beijing: China International Press.

Smith, R. J. 1975. The Employment of Foreign Military Talent: Chinese Tradition and Late Ch'ing Practice. *Journal of the Hong Kong Branch of the Royal Asiatic Society, 15*: 113-138.

Smith, R. J. 1976. Foreign-Training and China's Self-Strengthening: The Case of Feng-Huang-Shan, 1864–1873. *Modern Asian Studies, 10*(2): 195-223.

Smith, R. J., Fairbank, J. K., and Bruner, K. F. 1991. *Robert Hart and China's Early*

Modernization: His Journals, 1863–1866. Cambridge: Council on East Asian Studies.

Stevens, K. 1998/1999. The American Soldier of Fortune Frederick Townsend Ward Honoured and Revered by the Chinese with a Memorial Temple. *Journal of the Kong Kong Branch of the Royal Asiatic Society*, *38*: 285-291.

Swisher, E. 1958. Chinese Intellectuals and the Western Impact, 1838–1900. *Comparative Studies in Society and History*, *1*(1): 26-37.

Wang, C.-C. 1994. Li Hung-Chang and the Peiyang Navy. In S. C. Chu, and K.-C. Liu (eds.), *Li Hung-Chang and China's Early Modernization*. New York: M.E. Sharp, Inc.

Wang, H.-C. 2015. Merchants, Mandarins, and the Railway: Institutional Failure and the Wusong Railway, 1874–1877. *International Journal of Asian Studies*, *12*(1): 31-53.

Wright, S. F. 1950. Hart and the Chinese Customs. Belfast: W. M. Mullan & Son (Publishers), Ltd.

Zhang G. H. 1997. The Emergence and Development of China's Modern Capitalist Enterprises. In F. Wakeman Jr., and X. Wang (eds.), *China's Quest for Modernization: A Historical Perspective* (pp.234-249). Berkeley: The Regents of the University of California.

陈成沛. 2014. 福建船政学堂：以一校敌日本一国. 07–25. 海西晨报.

蒋廷黻. 2014. 近代中国外交史资料辑要：上中册. 北京：东方出版社.

王晓秋. 2014. 船政学堂的留欧学生. 08–04. 北京日报.

魏源. 1998. 海国图志. 长沙：岳麓书社.

约翰·濮兰德. 2010. 李鸿章传. 张启耀，译. 天津：天津人民出版社.

[illegible] Cambridge: [illegible]

[illegible] The American [illegible] [illegible] and Revered by the Chinese with a Memorial Temple [illegible]

Swisher, E. (1958). Chinese Intellectuals and the Western Impact, 1838–1900. *Comparative Studies in Society and History*, [illegible]

Wang, [illegible] In [illegible] Modernization. New York: [illegible]

Wang, [illegible] and the Railway [illegible] *International* [illegible]

Wright, [illegible]

[illegible] Modern Capitalist [illegible] Berkeley: The Regents of the University of California.

[illegible]

[illegible]

[illegible]

[illegible]

[illegible]

Chapter Seven

The Translation Department of Jiangnan Arsenal

江南制造局翻译馆

本章介绍 19 世纪西学东渐时，清代引进西方科学的过程。重点讨论徐寿、徐建寅、华蘅芳、李善兰和傅兰雅、伟烈亚力、艾约瑟等中西方译员，在江南制造局翻译馆译书的中外知识分子如何为各个学科的专有名词尤其是化学名词命名以及在建立格致书院过程中中西思维差距导致其功能受阻等现象。

7.1 The Background 背景介绍

In the Chinese history, there were three periods when Western learning was introduced to China, i.e. during the 16th and the 17th centuries, from the late 19th century to the early 20th century, and since 1978 when the policy of reform and opening to the outside world was adopted. The first wave was between 1582 and 1723 when Matteo Ricci, Adam Schall (汤若望), and Ferdinand Verbiest (南怀仁) came to China and spread Christianity via scientific knowledge and it lasted 141 years (孔国平等, 2012). Xu Guangqi, the Chinese literatus, and Ricci, the Italian Jesuit translated the first six chapters of Euclid's *Elements* into Chinese. Schall, the German Jesuit, revised and compiled the Chinese Shixian Calendar (时宪历) based on Gregorian Calendar (格里历 / 公历) and determined the "24 solar terms" (二十四节气) in the lunar calendar (佚名, 2018). The Belgian Jesuit Verbiest helped Emperor Kangxi with producing cannons and explosives in fighting against Wu Sangui (吴三桂) and the rebels in 1673 (严雄飞, 雷玉明, 2003). During this period of time, the tellurion (地球仪), world map, mechanical clock, prism (三棱镜), and Madonna (圣母像) brought by Matteo Ricci attracted the Chinese a great deal. Ricci also introduced to China the painting method of the light and shadow perspective (光影透视法), manual computation vertical (笔算竖式法), and the Roman alphabet phonetic method (罗马字母注音法), as well as cartography, astronomy and the Western calendar. The Jesuits' activities in China were called to an end due to the disputes between Emperor Kangxi and Roman papacy regarding rituals. Previously, in order to better spread Christianity, Ignatius Loyola (罗耀拉), the head of the Society of Jesuits instructed the Jesuits in China to adapt to the customs of the local people. Thus, the Jesuits began to wear the Confucian robe and allowed converts to worship their ancestors at the same time. But this practice changed due to the Vatican order, which tremendously disturbed Emperor

Kangxi. The latter in 1706 ordered to stop the spreading of Christianity in China. The complete ban began to be implemented from the reign of Emperor Yongzheng and the suspension lasted more than 130 years between 1706 and 1840 when the First Opium War began (董丛林, 2018).

The second wave of introducing Western learning began in the first half of the 19th century when English Protestant Robert Morrison came to China in 1807. He witnessed the forced opening of China's gate to the outside world in 1840. But Chinese literati officials did not realize the need to learn from the West until twenty years after the First Opium War in 1840. Having established Zongli Yamen, the foreign affairs office, Tongwen Guan, the interpreters' college, Jiangnan Arsenal and Fuzhou Shipyard, the scholar officials also saw the importance of introducing Western learning via translation. Xu Shou, an employee in Jiangnan Arsenal proposed to Zeng Guofan that a translation department should be built in order to gain and spread Western learning. Initially, Zeng Guofan did not realize its importance. But under Xu Shou's repeated requests, Zeng Guofan saw the necessity of it. Therefore, he ordered the establishment of the Translation Department in Jiangnan Arsenal as he said that translation was essential to manufacturing in China (翻译一事，系制造之本) (熊月之, 2016: 393).

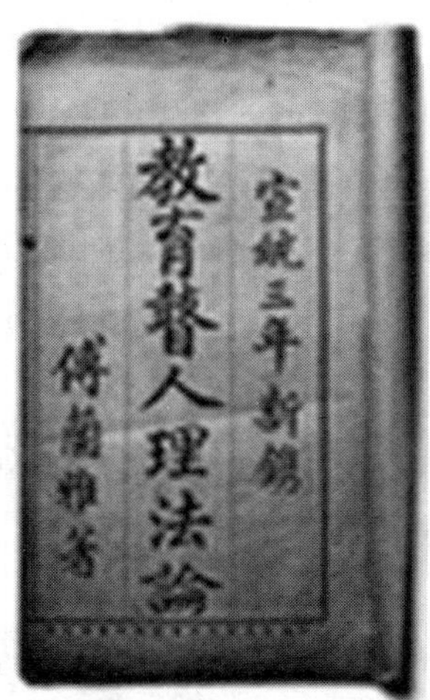

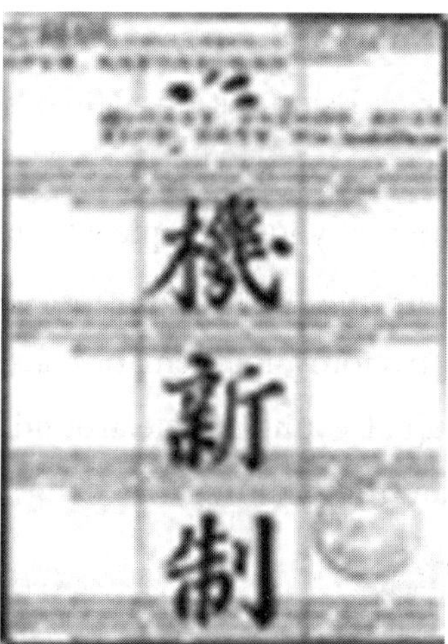

Fig. 7–1 傅兰雅著译

While the 17th and 18th century science was brought to China by Catholic missionaries, the 19th century science was mainly introduced by Protestant missionaries (Peake, 1934). John Fryer was one of them and he was appointed in 1868 as Director of the Department for the Translation of Scientific Books in Jiangnan Arsenal (Wright, 1995). He went back to England and bought about fifty science books, in an attempt to prepare a complete encyclopedia similar to the Encyclopedia Britannica to educate the Chinese people (Chun, 2005; 熊月之, 2016). His colleagues included both the Westerners and the Chinese, such as Alexander Wylie, Carl T. Kreyer (金楷理), Young John Allen (林乐知), Xu Shou, Hua Hengfang, Xu Jianyin (徐建寅), Shu Gaodi (舒高第), and Zhao Yuanyi (赵元益). Fifty-nine scholars including fifty Chinese and nine foreigners, were employed to co-operate in translating Western works of science and technology, i.e. mathematics and measurement (算学测量), steam turbine (蒸汽机), chemistry, palegeology (地质地理), astronomy, navigation, natural science (博物), medicine, technology, shipbuilding and art of war (兵法), etc. (熊月之, 2016). Although Li Shanlan was not employed by the Translation Department, he had engaged in translation work much earlier, i.e. in 1857 in the Mohai Shuguan or the Inkstone Press run by the London Missionary Society (Wright, 1995) and played an important part in the dissemination of Western learning. In the following session, several important figures will be introduced, i.e. Xu Shou, Li Shanlan, John Fryer, Xu Jianyin and Hua Hengfang.

7.2 Xu Shou and Li Shanlan 徐寿与李善兰

As we know, in the late Qing Dynasty, the thirst for becoming a civil servant was pervasive all over China and the essential method to achieve such a goal was to pass the Imperial Civil Service Examination, which required each examinee to learn by heart all the Confucian classics, i.e. the Four Books and the Five Classics. Yet in Wuxi, Jiangsu Province, a tiny group of young people who failed in the exams turned to natural sciences. The prominent figure among this group was Xu Shou, who showed tremendous interest in the subjects like astronomy, mathematics, acoustics, chemistry, mining and medicine and he attracted a group of young people around him, i.e. Hua Hengfang, Xu Jianyin, his son, and later Li Shanlan from Haining, Zhejiang Province.

Fig. 7-2 徐寿

Fig. 7-3 李善兰

Fig. 7-4 华蘅芳

They made experiments and checked the results based on the recently published book titled *Bowu Xinbian* (《博物新编》) in 1855, a new account of natural philosophy by Dr Benjamin Hobson (合信), an English medical missionary. The book, devoted entirely to modern science and written in Chinese, contained knowledge in physics, chemistry, astronomy, geography and zoology (Wright, 1995). The three, i.e. Xu Shou, Xu Jianyin and Hua Hengfang got together, discussing the problems and solutions described in *Bowu Xinbian*, as John Fryer recorded as follows:

> The book, although of a very elementary character, was like the dawn of a new era upon their minds, enabling them to leap at one bound across the two centuries that had elapsed...and bring(ing) them face to face with the results of some of the great modern discoveries. Apparatus was extemporized at their homes to perform the various experiments described in its pages, and every new theory or law put to the test as far as their limited means would permit. Frequent papers were written and circulated from one to another, while queries were continually started by individuals asking for more information on difficult subjects. A pile of such manuscripts accumulated in the house of Mr Hsü (Xu Shou), who with his son formed a sort of centre for this little oasis in the midst of a vast desert of ignorance. (Wright, 1995: 56-57)

The above activities engaged by Xu Shou and his friends remind us that the amateur scientists regularly presented their findings to a group of college professionals in what had later become the Royal Society in England during the 17th century. Curiosity and impetus for gaining the truth drove those inquiring minds in the 19th century China and the 17th century England to observe nature and study science. By doing so, they not only derived spiritual pleasure but also satisfied their curiosity about the natural world. In fact, that instinct of exploring the natural world was deeply entrenched in every human being and the enthusiasm could only be released in a free and relaxed environment. Yet the Imperial Civil Service Examination guided the Chinese with ambition to climb up in the social ladder and becoming a member of the officialdom was the sole aim for them to pursue. Few people showed interest in studying science as it neither offered profits nor promised a bright future like the Imperial Civil Service Examination. In this way, it greatly restrained people's mind and creativity as few people were willing to study something that was unpractical and unprofitable. In a sense, utilitarianism and practicality were something that hindered China from moving fast to modern society. As Confucianism did not contain science and regarded science as something like alchemy or quackery, the pursuit of science must be in conflict with Confucian ideology, which considered one's moral behavior as the most important. As was illustrated in Xu Shou's case, Xu Shou thought negatively of the Chinese traditional beliefs like *yin* (阴) and *yang* (阳) and he was also skeptical about some parts of Western thought. That was extremely rare in the late Qing society. The following was what Xu Shou said about Chinese traditional culture:

> Do not be two-faced, do not speak wildly, talk to people to establish the truth (of the matter) (...) Do not spread rumours, do not speak of things of which you have no experience, do not talk of horoscopes, nor of *fengshui* (siting; sometimes called "geomancy"). Do not speak of sorcery and prophecy. Do not use *yin* and *yang* to select the day for marriages and funerals. In sacrifices for the Four Seasons, sacrifice to your own ancestors, not to external spirits. In managing funerals do not use Buddhist monks and Daoists to perform rituals or musicians to beat (drums) and blow (shawms). In siting dwellings, there is no need to consult *fengshui* practitioners; simply discuss it with other people. Never speak of the production and destruction of the *wuxing* (五行), nor talk of the superficial ideas of *li* and *qi* (气). Always ascertain the truth of the matter by reference to the actual facts (以事实证). (Wright, 1995: 60)

As we can see, Xu Shou did not believe in those traditional concepts like *yin*, *yang*, *wuxing*, and *fengshui* because all the hypotheses were based on imaginations and could not be proved by experiments or facts. What's more, the traditional belief was likely to cause superstition and ignorance. Xu Shou thought that seeing was believing and everything was based on observations and facts. Xu Shou was really someone who possessed the qualities that a scientist had, such as skepticism and belief in truth. Like many Chinese, Xu Shou was an atheist and did not believe in religion and the afterlife world. This was different from what some Western scientists did. For instance, Isaac Newton's scientific drive was derived from his strong religious belief and his urge to prove what he believed.

In the Translation Department of Jiangnan Arsenal, Xu Shou co-operated closely with John Fryer to translate many science books into Chinese. The way they did the translation was like this: as the book was written in English, Fryer needed to verbally render it into Chinese before Xu Shou turned it into proper written Chinese. The reason was that John Fryer's written Chinese was not that good and Xu Shou did not understand English. But since Xu Shou himself was a scientist, he found it quite easy to understand what Fryer interpreted to him from the book and render it into good Chinese. According to Wright

(1995: 67-68), the English books of science and technology Xu Shou and Fryer translated included *Manual of the Steam Engine* (《汽机发轫》, 1871), *The Mirror of Chemistry: A* Source-Book (《化学鉴原》, 1872), *A Sequel to* The Mirror of *Chemistry: A Source-Book* (《〈化学鉴原〉续编》, 1875), *On Medicine* (《医学论》, 1876), *A Chinese-English Glossary of the Names of Chemical Substances* (《化学材料中西名目表》, 1885), and many others. *The Mirror of Chemistry: A Source-Book* outlined some chemical principles and the nature of various elements. *A Sequel to* The Mirror of Chemistry: A Source-Book was concerned with organic chemistry. *A Supplement to* The Mirror of Chemistry: A Source-Book (《〈化学鉴原〉补编》, 1879) dealt with inorganic chemistry.

One of the most distinguished things about Xu Shou was that he was the first Chinese who "published" in the scientific journal *Nature*. Because of his skepticism, Xu Shou detected some defects in a Westerner's calculation in musical instrument, so he began to do experiments and calculate it again. Eventually, he reached the conclusion that the previous result was wrong. Once he read the Chinese version of the book *Sound* by John Tyndall and jointly translated by John Fryer and Xu Shou's son Xu Jianyin, he found some errors. The book said that "the length ratio of an open pipe to another which sounded exactly one octave higher was 2: 1", but "Xu Shou already knew from his own experiments that this was not the case, and had established a ratio of 9: 4" (Wright, 1995: 69). Thus, John Fryer wrote to the writer John Tyndall asking about it and at the same time he sent a copy of the letter to the journal *Nature*. Although Tyndall did not reply, the editor of *Nature* highly praised Xu Shou's finding and gave positive remarks:

> It will be seen that a really scientific modern correction of an old law has most singularly turned up from China, and has been substantiated with the most primitive apparatus. (Wright, 1995: 71)

Thus, John Fryer's letter to *Nature* was published in the journal and Xu Shou became the first Chinese who reported his findings and corrected the previous error in a prestigious academic journal of the West. From this we can see that the Chinese like Xu Shou and others were talented with scientific discoveries and they were driven by their pure interest instead of practical needs.

There was another group of Chinese in Zhejiang Province who were active in scientific studies and the leader was Li Shanlan, who began to be interested in *Jiuzhang Suanshu* or *The Nine Chapters on the Mathematical Art* (《九章算术》) at the age of nine and later taught himself Euclid's *Elements* translated by Matteo Ricci and Xu Guangqi.

Around 1845, Li Shanlan set up a school in Jiaxing (嘉兴) to teach young people, where he got in touch with some mathematicians, such as Gu Guanguang (顾观光), Zhang Wenhu (张文虎), and Wang Yuezhen (汪曰桢). They often gathered together discussing mathematic problems. During this time, Li Shanlan wrote books regarding "sharp technique" (尖锥术) including *Fangyuan Chanyou, Hushi Qimi, Duishu Tanyuan*, etc. (王渝生, 2015). *Jiuzhang Suanshu* edited by Liu Hui (刘徽) in the Eastern Han Dynasty, summarized the mathematical achievements since the Warring States Period, the Qin and Han dynasties in China. It was the first to mention the score problem and to record surplus and deficit (最早提出分数问题，记录了盈余不足等问题). It also described for the first time negative numbers and their addition and subtraction algorism in mathematics history (佚名, 2019b). *Elements* was a great geometry book written by ancient Greek mathematician Euclid, in which for the first time man's understanding of space had been completed (佚名, 2019a).

In 1852, Li Shanlan began his translation career in Mohai Shuguan. He showed his books to Alexander Wylie and other colleagues. The missionaries highly praised Li Shanlan for his interesting books. His first joint effort with Wylie was to translate the last nine chapters of Euclid's *Elements*, which was unfinished by the Jesuit Fathers during the late Ming Dynasty. Then, Li Shanlan co-operated with Joseph Edkins (艾约瑟) and translated the book *Zhongxue* (《重学》), introducing for the first time Newton's Three Laws of Mechanics (牛顿力学三大定律). The other translated books like Augustus de Morgan's *Elements of Algebra* (《代数学》), Elias Loomis's *Elements of Analytical Geometry and of Differential and Integral Calculus* (《代微积拾级》), John F. W. Herschel's *Outlines of Astronomy* (《天文学纲要》), *Philosophiæ Naturali Principia Mathematica* (《奈端数理》) were also joint efforts between Li Shanlan and other missionaries like Alexander Williamson (威廉姆逊), John Fryer, and Alexander Wylie (李善兰, 2015; Martzloff, 1224). When Li Shanlan was employed in 1861 by Zeng Guofan in Anqing Arsenal (安庆军械所), he requested Zeng Guofan to publish the Chinese version of Euclid's *Elements* and four years later in 1865 other mathematics books written by Li Shanlan and Euclid's *Elements* were published sponsored by Zeng Guofan.

Science is a term originated from ancient Greece and it has two characteristics: non-utilitarian and truth-seeking. Aristotle once commented that people loved science only for the sake of science, but did not have any specific purpose for it. It is purely out of fun and interest. "The ancient Greeks regarded useless, free, pure science as true science." (吴国盛, 2018). This is quite different from the Chinese way of thinking. The Chinese tended to do everything for the purpose of its usefulness and practicality. The appearance of *Jiuzhang Suanshu* was out of the need of measuring and calculating agricultural fields.

The sad truth was that the effort made by these two tiny groups of inquiring people was too insignificant to change the situation in the late Qing Dynasty when the majority of the people were still attracted to the official career via passing the Imperial Civil Service Examination. It was a necessity to have some contacts in the government to get books published. In this case, Zeng Guofan helped Li Shanlan to publish his books. The science genius Xu Shou also had some flaws in his personality as he refused to use the Shanghai Polytechnic Institute for public purpose. He took it as his own property and moved his family members into the institute while leaving no room for its original purpose, i.e. public education set by his partner John Fryer. When the institute was founded, it attracted a lot of donations from the Westerners including facilities and equipment, and various samples of plants and animals. It was intended by the co-sponsor John Fryer to spread scientific knowledge to the public. Yet unexpectedly, it was not supported by Xu Shou, thus causing some conflicts between them. Xu Shou's behavior was characteristic of the Chinese gentry class, who paid attention to the character cultivation while ignoring their social responsibilities. It was not until the turning of the century when Liang Qichao publicized the public spirit or public virtues (公德) to the whole society that the Chinese began to take notice of this aspect of humanity.

7.3 John Fryer 傅兰雅

As one of the major channels to disseminate knowledge of science and technology, translation played an important role, in addition to the London Missionary Society (1843) and the Shanghai Polytechnic Institute (1870). Added as a department to Jiangnan Arsenal three years after its establishment in 1868, the Translation Department was aimed at introducing Western science and technology. Zeng Guofan, the high-ranking official, realized its importance and wrote a memorial to the throne:

> Now translation is the foundation of modern manufacture. Mathematics is used by foreigners as the mother of manufacturing science. Its wonder is explained by works and drawing. Being handicapped by the difficulty of language, although we know how to manufacture things, we are unable to understand the principles of manufacturing...When the translation bureau is set up, capable and intelligent students will be selected to be trained as translators...(Bennett, 1967: 21)

What Zeng Guofan was concerned with was the method of manufacturing, but the real impact was far from it. As Director of the Department, John Fryer's leading role was to be discussed. Having taken two different posts, i.e. teaching and editing, John Fryer decided that translation was something he loved best and he stayed in the Department for twenty-eight years.

Since his college major was in education, not in science, Fryer needed to teach himself those subjects while doing the translation. "I have begun by studying and translating three subjects at once. In the morning I take coal and coal mining in all its details, in the afternoon I dig into chemistry and in the evenings acoustics." (Bennett, 1967: 23-24) It seemed that he had dual purposes: one was to help this ancient nation to move forward via scientific and technological knowledge and the other was to get promoted through his hard work. It turned out that Fryer had reached his first goal, but not the second one.

Initially, John Fryer had three Western colleagues, i.e. Alexander Wylie, Dr John MacGowan (玛高温) and the Reverend Carl Kreyer and three Chinese ones, i.e. Xu Shou, Hua Hengfang, and Xu Jianyin. As a matter of fact, the Translation Department was initiated by the three Chinese because all of them saw the urgent need to learn from the West. In addition, the three were all keen on reading books of science and technology and benefited from it. It is because of them that Zeng Guofan proposed to the throne in adding the Translation Department to the arsenal.

Having been given the freedom to choose the books for translation, John Fryer ordered over 148 books from England, among which "twenty-nine were in the military area, twenty-eight were in the field of shipbuilding and navigation, twenty-eight in the field of manufacturing, thirteen in geology, ten in chemistry, six in mathematics, three in medicine and thirty-one on general scientific topics" (Bennett, 1967: 28-29). Since it required a joint work from two colleagues, it took one year to finish translating just one book. The most difficult task was how to give nomenclature to different scientific terminology, especially chemistry. A terminology committee was organized by Fryer among the missionaries who were engaged in the translating tasks in order to standardize terminology. His idea was that the committee should collect existing terms used by translators, such as the Jesuits and Protestants of the 16th and 17th centuries and compile a list of terms which were acceptable. He said that "all writers of technical books already published be communicated with and asked to alter their terminology in all future editions to conform to the fixed standard" (Bennett, 1967). The three methods Fryer used in translating terminology were to find a term that already existed, to coin a new one, and to invent a term or phoneticize the foreign term. His method sounded reasonable, but his colleagues in the committee disagreed with him because different Chinese characters indicated different matters or substances but the sound or pronunciation was all the same. That would cause confusion to the reader.

With regard to terminology for the Periodic Table of the Elements (元素周期表), Xu Shou contributed a great deal by using two methods: transliteration (谐音) and semantic translation (会意). If you use the first method of transliteration, you have the nomenclature of the elements 氦 for helium, 氩 for argon, 锂 for lithium, 砷 for arsenic, and 碲 for tellurium. If you use the second method of semantic translation, you have 氢 for hydrogen, 氯 for chlorine, 氧 for oxygen, and 氮 for nitrogen (佚名, 2017). In the travel book written by Hua Hengfang, we can read special terms like "淡轻四绿" (four nitrogen hydrogen chloride), "铝二养三" (aluminum two oxygen three), etc. Modern people refer to those chemical terms as $(NH)_4CI$ and AL_2O_3 as 氯化铵 and 三氧化二铝. But previously Xu Shou used the character 淡 and character 养 to stand for the chemical elements N and H (钟叔河, 2010: 290).

The sale of the first translated books between 1870 and 1880 was more than 30,000 copies and it kept increasing until the 1890s. Kang Youwei was greatly influenced by those books when he bought all the books published by Jiangnan Arsenal in 1882 and that certainly had much to do with his initiation of the Gongche Shangshu (公车上书) in 1895 and the One Hundred Days Reform in 1898. In addition, Liang Qichao also purchased many of the Jiangnan Arsenal publications, i.e. *Gezhi Huibian* (《格致汇编》). Similarly, Tan Sitong (谭嗣同) also read *Gezhi Huibian* and he even visited John Fryer in 1893 and was shown many fossils and photographic equipment (Bennett, 1967).

John Fryer published several hundred Chinese volumes, and some became textbooks at Beijing University and in some mission schools. In 1870, together with Xu Shou, John Fryer co-built the Shanghai Polytechnic Institute and helped to publish *Chinse Scientific Magazine* (《中国科学杂志》) in Chinese. Fryer founded in 1884 *Chinese Scientific Book Depot* (《书库》) in Shanghai and published *Gezhi Huibian* (Chun, 2005). At the age of 57 in 1896, Fryer took the employment as Professor at Berkeley, University of California, devoting himself to Oriental Cultural Studies in the US.

During his stay in China, John Fryer cherished hope for China to become stronger despite of some depressions he suffered. "...The system of ignoring everything but the Four

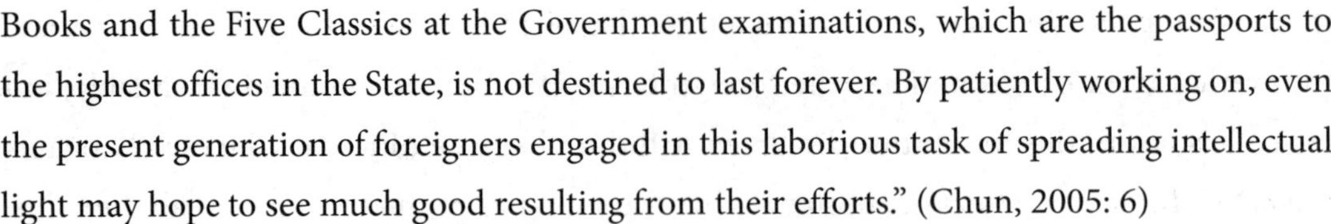

Books and the Five Classics at the Government examinations, which are the passports to the highest offices in the State, is not destined to last forever. By patiently working on, even the present generation of foreigners engaged in this laborious task of spreading intellectual light may hope to see much good resulting from their efforts." (Chun, 2005: 6)

7.4 Xu Jianyin and Hua Hengfang 徐建寅与华蘅芳

Unlike his father Xu Shou, Xu Jianyin was successful in the Imperial Civil Service Examination and was promoted to various official posts. One of the important position he held in 1879 was the Second Councilor to the Chinese Legation in Germany (驻德国二等参赞) and Xu Jianyin paid technical visits to more than eighty factories in Germany, France and Britain in order to purchase ironclads. By carefully comparing the ironclads made in Britain and Germany, Xu Jianyin spot some drawbacks in the former shipyard and decided to order two from the German Vulcan Shipyard (伏尔铿造船厂) (钟叔河, 2010). The two well-known ironclads Zhenyuan and Dingyuan were manufactured under Xu Jianyin's supervision in Germany for Li Hongzhang who was developing the Beiyang Fleet modeling after the German Navy. Xu Jianyin's experience in Europe left him a deep impression that China was far left behind by the Western countries in technological advancement and if China intended to catch up, it must implement political reform. Otherwise, the enormous gulf between China and the industrialized countries could hardly be bridged. Japan's success was a good case in point. By having a thorough reform in politics during the Meiji Restoration, Japan leapt to an industrialized country within a short time (Wright, 1995). Xu Jianyin recorded in greater detail his activities and thoughts during the twenty months traveling in Europe in the book *The European Travels* (《欧游杂录》).

Accompanied by his father, Xu Jianyin came to work in the Translation Department of Jiangnan Arsenal in 1868. John Fryer, the director, knew Xu Jianyin previously and both had a very good time co-operating in translating books of science and technology. Only six years younger than Fryer, Xu Jianyin regarded him as his own brother and told everything about him to Fryer and they became close friends. According to Wright (1995), the books translated by John Fryer and Xu Jianyin included *Practical Geometry* (《运规约指》, 1870), *Chemical Analysis* (《化学分原》, 1872), *New Types of Steam Engines* (《汽机新制》, 1872), *The Engineer and Machinist's Drawing Book* (《器象显真》, 1872), etc. From the publication years shown above, we can see that most of the books translated into Chinese exhibited the state-of-the-art science and technology during that period of time. Both Xu

Shou and Xu Jianyin did their part in promoting modernization in China. Unfortunately, while Xu Jianyin was making great efforts in experimenting with smokeless ammunition in Wuhan Arsenal run by Zhang Zhidong, he died in an explosive accident.

As a close friend and co-operator of Xu Shou when working in Anqing Machinery Bureau, Hua Hengfang designed the first China-made steamship Huanghu (黄鹄) under the supervision of Xu Shou. Like Xu Shou, Hua Hengfang began to be interested in mathematics at a very early age. He could make a comparison and contrast between *Jiuzhang Suanshu* and Euclid's *Elements* and pointed out that geometry was more useful than arithmetic. The ability of doing calculations was not sufficient to understand the relations between points and lines while a thorough understanding of geometry helped people master the four rules of arithmetic (四则运算).

> 《几何原本》为西法中最古之书，不言法而言理，不言数而言象，盖彻乎立法之源。凡《九章》所不及者无不赅也。不读几何则不能明点线面体之理，而于加减乘除开方之用终不能了然于心。(孔国平、佟健华、方运加，2012：39)

In 1867, Hua Hengfang together with Daniel Jerome MacGowan, an American missionary translated *Manual of Mineralogy* (《金石识别》) written by J. D. Dana (代那) and published it in 1872. The second book he jointly translated with MacGowan took place in the Translation Department of Jiangnan Arsenal in 1868. The book title was *Elements of Geology* (《地学浅释》) written by the English geologist Charles Lyell (赖尔). The book was renown at the time and enjoyed the world-class status. But the process of translation was frustrating because Hua Hengfang was ill, suffering from diarrhea, which made him extremely painful. To make the matter worse, MacGowan needed to stop his translation from time to time because as a private physician, he had patients to attend to. That gave Hua Hengfang a very difficult time and he had to continue with the correction and proofreading while waiting for his partner to come back. Since the content of the book was unfamiliar to Hua Hengfang, some descriptions of the cataclysmic geological events caused nightmares for him and almost made him sick. On many occasions, Hua Hengfang had to make guesses of the real meaning by "looking at MacGowan's facial expressions and observing his gestures" because neither of the two was proficient in his target language. Hua Hengfang did not speak English and MacGowan's knowledge of Chinese language and culture was very limited (Wright, 1998: 664).

玛（高温）君于金石之品知之最祥，因以医为业，不能延至制造局。故余僦屋于外，日至其家，俟其为医之暇，则与对译此书。书中所论之物有中土有名者，有中土无名者，有中土虽有名而余不知其名，一时不易仿究者。每译一物，必辨论数四。其有名者，则用中土之名；其无名者及不知其名者，则将西国之名译其意义；又有以地为名、以人为名并无意义可译或其名鄙俚不可译其意义者，则用中土之字以写西国之音，故其名佶屈聱牙、不能以文意相贯，多至五六字、七八字者，往往有之。（孔国平、佟健华、方运加，2012：94）

The hardship of translating scientific books into Chinese was vividly described by John Fryer. It was "perhaps about as dull and unthankful a task as any foreigner could engage in especially in such a secluded place as the Kiangnan[1] Arsenal, and under the depressing influences of the climate of this part of China. Nothing but a strong sense of duty and a firm belief that this kind of labour is one of the most effective means...has sufficed to render endurable the long weary years of close and continuous application which it has involved" (Wright, 1998: 664).

Given all the difficulties and hardships both English and Chinese translators were dedicated to their work, hoping that one day China would become as strong as the industrialized countries. Indeed, their efforts were not made in vain. Not long afterwards, reformers like Kang Youwei, Liang Qichao, and Tan Sitong were tremendously inspired by those translated books and they began to engage themselves in making changes to the Qing government and the One Hundred Days Reform did take place in 1898. In spite of the fact that this reform only lasted about three months, the foundation of the old regime was definitely shaken and China had quickened its pace to a modern society.

To summarize, we discussed in this chapter how John Fryer, Xu Shou, Li Shanlan, Xu Jianyin and Hua Hengfang co-operated to translate the Western works of science and technology, the difficulties they came across and overcame, and how Kang Youwei and other reformists benefited from reading those books.

◆ Topics for Discussion

1. Why was there a long interval between the Jesuits and the Protestant missionaries when the latter came to China?

1 Kiangnan 指江南，是 Jiangnan 的威妥玛式拼法。

2. Why weren't there many Chinese men of letters who had the curiosity to explore the natural world?

3. Could Chinese scientists like Li Shanlan, Xu Shou, and Hua Hengfang do more in promoting science and technology?

4. Your comment on *li* and *qi*.

5. The prerequisites for scientific work.

6. Academic environment and research discoveries.

7. The importance of logic in science.

8. The traditional Chinese way of thinking and scientific development.

◆ Reading Assignment

Dolezelova-Veligerova, M., and Wagner, R. G. (eds). 2014. Chapter 1 and 2 of *Chinese Encyclopedias of New Global Knowledge (1870–1930)*. New York: Springer-Verlag Berlin Heidelberg.

◆ Bibliography

Bennett, A. A. 1967. *John Fryer: The Introduction of Western Science and Technology into Nineteenth-Century China*. Cambridge: The East Asian Research Center.

Bennett, A. A. 1983. *Missionary Journalist in China: Young J. Allen and His Magazines, 1860–1883*. Athens: The University of Georgia Press.

Chun, D. S. 2005. John Fryer, the First Agassiz Professor of Oriental Languages and Literature. Berkeley: Chronicle of the University of California.

Li, H.-T'I. 2014. Late Qing Encyclopaedias: Establishing a New Enterprise. In M. Dolezelova-Velingerova, and R. G. Wagner (eds.), *Chinese Encyclopaedias of New Global Knowledge (1870–1930)* (pp.29-53). New York: Springer-Verlag Berlin Heidelberg.

Martzloff, J. 2008. Li Shanlan. In Selin H. (eds), *Encyclopaedia of the History of Science, Technology, and Medicine in Non-Western Cultures* (pp.1224-1226). Dordrecht: Springer.

Peake, C. H. 1934. Some Aspects of the Introduction of Modern Science into China. *Isis*, *22*(1): 173-219.

Wright, D. 1995. Careers in Western Science in Nineteenth-Century China: Xu Shou and Xu Jianyin. *Journal of the Royal Asiatic Society*, *5*(1): 49-99.

Wright, D. 1996. John Fryer and the Shanghai Polytechnic: Making Space for Science in Nineteenth-Century China. *The British Journal for the History of Science*, *29*(1): 1-16.

Wright, D. 1998. The Translation of Modern Western Science in Nineteen-Century China, 1840–1895. *Isis*, *89*(4): 653-673.

董丛林. 2018. 晚清教案危机与政府应对. 北京：中华书局.

孔国平，佟健华，方运加. 2012. 中国近代科学的先行者华蘅芳. 北京:科学出版社.

王杨宗. 2012. 过渡时代的奇人徐寿的故事. 长春：吉林出版社.

王渝生.2015. 李善兰. 08–01. 个人图书馆.

吴国盛. 2018. 我们对科学有多少误解? ——人文清华讲坛吴国盛演讲实录. 11–02. 爱思想.

夏晶. 2012. 傅兰雅和狄考文——西学译介的两种态度. 04–28. 中国人民大学清史研究所.

熊月之. 2016. 译术与西学东渐. 王建朗，黄克武. 两岸新编中国近代史：晚清卷下. 北京：社会科学文献出版社.

严雄飞，雷玉明. 2003. 西方传教士南怀仁在华活动述略. 山东农业大学学报，5（4）: 79–82.

佚名. 2014. 江南制造局翻译馆. 04–11. 中国国家图书馆网站 / 中国社会科学网.

佚名. 2015a. 傅兰雅. 06–10. 互动百科.

佚名. 2015b. 傅兰雅. 06–10. 华人基督教史人物辞典.

佚名. 2015c. 李善兰. 08–01. “科普中国” 百科科学词条编写与应用工作项目审核.

佚名. 2017. 化学元素命名. 08–04. 高中化学元素周期表——为什么化学命名中有那么多生僻字? ——教育文化.

佚名. 2018. 科学精神与汤若望的中国农历——有点意思的历史. 12–26. 简书.

佚名. 2019a. 几何原本. 02–15. 360 百科.

佚名. 2019b. 九章算术. 02–15. 360 百科.

钟叔河. 2010. 走向世界：中国人考察西方的历史. 北京：中华书局.

Chapter Eight

Young John Allen and Chinese Language Newspapers
林乐知与中文报纸

媒体的出现是社会步入现代的标志。本章主要讨论西方启蒙时代的成果之一报刊是如何被介绍到中国的。讲解中国的第一份报纸《申报》的出现和第一位报人王韬的贡献，同时介绍美国传教士林乐知主办《教会新报》和《万国公报》的经历，并探讨信息媒介的出现对中国进入现代社会所起的作用。

8.1 The Background 背景介绍

As one of the public sphere institutions proposed by Jürgen Habermas (于尔根·哈贝马斯), newspaper was a product of European enlightenment. In order to inform and criticize, the role played by the press media was to awaken people to the public to use their reason by being engaged in rational-critical debate on public issues. In *The Structural Transformation of the Public Sphere* (《公共领域的结构转型》, 1989), Habermas made a case study on Britain and pointed out that the institutions of the public sphere in the 17th and the 18th century Britain included the novel, the newspaper, the lending library, and coffeehouses. The first group of the British who made use of the public sphere to criticize were novelists and poets like Johnathan Swift (乔纳森·斯威夫特), Daniel Defoe (丹尼尔·笛福), and John Milton (约翰·弥尔顿). They were both literary writers and public intellectuals. Swift not only wrote novels like *The Gulliver's Travels* (《格列佛游记》), but also criticized the Irish government using his pamphlet *A Modest Proposal* (《一个温和的建议》). In the same manner, *Robinson Crusoe* (《鲁滨逊漂流记》) was not the only genre of writing Defoe engaged in, but he also published *Review*, a magazine to discuss and debate on public issues. Milton, in addition to *Paradise Lost* (《失乐园》), a long narrative poem, also published a pamphlet *Areopagitica: A Speech for the Liberty of Unlicensed Printing* (《论出版自由》) in 1644, championing the right of free speech.

The journals run by Joseph Addison and Richard Steele including *Tatler* (《闲谈者》, 1709–1711), *Spectator* (《旁观者》, 1711–1714) and *Guardian* (《卫报》, 1713) became the public sphere for political debates, which, according to Habermas (Cowan, 2004: 346, 351), was not only introduced by the Whigs to the Parliament, but also made use of by its opposition party the Tories to resist the former. Thus, the real democracy in the Parliament was formed.

Another important type of the public sphere was coffeehouses, where people of all walks of life engaged in critical public debates. According to Parker and Michael, the Boston Tea Party (波士顿倾茶事件) of 1773, the Anti-Stamp Act (反印花税法案) event of 1765, and the overthrowing of the Bastille of 1789 were all attributed to the discussions in the coffeehouses. It seemed that the coffeehouses, such as the Green Dragon Inn, Tavern and Coffeehouse were the public sphere for the Americans to brew and discuss the Party. Since they hated the British who imposed high tax on tea, the Americans considered coffee as their national drink. Regarding the Anti-Stamp Act of 1765, the decision was also made in Charlton's Coffeehouse in Williamsburg, Virginia and the rebels protested the collector sent by the royal governor, leading to the resignation of the collection and the abrogation of the Act by the British Parliament. Even *Declaration of Independence* was first read in a coffeehouse called the City Tavern, which was the venue for the newly formed Continental Congress (大陆会议). In France, coffeehouses were also frequented by philosophers and political leaders. It was said that the French revolutionaries initiated the destruction of the Bastille on July 14, 1789 in a Paris coffeehouse named the Café de Foy (勒塔耶尔, 2018). Voltaire and Montesquieu (孟德斯鸠) often went to a coffeehouse named Cafe Prokopis (普罗科普咖啡馆) and Diderot's idea of publishing an encyclopedia was inspired by his argument with d'Alembert (达朗贝尔) in the same café (勒塔耶尔, 2018).

Obviously, the public sphere represented by the novel, the newspaper, the lending library, and coffeehouses facilitated the social change and advancement because the wisdom and intellect gathered from different individuals and communities were more comprehensive, more reasonable, and more sensible than that of a single person. Public opinions reflected a collective intelligence that played a more important role in helping the government to modify its policy so as to promote people's consensus, happiness and a sense of fulfillment. In the next section, the Chinese language newspapers will be introduced.

8.2 Chinese Language Newspapers in the Late Qing Period 晚清时期的中文报纸

When addressing the question why the public sphere in modern China first took place in Shanghai, Xu Jilin (许纪霖, 2017) explained that people in Shanghai enjoyed more freedom compared with those of Beijing and Changsha due to the presence of the public sphere. Shanghai people developed a certain space through books, magazines and newspapers where they could freely exchange ideas concerning social and political issues. For instance, the Translation Department of Jiangnan Arsenal was situated in Shanghai and many Western books of science and technology were translated into Chinese. Shanghai Tongwen Guan or Guang Fangyan Guan (广方言馆) ran smoothly by using the modern curriculum while Tongwen Guan in Beijing experienced a chaotic period when new subjects of science and astronomy were being added to its curriculum. In addition, the Shanghai Polytechnic Institute served as an incubator for demonstrating and spreading modern knowledge to ordinary people. However in Beijing and Changsha, there was no such institute present. In this section, we will discuss two Chinese language newspapers in Shanghai and Hong Kong. One was *Shen Bao* (《申报》, 1872–1949) invested by British merchants and the other was *Xunhuan Ribao* (《循环日报》, 1874–1949) purely sponsored by a Chinese named Wang Tao (王韬). Both newspapers enjoyed a long presence spanning from the late 19th century to the mid 20th century.

8.2.1 Shanghai *Shen Bao* 上海《申报》

Shen Bao was the first commercial Chinese language newspaper published by the British businessman Ernest Major who jointly invested in 1872 with three other British in the newspaper. The aim of this newspaper was to make China better by using Western institution of media, in addition to profit making. The target readers were set for the ordinary Chinese and the layout followed the pattern of Europe, including leaders, leaderettes (编者按), news items, telegraphs, scraps of general information and advertisement (Anon, 2017). Several Chinese were employed for the newspaper and they were given the liberty to choose to publish whatever interested Chinese readers. Jiang Zhixiang (蒋芷湘), Wu Zirang (吴子让), He Guisheng (何桂笙), and Qian Xinbo (钱昕伯) were from Jiangnan and worked as editors. Zou Tao (邹韬), Li Shifen (李士芬), Cai Erkang (蔡尔康) and Shen Yugui (沈毓桂) were also added to the team. Most of them were friends of Wang Tao who was in Hong Kong and established his own newspaper *Xunhuan Ribao* in 1874, two years after *Shen Bao*. All the Chinese editors in the early stage of the Shanghai press market had connections with the missionaries of the London Missionary Society, Young John Allen, and Timothy Richard (李提摩太) and thus had knowledge of the West (Wagner, 2007).

Since *Shen Bao* was based in the International Settlement of Shanghai, it enjoyed more freedom even than that in Britain. Governed by the Municipal Council, *Shen Bao* was independent from the Qing government and the regulations set for the newspaper

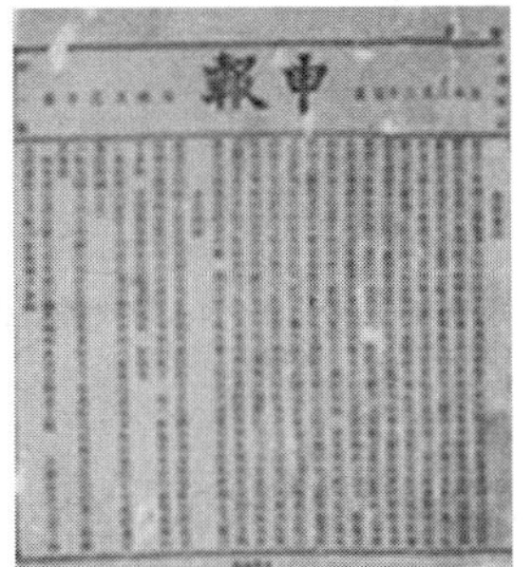

Fig. 8-1 《申报》

were not strict. The newspaper had its own informants inside the court and when Emperor Guangxu was severely ill, the reports regarding his condition were frequently released to the public and for half a year it met with no interruptions from the Qing government. Due to the truthfulness of its reports, the newspaper enjoyed a large readership which had brought profits to the institution as well. Apart from sensational news that attracted people's attention, *Shen Bao* also exposed and criticized the dark side of the society, functioning as one of the public sphere institutions. For instance, when the illicit prostitution at opium dens where young women were disguised as waitresses was revealed by *Shen Bao*, the women were released from the dens and the practice was banned. On other issues, *Shen Bao* also showed great concern over women's education and by using advertisements, editorials, and news reports, women as a group began to attract social attention (Anon, 2017).

In 1873, only a year after the appearance of *Shen Bao*, an unjust case took place in Yuhang (余杭), Zhejiang Province where Yang Naiwu (杨乃武) and Xiao Baicai (小白菜) were illegally punished and sentenced to death under the alleged crime of collaborating a murder of the latter's husband Ge Pinlian (葛品连). The story went like that: the newly wedded couple Bi Xiugu (毕秀姑), i.e. Xiao Baicai and Ge Pinlian rented a room in Yang Naiwu's house. Yang Naiwu, a *Juren*, a successful candidate of the Imperial Civil Service Examination at the provincial level, offended Liu Xitong (刘锡彤), the county magistrate (知县) for Yang Naiwu's character of uprightness and justice upholding. It so happened that a few months after marriage, Xiao Baicai's husband died, but his relatives suspected that Ge Pinlian might have been poisoned by the host of the house because some blood was seen flowing out of the dead body's nose and it was thought to be a joint plot between Ge Pinlian's wife and the host for their extramarital love. Thus, both were brought to court and after the inquisition by torture, both confessed the crime that they had never committed. The two innocent people were facing death punishment. However, Yang Naiwu's sister never believed that her brother had committed such a crime and she brought the case to the government court. Having gone through complicated procedures, Yang Naiwu and Xiao Baicai were proved to be not guilty. But three years had already passed and both were not in good health because of the torture at prison. In the course of the three years, *Shen Bao* played a pivotal role in reporting and tracking the case, which aroused people's attention and eventually attracted the attention of Dowager Cixi who agreed to review the case (佚名, 2017b).

Finally, *Shen Bao* also promoted Chinese literature by publishing a supplement called "Free Talk" (《自由谈》) to its newspaper. When Lu Xun (鲁迅) and Mao Dun (茅盾) were invited to write for the column, many young and old educated people were attracted to this newspaper and published their articles. They were Chen Wangdao (陈望道), Xia Mianzun (夏丏尊), Zhou Jianren (周建人), Ye Shengtao (叶圣陶), Lao She (老舍), Shen Congwen (沈从文), Yu Dafu (郁达夫), Ba Jin (巴金), Zhang Tianyi (张天翼) (佚名, 2017a), to name but a few. It was a period of vigorous thought and bloom of Chinese literature.

The newspaper, a product of the enlightenment and modernity, when introduced to China functioned as a bridge between the Qing court and local people. The message conveyed by the newspaper was that the government had the responsibility to take care of its people, to know their plight and difficulties so that they could take measures to help the people and solve their problems. With the appearance of the public sphere, the Qing court was beginning to take notice of the people's problems and difficulties and fulfill its duty as the ruler. Next, we will take a look at another Chinese media in Hong Kong.

8.2.2 Hong Kong *Xunhuan Ribao* 香港《循环日报》

Xunhuan Ribao was the first Chinese newspaper run by a native Chinese Wang Tao. Wang Tao's exile experience proved to be useful in directing him to become a newspaper man. In 1862, when Li Xiucheng (李秀成), one of the Taiping Movement leaders declared to attack and occupy Shanghai where Wang Tao was working at Mohai Shuguan to help Dr Walter Henry Medhurst to translate the Bible into Chinese since 1849, Wang Tao wrote a letter to the Taiping official Liu Zhaojun (刘肇钧) advising him to avoid confrontations with foreigners in Shanghai, but focus on the upper reaches of the Yangtze River. He also asked Liu Zhaojun to pass the message to Li Xiucheng. In the letter, Wang Tao also showed the group how to strategically deploy his army and eventually occupy Shanghai (柯文, 1998). Unfortunately, this letter was intercepted by the Qing army and Wang Tao thus became a wanted man. He had to leave Shanghai for Hong Kong under the protection of the British consulate Frederick Bruce and missionaries.

Fig. 8–2 王韬

In Hong Kong, Wang Tao was invited by the head of the Anglo-Chinese College (英华书院) and the English missionary James Legge (理雅格) to proofread the English version of Chinese classics, such as *The Book of Songs*, *The Book of Changes*, *The Book of Rites*. As a Sinologist, James Legge translated the Four Books and the Five Classics into English during the twenty-five years from 1861 to 1886 and published twenty-eight volumes in all (钟书河, 2010; 佚名, 2019). In addition, he also translated many other important Chinese books into English. In 1875, Legge was employed as Professor of Chinese studies at Oxford University (赖某深, 2017). James Legge spoke Chinese and Wang Tao's job was to help the former fully understand the meaning of the Chinese books before he turned it into English.

Wang Tao's unique work experience with Dr Medhurst and James Legge made him a disseminator of English culture to the Chinese people and at the same time a transmitter of Chinese culture to the English people. Apart from doing the translation, Wang Tao was also working part time as the editor in chief for the newspaper *Chinese Mail* (《华字日报》), providing information for the Qing court and also reporting news about Guangdong and Hong Kong (杨之, 2016). Those experiences showed to him that media in terms of press and newspaper played an important role in bridging the distance between the emperor at the top and the people at the bottom. Thus, when James Legge decided to go back to Britain in 1873, Wang Tao, with the help of Huang Sheng (黄胜), who supervised Hong Kong Mohai Shuguan, spent 10, 000 Mexican eagle (墨西哥鹰洋), a currency used by Mexicans to have jointly bought Mohai Shuguan and turned its name into China Printing Bureau (中华印务总局) and in the beginning of 1874, *Xunhuan Ribao* came into being (柯文, 1998). The Chinese characters 循环 means circulation and essentially they implied that the newspaper like many other things would be continuous and kept alive forever.

Xunhuan Ribao was original because it frequently published editorials in addition to news regarding people's daily life. In Wang Tao's opinion, a newspaper should also become a tool for political criticism apart from its common functions. By contacting foreigners, Wang Tao understood the importance of the role media played in informing and educating the public and criticizing and guiding the government. Wang Tao began to use *Xunhuan Ribao* to publish his own opinion and comment on current affairs for the purpose of pushing China to modernize. Those news commentaries published in Hong Kong were compiled by Wang Tao into a collection named *Taoyuan Wenlu Waibian* (《弢园文录外编》). His commentaries often focused on political reform, self-strengthening and education.

For instance, in the article titled "On Scholars" (《原士》), Wang Tao criticized the Imperial Civil Service Examination by pointing out its inefficacy and failure to screen the real talents.

> 往往有髫龄就学，皓首无成，而士之受其愚者不少矣。呜呼！此徒以功名富贵，鼓舞其心志，虽有奇材异能，非是莫由进身，其愚黔首之心，实无异乎祖龙之一炬也！（王韬，2012：10）

The people who passed the exam were incapable of doing the job because they had no idea about how to plan a budget or till the land. When being asked about military or law, they became bewildered and puzzled. Very few successful candidates were competent for management.

> 何至所习非所用，所用非所长，问以钱谷不知，问以兵刑不知，出门茫然，一举步即不识南北东西之向背哉？（王韬，2012：10）

Wang Tao criticized the eight-legged essays not because he himself failed in the exam but because he really found it useless in turning China into a stronger country. In the end of the article, Wang Tao highly recommended that science and mathematics should be the subjects for choosing able people (王韬, 2012: 10-11).

In another essay "On Reform"(《变法》), Wang Tao stated that the reason why China was left far behind by Western countries was mainly the backwardness of people's mind. He listed some examples, such as conformism (因循守旧), drifting along (苟且), deception (蒙蔽), whitewashing (粉饰), greed (贪罔), hypocrisy and unreasonableness (虚骄). The method of dealing with it was to reform the Imperial Civil Service Examination system because incompetence existed everywhere in military, administration and manufacture. The suggestions he made included being practical, realistic, and open-minded, emphasizing talent while abandoning nepotism (王韬, 2012). Wang Tao's insight lay in his emphasis on human ability instead of pure technology. That was quite different from those self-strengtheners, such as Zeng Guofan and Li Hongzhang who aimed to learn Western technology of manufacturing armories and warships but ignored the crucial role played by humans per se.

In his third essay "Caring for the People" (《重民》), Wang Tao argued that neither monarchy nor democratic institution was suitable for China, but the combination of the two would work. Previously, the emperor did not communicate effectively with people and he failed to know what their needs were. Thus, a bridge needed to be built between the two with hearings from both sides before the decision was made.

> 论者谓：君为主，则必尧、舜之君在上，而后可久安长治；民为主，则法制多纷更，心志难专一。究其极，不无流弊。惟君民共治，上下相同，民隐得以上达，君惠亦得以下逮。都俞吁咈，犹有中国三代以上至遗意焉。（王韬，2012：23–24）

The real problem was not that the common people refused to communicate with the people at the top but that the emperor did not pay attention to his people. Thus, what Wang Tao implied was that the emperor should be able to detect what people thought and what difficulties or problems they had so as to provide solutions to the problems. Democracy in China should be upheld in that people's sufferings or voice should be heard by the people at the top.

The fact that Wang Tao was able to offer such frank remarks on China's politics was because he stayed in Hong Kong. Therefore, he had the courage to make sharp criticism of the Qing government and offer his own advice. As we can see, much of his criticism overlapped with what Robert Hart had presented to the court in his memorial of 1865 titled "A Bystander's View" and Thomas Wade's "A Brief Discussion on the New Proposal" of the same year. The difference was that the two memorials were written by foreigners while Wang Tao's criticism was made by a native Chinese, which showed that Chinese intellectuals began to confront the problems existing in the government and tried to bring it to the attention of the court.

8.2.3 Young John Allen: The Newspaperman in China 林乐知：驻华报人

Among different news publications which appeared in the late Qing period, the two magazines run by Young John Allen made great impact on China's modernization, i.e. *Church News* (《教会新报》, 1868–1874) and Chinese *Globe Magazine* (《万国公报》). As an American Protestant, Allen came to Shanghai, China in 1860 in an attempt to spread Christianity and convert as many Chinese as possible. Yet during the process, he met insurmountable obstacles carrying out his missionary job properly. Due to the American Civil War (1861–1865), Allen's funds were cut off from the Board of Methodist Episcopal

Fig. 8-3 林乐知

Church, South and Allen lost the orientation of his missionary work. He had to find other avenues in order to make a living and at the same time continue his missionary obligations. By teaching English at Shanghai Tongwen Guan since 1867 and translating Western books of social and natural sciences into Chinese since 1871 at the Translation Department of Jiangnan Arsenal, Allen was able to support his family through the working days and continue his missionary work during Sundays. The two paid jobs were of the government employment. As if the two secular jobs were not enough to make him happy, Allen began a voluntary job as a newspaper editor and that made him extremely happy and feel rewarded because it was beneficial to the Chinese people especially the literati.

Since his arrival in China, Allen's contact with local people was via religious preaching and he had no way of reaching the literati who occupied a vital position in Chinese society. Once he began to publish newspapers and magazines, Allen found it a source of attracting the attention of the literati and that unexpected harvest made him joyful.

Different from Robert Hart who came to China as an interpreter and had formal employment with his own country, Young John Allen came to China as a missionary, relying solely on the Board for his financial support. Once the funds could not reach him, Allen felt desperate but at the same time he was left with much space for creativity. Having experienced different jobs, Allen found newspaper editing could reach Chinese learned people, who were the decisive factor for reforming China. As a matter of fact, through talking to Feng Guifen, the adviser to Li Hongzhang, Allen understood a small group of literati like Feng Guifen were more open-minded and wished to make a change to China. Thus being the editor of *Church News* and then *Globe Magazine*, Allen worked with great enthusiasm and found it truly worthwhile because the following reformers, such as Guo Songtao, Kang Youwei, and Liang Qichao were greatly influenced by the articles published in *Globe Magazine* and his translated works in Jiangnan Arsenal (Bennett, 1983: 58). In this sense, the modernity in China was initiated by modern media, such as newspapers, magazines, and published books translated from foreign languages into Chinese.

Allen's original purpose of becoming the editor of the newspapers was, according to Bennett, to use it as a link uniting the Protestant missionaries in China, and transmitting Western knowledge including secular news and science. It was also hoped to inspire a better government, to stimulate other newspapers and magazines, to introduce "new ideas on religion, morality, and conduct" (Bennett, 1983: 63).

Having witnessed with his own eyes the poverty, superstition, insanitation, and the gap between the rich and the poor, Allen resolved to make a change using his religious and scientific knowledge and he considered it his calling to do so. Now that the Board agreed to his proposal of engagement in secular work, Allen wanted to make good use of the media to fulfill his goal. This had much to do with the education he received at Emory University, and his firm belief in God. He was determined to serve God by spreading gospels to the heathen country.

8.2.4 Chinese *Globe Magazine* 中国《万国公报》

Young John Allen's decision of founding his own journal was stimulated by his editorship for *Shanghai Xinbao / Shanghai Daily News* (《上海新报》). He took up the job in 1868 from John Fryer because the latter would leave and take a new post of translation in Jiangnan Arsenal. The four months' experience of journalism motivated Allen to have a Chinese journal of his own in the same year aiming at the Chinese Christians and he considered it as part of his missionary work. He named the journal as *Church News*. Initially, the coverage of the journal devoted nearly half of the space to Christianity related news. Gradually, Allen extended the coverage to more secular news and scientific knowledge. In addition, criticism of government was also part of the content. Up to 1874, six years after the *Church News* publication, Allen decided to changed it into a weekly magazine, reporting mainly secular news and it was called *Globe Magazine*. The content of the journal covered five areas: news stories in China, Sino-Western relations, the West and its institutions, scientific and technological materials, and criticism and proposals. The first four areas were mainly concerned with information and events while the last one was about promoting a better government and the well-being of the people.

Fig. 8-4 《万国公报》

Next, we examine what Allen himself had written in *Globe Magazine* and how other Westerners, such as Robert Hart, Thomas Wade, and Timothy Richard echoed Allen's opinion on China's weak points and the areas to improve. In one of the columns titled "On Sino-Foreign Relations" ("中西关系略论") in the magazine published in the first year of Emperor Guangxu, i.e. in 1875, the opening article written by Allen discussed the existing problems in China regarding administration, military, finance, and Sino-foreign relations.

The title of Allen's article "On How to Get Rich" suggested that China was not rich. So what were the reasons?

The first drawback was encouraging agriculture and schooling rather than industry and commerce. This was problematic and absolutely wrong because people were not treated equally. In fact, people engaged in different kinds of trade played an important part in society and nobody could live without others' contributions. It was wrong to show respect for the learned people only and the fact was that they could do nothing except seeking remarkable sentences and culling model sentences. When you pressed them for the meaning of integrity (诚正), good manners (修齐), modeling peace (治平), they were puzzled and at a loss as if they had never learned it before. What they did was only to swallow the ancient learning without digesting it. This was something really ridiculous. Allen used Francis Bacon, the English philosopher, and Peter the Great (彼得大帝), Russian Emperor as examples to illustrate the importance of innovation and change. Bacon changed the ancient Greeks' ideas and used a new method named induction to seek truth. Peter the Great visited European countries and brought back the new technology and let his people imitate so that Russia became strong (李天纲, 2012: 160-161).

> 重耕读而轻工商，中国之弊，与西国当年相同。西国有贤者出，剔其弊而与其利焉。谓士聪明出众，只谋富贵于一身，而于农工商无与也。农以耕田糊口，工以手艺营生，商以贸易为业，其势分而其情不属，几如脉络之不相连矣，可乎哉？况农工商各有经营之事，而士则养尊处优，徒工文字，而待食于人。
>
> 中国则以率由旧章，为不违先王之道。而不知先王之道宜于古，未必宜今。今之时势，非先王之时势矣。中国士人何食古不化若斯哉？终年伏案功深，寻章摘句，以为束身于名教中也，而实为八股文章束缚其身耳。
>
> ……而今之中国士人，神理固不知矣，即格致亦存其名而已。所伪为知者，诚正修齐治平之事耳。言大而夸，问其何为诚正，何为修齐，何为治平，则茫乎莫解，与未学者等……中国开科取士，立意甚良，而惟以文章试帖为专长，其策论则空衍了事也。[1]（李天纲，2012：160–161）

Robert Hart in his "A Bystander's View" published in *Globe Magazine* in 1880 (光绪六年十月初二) emphasized the importance of building relations with the outside world and keeping promise after signing treaties. Although this memorial was passed around in Zongli Yamen in 1865 after Hart replaced Horatio Nelson Lay as Superintendent at

1 文章载于三百五十八卷，光绪元年九月十八日。文中自称本馆主，故判作者为林乐知。

the Customs House for a couple of years, there was little response from the high-ranking officials. Hart pointed out that the reason why China remained poor was the closed-door policy practiced by the Qing government...Hart referred to Emperor Xianfeng's refusal to allow foreign consuls settling in Beijing and the latter's refusal to ratify the treaty document. Both events caused wars staged by the British and the allied troops and ended up with greater losses of China (李天纲, 2012: 164-167).

> 所论中华，自有纪载以来历数千年，莫古于中国，而自四海各国观之，莫弱于中国，事之真也。自古不通于外国，近数十年各国渐渐与中国往来，若欲闭关拒绝，原所不易……
>
> ……惟条约所允，地方常有违背。今洋人怀疑，上司不知所致，而上宪不悟，无奈复动干戈，得有“随时赴京”明文方息。迨后，因可赴京，以为更妥。乃大臣初次北上，仍以夷相待，违约阻止，复致兴兵。在京换约，派常驻之大臣，致有庚申年之事。似此文事皆由智浅而欲轻人，力弱而欲服人。现在某事当行，某事不当行，已有条约可凭。一经背约，即有问故之患。所言外患由内召，此也。（李天纲，2012：164–165）

Against such background, Hart proposed that firstly, China should allow foreigners to teach them how to manufacture coins, build ships, and use telegraphs. Secondly, the emperor should agree to the audience of foreigners in order to build good relations. Thirdly, it was beneficial to send officials abroad. Finally, the government should permit foreign merchants to join Chinese traders to produce vehicles and motors (李天纲, 2012: 168).

> 凡有外国可教之善法，应学应办。即如铸银铸钱，以便民用，做轮车以利行人，造轮船以便涉险，置电器以通信。外国之好法不止四条，然旁观劝行之意不在此，系在外国日后必请之事。
>
> 大皇帝召见各国驻京大臣，若不允见，虽不便遽至失好，恐必籍他端而生事，不如先告以可见。
>
> 命大臣驻扎外国，于中国有大益处。在京所驻扎之大臣，若请办有理之事，中国自应照办，若请办无理之事，中国若无大臣驻其本国，难以不照办。
>
> 准洋商合华商会，制轮车电机等事。（李天纲, 2012: 168）

Thomas Wade, English Consul, echoed the point raised by Hart in his article titled “A Brief Discussion on the New Proposals” published in *Globe Magazine* on the same day of 1880 as Hart's “A Bystander's View”. In fact, this discussion was made in response to the

British Envoy to China, Rutherford Alcock's request to report the current situation and future prospect in China. That was the year 1866, just one year after Hart's "A Bystander's View" was passed around in Zongli Yamen. Having read it, Alcock found it really relevant and asked Wade to present it to the Qing government (王晓艳, 2016). The "new proposals" as shown in the title referred to the suggestions made by Wade to improve the situation in China.

Viewing that Britain had occupied Burma, France Annam, and Russia coveted Korea, China was extremely worried about the powers' invasion of its own country. Yet, in the eyes of Thomas Wade, it was not necessary to only worry about something that might happen. The point was that China should think about strengthening its own national power by following the new methods.

> 英国早得缅甸一分，法国亦得安南，俄国分在西路朝鲜之外，或闻三国皆有必占内地之心乎？……可虑者不在外国有无侵占之心，而在各处有易侵占之势。（李天纲，2012：177）

The new methods mentioned by Wade include opening railways, fly lines and mining hardware and coal; training land and sea armies; and cultivating talents in various disciplines including medicine. If China decided to adopt those above mentioned methods it would not only be beneficial to its own country but also welcome by other countries. If need be, the Chinese could always invite foreigners for help as in the case of the Customs House and foreigners would be willing to lend a hand.

Thomas Wade in his proposal emphasized the importance of open-mindedness and a friendly attitude to foreigners and he hoped that the Chinese could get rid of suspicion and collaborate with the people who wanted to help.

Thomas Wade wrote the piece in fluent Chinese. Having finished his position as British Envoy, Wade went back to Britain and became a sinologist at Cambridge University.

> ……如各省开设铁道，飞线及开采五金、煤矿，操练水陆各军，国用不足，约请借贷，医学各项，设馆教习。以上各新法。中华如定意试行，各国闻之无不忻悦，益固多焉……即如海关、税务司，自设以来，内外既免生事，税银亦见其增。此系管理通商，各官无不知，而税务司数员虽皆请外国人，在请办各员管理税务其权是否皆在中国，外国无一肯驳。更俟将来中华能悉外国语言规矩，至辞去外国各员，自理税务。中华具此材能，外国无不欣美之极。（李天纲，2012：175）

Like Young John Allen, Timothy Richard, the British missionary, came to China in 1870 and he firstly stayed in Shandong Province and then in Shanxi Province to be engaged in disaster relief. Later, he had close contact with Chinese reformers like Kang Youwei and Liang Qichao. Richard put great emphasis on education. Shanxi University was established under his suggestion to educate the Chinese people after the mass murder of Western missionaries in Shanxi Province took place during the Boxer Uprising in 1900. He published articles in *Globe Magazine* and one of them was titled "New Laws to Save People" in 1876 (光绪二年七月二十二日). Viewing the poverty of the Chinese people, Richard proposed in the article to develop economy according to the local situation. For instance, coal mining was one of the things that Qingzhou, Shandong could do because it was rich in mercury, coal and mineral. One thing that prevented people from exploiting the mine was superstition because they believed if they opened the mine, it would destroy *fengshui*. However, Richard had different opinions. He thought it better to become wealthy rather than starving. The products, such as potassium nitrate (火硝), indigo powder possessed by Qingzhou could be fully exploited in order to make magenta (洋红) and ultramarine blue (蓝靛) so that it was unnecessary to import them from other countries. The same was true with cotton. If China could manufacture its own cloth, it would be unnecessary for China to buy it from Britain which bought cotton from distant America and sold it to China. Even with long-distance transportation, Britain still made profits.

> 一、开矿亦救民之一法。地有矿而不开，犹之富家有钱，窖而不用，受风水之谜，宁肯饿死，闻之者莫不伤心。今中国各矿皆有，而青州亦有汞、煤等矿，若派老成、熟识之人专领是事，岂非富国富民之一善乎？
>
> 二、民有恒产，始有恒心。中国人多事少，丰年游民坐食无资，凶年更难维持。今若各按地产，各造机器，制办新货，则人皆有事业。
>
> 丰年固可安居，荒年亦能保护身家。有如青州出火硝、蓝靛，若用机器自造洋红、洋蓝，各省何必都用外国所来等物乎？……即如洋布一物，花本产自美国，距英国万里之遥。而英国采买织纨，又四万里，发至中国。除清本外，计有五万里之脚价，仍然获利。若中国自行置办，或至美国装花，水脚不过三万路程。[1]（李天纲，2012：184）

As we can see, *Globe Magazine* not only published reports on current affairs, such as the Wusong railway (吴淞铁路) sale, the cancelation of the Chinese Educational Mission,

1 文章载于四百零四卷，光绪二年七月二十二日。

and the case of *Su Bao* (《苏报》), but also made comments and proposals for some defects or drawbacks existing in Chinese society. The critiques and criticism were sometimes rather sharp but what the article contributors described and revealed was partially true. The point was that Chinese scholar officials should get rid of suspicions and anxieties, and have the courage instead to learn from the advanced countries. Only in this way could China eliminate poverty and superstition so that the Chinese people could live a better life. A change of mind was the most urgent thing to do. The above writers made it crystal clear that if China wished to keep its own autonomy and not to be bullied by stronger countries, it had to develop its own economy and make its people rich and that was the only way out for China.

As a matter of fact, Feng Guifen had already written proposals in the 1850s for the Qing government to consider and he named it "Jiaofenlu Kangyi" (《校分庐抗议》) and submitted it to Zeng Guofan wishing to get it published. However, Feng Guifen did not get response from Zeng Guofan so he had to pass it around within a small circle of friends and family members (冯桂芬, 2015). Compared with *Globe Magazine*, Feng Guifen's ideas, no matter how brilliant they were, could not reach a wider audience like what the news media did. Therefore, the impact of the public sphere or media was tremendous and it was after reading the articles published in *Globe Magazine* that Kang Youwei and Liang Qichao decided to reform and initiate the Gongche Shangshu Movement and opened a new chapter in the Chinese history.

To sum up, in this chapter, we discussed three major Chinese language newspapers, i.e. *Shen Bao*, *Globe Magazine* and *Xunhuan Ribao*, and their publishers. With the appearance of the public sphere and the critiques made by the media, the Qing rulers realized what problems and difficulties the Chinese people were facing and what obligations they had and in what way they could make people's life better. Freedom of press allowed China to enter the modern society one step further.

◆ Topics for Discussion

1. The introduction of the public sphere to the Qing Dynasty.

2. The impact of *Globe Magazine* on China's modernity.

3. What was the intention of the article contributors when they wrote the memorials to

the Qing government?

4. What do you think of the Westerners' critiques of China's problems?

5. Were valuing money over loyalty (重利轻义), pomposity (浮夸), and incompetence of the scholar officials the main problems?

6. The new writing style created by Wang Tao.

7. The role played by *Shen Bao* and *Xunhuan Ribao*.

8. A civil society based on the public sphere.

9. The relation between the enlightenment and the public sphere.

Reading Assignment

Volz, Y. Z., and Chin-Chuan, L. 2009. From Gospel to News: Evangelism and Secularization of the Protestant Missionary Press in China, 1870s–1900s. *Journalism*, *10*(2): 171-195.

Bibliography

Anon. 2017. *Shen Bao*. 11–05. From Wikipedia website.

Bennett, A. A. 1983. *Missionary Journalist in China: Young J. Allen and His Magazines, 1860–1883*. Athens: The University of Georgia Press.

Cowan, B. 2004. Mr. Spectator and the Coffeehouse Public Sphere. *Eighteenth-Century Studies*, *37*(3): 345-366.

Habermas, J. 1991. *The Structural Transformation of the Public Sphere*. Cambridge: MIT Press Paperback Edition.

McComb, S. 2015. *Fostering Enlightenment Coffeehouse Culture in the Present*. Austin: The University of Texas.

Wagner, R. G. (ed.). 2007. *Joining the Global Public: World, Image, and City in Early Chinese Newspapers 1870–1910*. Albany: State University of New York Press.

冯桂芬. 2015. 校分庐抗议汇校. 冯凯，整理. 熊明心，校对. 上海：上海社会科学院出版社.

柯文. 1998. 在传统与现代性之间——王韬与晚清改革. 雷颐，罗检秋，译. 南京：江苏人民出版社.

赖某深. 2017. 向世界传播中国文化的先驱——王韬. 09–20. 中华读书报.

李天纲. 2012.《万国公报》文选. 上海：中西书局.

热拉尔·勒塔耶尔. 2018. 巴黎咖啡馆史话. 刘宇婷，译. 重庆：西南师范大学出版社.

王韬. 1994. 弢园文录外编. 楚流，书进，风雷，选注. 沈阳：辽宁人民出版社.

王韬. 2012. 弢园文新编. 李天纲，编校. 上海：中西书局.

王晓艳. 2016.《新议略论》述评. 黑龙江史志，(6)：41–47.

许纪霖. 2017. 近代中国的公共领域为什么诞生在上海?. 03–19. 爱思想

杨之. 2016. 清报先驱——王韬. 11–09. 北京晚报.

佚名. 2017a. 申报. 11–05. 360 百科.

佚名. 2017b. 杨乃武与小白菜这个清末冤案的真实故事是怎样的?. 04–16. 搜狐网.

佚名. 2019. 理雅格. 09–15. 搜狗百科.

钟叔河. 2010. 走向世界：中国人考察西方的历史. 北京：中华书局.

Chapter Nine

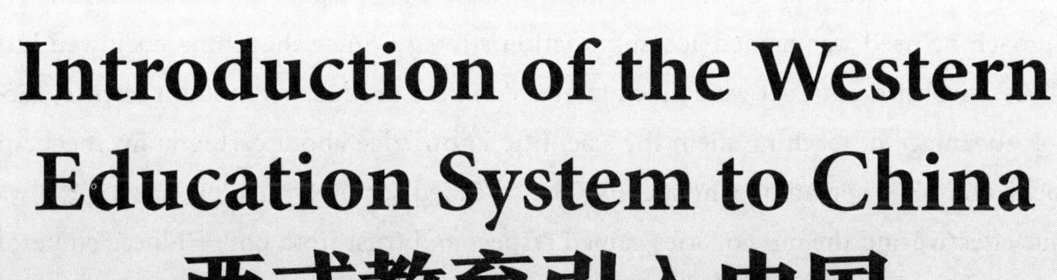

Introduction of the Western Education System to China

西式教育引入中国

本章介绍西学东渐时传入中国的两种西式教育——普通教育和医学专科教育。前者以英国伦敦教会的新教教徒马礼逊为代表。他不辞劳苦地在中国开放之前来到广州，学习汉语、编纂《华英字典》、翻译《圣经》、传播福音、设立印刷所、创办英华书院，为今后的传教士开辟了道路。后者的代表是美国实业家洛克菲勒，他在中国兴办慈善事业、创建协和医学院，培养了一些高精尖的西医医生，为中国的医学教育奠定了基础。

9.1 The Background 背景介绍

In the Chinese history, Western learning was introduced to China for three times. As has been discussed, the first group of Christians who came to China in the late Ming Dynasty were called the Jesuits and they were Catholics. Knowing that the Chinese thought highly of their own culture while disregarding other cultures, Matteo Ricci, the representative of the Jesuits, tried hard to adapt to Chinese culture by wearing the Confucian robe, learning Chinese language, and showing respect for Confucianism. The approach he used was named accommodation strategy. Since the Chinese showed little interest in Christianity, yet were much interested in the products of modern science, Ricci took advantage of teaching them the scientific knowledge about cartography, mechanic clocks, etc. while spreading Christianity. The so-called scholarly mission (学术传教) was quite effective and the missionaries gained respect and trust from both Chinese emperors and officials. For instance, the world map brought by Ricci dispelled the Chinese old view on the world, that was, "The sky is round and the earth is square" (天圆地方) or China as the center of the world. The new notions like earth, five continents, the Pacific Ocean, the Atlantic Ocean, and the Mediterranean Seas shown in the Kunyu Wanguo Quantu (坤舆万国全图) drawn by Matteo Ricci clearly indicated that China was only a part of the world, but not the center of the world. Since the previous cosmology the Chinese held was the foundation of Chinese centralism, people's perception of the Hua-Yi distinction began to falter (张西平, 2010). The Jesuits after Matteo Ricci, i.e. Adam Schall and Ferdinand Verbiest helped the Chinese change to a new calendar and build a modern observatory. Schall became a close friend of Emperor Shunzhi and the latter was almost converted. Verbiest helped build cannons for China's military and became the imperial astronomer (钦天监正监).

Fig. 9–1 利玛窦与南堂（北京宣武门）

However, during the reign of Emperor Kangxi, the Vatican changed their mind and stopped the Jesuits from accommodating Chinese culture. All the converts were not allowed to worship Confucius any longer because God was the only one they should venerate. The so-called Rites Dispute (礼仪之争) led Kangxi to ban the Jesuits from coming to China and the following emperor Yongzheng completely banned the Christians from coming to China. The interruption lasted more than one hundred and thirty years as discussed in Chapter Eight and it wasn't until the early 19th century when Robert Morrison came to China that renewed the Christian missions to China. But this time, they were mostly Protestant missionaries. Robert Morrison was the first Protestant who came to China in 1807.

While foreign mission was one of the Jesuits' obligations, the arrival of the Protestant missionaries had much to do with the Evangelical Revival (福音复兴运动) in Britain from 1730 to 1740. In the 18th century, Britain had become increasingly secular due to the enlightenment and the Industrial Revolution. People seemed to take interest in secular life and had little religious restraint. Card playing, bear baiting, and cock fighting could be seen everywhere. The public were even willing to buy tickets watching people fighting and killing each other, which reminded people of the ancient Romans. Bad habits, such as drinking, gambling and fighting were rampant and the level of social morality was at its lowest (Anon, 2016). The person who wanted to reverse the situation was called George Whitefield, a preacher, who began to preach in the open air to those non-church goers. Following him was John Wesley (约翰 · 卫斯理) and his brother Charles Wesley (查尔

斯·卫斯理), who followed a similar itinerant approach to preaching and traveled all over Britain. Gradually, more and more people came to listen to the Gospel and this movement was called the Evangelism Revival. In fact, the Wesley brothers built the Church of Methodism (卫理公会教堂), meaning to follow exactly what the Bible has said and their method appeared to be effective.

The essence of Evangelicalism was "a unique eschatological (末世论的) theology which concerned itself with the fear of an approaching millennium and the calling of evangelicals to be the rational and responsive agents of divine providence" (Daily, 2013: 18). With the expansion of the British Empire, there was a need for the heathen world to be in touch with the message of God. Thus, in 1795, the London Missionary Society was formally established with a Board of Directors and they intended to fulfill this task through turning the Bible into the language of the target countries (Daily, 2013). It was against such a background that Robert Morrison entered Gosport Academy, a theological school designed for the London Missionary Society, to be trained as a foreign missionary and the target country was China.

David Bogue, the head of the Gosport Academy, was a liberal-minded person. His objective for this three-year training school was to prepare the would-be missionaries with four qualifications when they were abroad. They should be able to master the heathen language, translate the Bible into the native language, own a printing press to print the translated materials, such as the tracts and the Testaments, and finally set up schools in order to produce more competent ecclesiastical workers in the target countries. In order to achieve such a goal, the candidates must meet the criteria for personality, knowledge, disposition, and a hold on to the principles. For instance, "a good temper, sagacity, firmness and intrepidity, and ability to endure hardness" were about one's character. Understanding of the native people, the approach to passing Christian doctrine and familiarity with the native language were about knowledge. Patience, humility, gentleness, and a spirit of Martyrdom were concerned with one's disposition. The principles referred to a firm hold on to "general, liberal and just" stand in devoting to the missionary cause (Daily, 2013: 49-50).

Bogue's purpose of setting up schools in the local area was to cultivate more native people to be future missionaries. In this way, the Gospel could reach an increasingly large number of people. In designing the school's curriculum, Bogue took a liberal approach. Instead of choosing the courses related to Christianity only, he put emphasis on both general education and special missionary education as he fully understood that the more extensive one's knowledge range was, the easier for the missionary to survive in an unexpected condition because he could find a job using his knowledge so as to carry on his mission. This humanistic teaching approach had much to do with the slogan of the enlightenment, i.e. "Knowledge is power" and a practical mind advocated by Thomas Reid in his theory of realism.

Since the encyclopedic knowledge was the foundation for the missionaries to accomplish their responsibilities, the curriculum for general education included astronomy, theology, geography, philosophy, history, rhetoric, and linguistics. Specifically, the knowledge of geography and history helped the missionary to understand the native people better so that he could shorten the distance when trying to preach. Rhetoric and linguistics promoted the missionary's confidence in making himself understood and gaining agreement from the audience.

During the process of teaching, Bogue trained the learners' ability of autonomous learning by letting them read the assigned materials and then demonstrate in class how much they understood the materials. As for the three classical languages Greek, Latin and Hebrew, Bogue adopted a similar teaching approach, asking his students to learn by themselves and come back for examination. In this way, they would find it a lot easier to learn the heathen language on their own. Just as what had been described by Bogue himself, "The aim of this pedagogy was 'not to think for the pupil, but to make him think for himself'". In class, "he frequently stopped them, proposing questions by which he could discover their industry and judgment; whether they had a proper understanding of the subject, whether they had read the books, whether they had made extracts, and whether they were to the purpose" (Daily, 2013: 51-52).

Bogue's approach reflected the essence of Western education, i.e. to cultivate independent thinking and autonomous learning with a wide range of knowledge as the foundation and on this foundation solid knowledge structure could be built that enabled the learner to carry out a specific task independently. Oratory was a necessary ability for a missionary to get across his Gospel message to his audience. Robert Morrison was taught this way and he obtained the ability expected of the education. Upon his arrival in China in 1807, Morrison meticulously followed the instructions given by David Bogue at Gosport Academy. The first thing Morrison did was to find a native Chinese to teach him the language.

9.2 The Impact of Robert Morrison's Activities on China's General Education 马礼逊的活动对中国普通教育的影响

Fig. 9-2 马礼逊（右）学习中文

Upon arriving in China, Morrison exactly followed what Bogue had taught him to do in class. To master Chinese language, he was taught by the native Chinese. In the meantime, Morrison was trying to translate the Latin-English dictionary into the Chinese-English dictionary. Besides, he asked the person employed to buy Chinese books of classics so as to learn by himself. Within seven years (1808–1815), Morrison completed the dictionary editing. The hardship he experienced in the process was beyond description.

Robert Morrison came to China during the reign of Emperor Jiaqing who followed his father Qianlong's footstep by adopting a seclusion policy. The edict issued by him stipulated that no Chinese was allowed to teach foreigners the language and once found out, the person would be sentenced to death. Some Chinese language teachers took advantage of the edict by cheating Morrison or running away with money without saying a word. In addition, he had to pretend to be an American because it seemed that Americans were more welcome by the Chinese than the British. Although he was employed by British East India Company in 1809 as an interpreter, Morrison was not allowed to socialize openly. Besides, the Catholics in Macau supported the Qing court's decision not to allow the Christians to distribute tracts and the Testaments to the people in interior China and this order was pointed at Morrison (Anon, 2014).

So for many years, Morrison lived alone in an old French house and suffered from loneliness and the cutoff from his Board at home. Yet with the determination to bring the Gospel to the heathen people, Morrison put up with the difficulties and finished compiling *The Chinese English Dictionary* (《华英字典》, 1815). Initially, the dictionary was prepared for the future missionaries who would use it to learn Chinese, but in fact it was made use of by the Chinese students at the Anglo-Chinese College (英华学院) as well. Other works Morrison finished were *Grammar of the Chinese Language* (1815) and *A Dictionary of the Chinese Language, in Three Parts* (1815–1823) (Morrison, 2015). They all became useful teaching materials later at Anglo-Chinese College.

The second major task for Morrison was to translate the Bible into Chinese so that the local people could read on their own. In order to carry out the task, Morrison needed to understand Chinese culture first because language and culture were closely connected and that was made clear by David Bogue at Gosport Academy. So Morrison started to read Chinese classics bought by his servants including philosophy, science, and government. Morrison also purchased a forty-volume set on the history of China (Daily, 2013). The knowledge of China equipped Morrison with much facility when he did the translation. But Morrison still came across difficulties in rendering English into proper Chinese due to his belief in the word-for-word translation approach. For instance, when translating the sentence in Genesis 1:2, Morrison turned the phrase "darkness was over the surface of the deep" into "暗在深之面上" in "Now the earth was formless and empty, darkness was over the surface of the deep, and the Spirit of God was hovering over the waters", and turned the phrase "Zeal for your house will consume me" in John 2:17 into "尔室之勤烈，尽吃我焉". Yet the correct versions should be "渊面黑暗" and "我为你的殿心里焦急" (郑诗亮, 2018).

It was really hard for an English speaker to translate the Bible into Chinese within such a short time of learning Chinese language. Some Westerners during that period of time even claimed that "...no translation of the Holy Scriptures could be made into the Chinese language...the nature of the language would not allow of any translations whatever to be made into it" (Daily, 2013: 88).

According to Bogue's instruction, once the written materials were finished, they should be printed out immediately so that the local people had something to read. So Morrison set up a small printing press and printed the materials first using the woodblock printing technique (雕版印刷术).

Finally, Robert Morrison established a school in 1818 named Anglo-Chinese College. In the same manner, Morrison wanted to make a copy of the Gosport curriculum onto Anglo-Chinese College. Considering the situation in China, Morrison decided to set up the school in Malacca first, aiming at Chinese students. But there was a severe lack of books at first. It needed English resources in theology, rhetoric, mathematics, history, geography, etc. In order to build a library with sufficient resources for the school, Morrison went back to London in 1824 raising funds and received three hundred volumes of valuable books from Lord Kingborough, in addition to £1, 520 donated by him. Morrison himself also spent more than £1, 000 of his salary and bought English books for the library. In the meantime, he also brought back a thousand copies of Chinese books to Britain and those books could be found in SOAS-School of Oriental and African Studies, University of London later. The curriculum designed for Anglo-Chinese College followed the Gosport example and teach "reading, writing, singing...arithmetic, geography, history of the world, etc." (Daily, 2013: 180). Morrison did not live to see full functioning of the school because he died in 1834. But his pedagogical idea was passed down to the following schools built by the Morrison Fund (马礼逊基金) donated by Elijah Coleman Bridgman, Lancelot Dent (颠地), William Jardine, David W. C. Olyphant (奥立芬), John Morrison and others to support education in China.

The first Morrison School was set up in Macao in 1839 and headed by the Reverend Samuel Brown (布朗牧师), an American Protestant. In his school were students like Tang Tingshu (唐廷枢), Yung Wing, Huang Kuan (黄宽), and Huang Sheng, who became successful in their future careers. Mr Brown had his own ideas of education. Having evaluated the effect of Chinese education, he pointed out that traditional Chinese education was in conflict with Western education as it put emphasis on rote learning and students were required to learn all the materials by heart without understanding the meaning of them. This hindered them from developing creative thinking and independent thought. In view of this, Brown wanted to change students' superstition and idolatry and train them to think independently. In this way, the Reverend Brown inherited what Robert Morrison had advocated in pedagogy.

Interestingly, the first step that Brown took was from the boys' living environment and the acquisition of Western etiquette (Smith, 2005). The boys were given individual space for living at the school and that gave them a sense of ownership for cleaning the room, taking care of personal hygiene and cultivating a sense of responsibility. It was intended that this sense of responsibility could be transferred to their studies. Secondly, the boys were given the opportunities of observing how the Browns received and sent their guests and how the guests behaved in front of the boys. Gradually, the boys also picked up the manners and etiquette needed for public presence.

Yung Wing was one of the students in the Reverend Brown's class and he became the first Chinese graduate from Yale University of the United States. When he came back to China, Yung Wing was actively engaged in the Self-Strengthening Movement and helped buy machines from the United States and made a proposal of sending the first batch of the Chinese teenagers to study in the United States, which will be discussed in Chapter Ten. We can see the effect of Brown's instruction from what Yung Wing had written in one of his compositions:

> The Chinese have schools, but they learn but few things, and their learning is different from that of other nations. They only repeat their lessons, without thinking or understanding them. When they have learned five or six years, their teacher explains to them a little out of the book. I think there is not one school in China as good as the schools in the United States or in England. There are a great many Chinese boys and girls not educated as in your country, because the Chinese are stingy fellows. That is the reason they can't have good education. (Smith, 2005: 24)

Here we can see the Chinese students at Morrison School developed a habit of observation and critical thinking and they could make a comparison and contrast between the two different education systems and came up with their own conclusion. The missionary schools represented by Morrison School introduced the Western education system in terms of the curriculum and teaching approach. The adoption of class hours, division of class, the use of class materials, laboratories and experiments, departmental teaching, grade systems, equal opportunities for both boys and girls, addition of physical and musical education, etc. were all something new to the traditional Chinese education (龚鹏程, 2018). By adopting the Western education system, Chinese youths began to get in touch with scientific and engineering subjects in addition to humanity subjects, which broadened the learners' horizons and nurtured their critical and independent thinking.

The role played by Morrison School was summarized by Zhang Weibao as follows (张伟保, 2012). It led to the termination of Chinese old-style private education (私塾教育), adopted the modern education system in terms of division of classes, course objectives, course content, approaches, and abolished the Imperial Civil Service Examination (废除科举考试).

In conclusion, the original purpose of Protestant missionaries who came to China was to propagate Christianity and everything they did was pointing at the same goal. But the byproduct of those activities was a complete introduction of the Western education system, printing press, and the way of thinking to the Chinese people so that China's modernization was promoted through this kind of cultural exchanges and the person who made the pioneering contribution was Robert Morrison. After his death, Morrison School became a model for general education and began to flourish in China.

9.3 The American Medical Missionaries 美国医学传教士

Following the introduction of general education to the 19th century Qing Dynasty, professional education, i.e. medical education also entered China, but it was accompanied by the medical missionary introduced by American Protestants, such as Peter Parker. Like evangelicalism which happened in the early 18th century Britain, the Revival Movement took place in America, which underwent several stages, i.e. the First Great Awakening (1730–1755), the Second Great Awakening (1790–1840), the Third Great Awakening (1850–1900), etc. (Anon, 2018b). Peter Parker was the first American who was stimulated by the Revival Movement when he studied theology and medicine at Yale University. By attending an annual meeting of the United Foreign Missionary Society (外方传教联合会), Parker was determined to carry out foreign mission and serve the Chinese people using the medical knowledge obtained. Thus, Parker was ordained by the ABCFM, i.e. the American Board of Commissioners for Foreign Missions (美国公理会海外传教差会) to be a medical missionary in China (吉利克, 2008). He was given three tasks, i.e. to get familiar with Chinese language and customs, to circulate and preach the Gospel, and to "use his medical training to relieve physical suffering and to introduce knowledge of Western 'arts and sciences'" (Anon, 2017e).

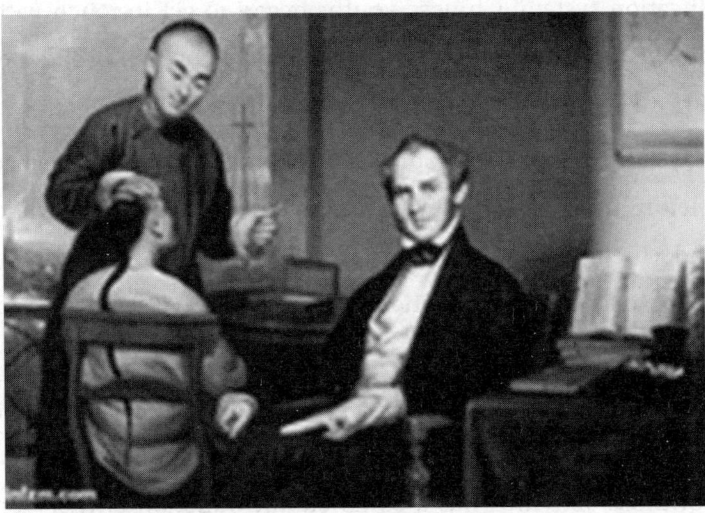

Fig. 9-3 伯驾医生

Unlike the hard time Robert Morrison had experienced when Peter Parker first came to China in October 1834, he was lucky enough to stay in Guangzhou with three of his American colleagues to work with. They were Elijah Coleman Bridgman, Samuel Wells Williams, and Edwin Stevens all sent by the American Board. The former two used to be co-workers of Morrison while the latter was Parker's Yale friend. In November 1835 only one year after Parker's arrival, he opened Ophthalmic Hospital in Guangzhou and began to treat his patients' eye diseases. The treatment was given free of charge and many patients came to the hospital. For the first seventeen days, Peter Parker treated 240 patients. Due to the high demand from the Chinese, most of the Parker's time was occupied by receiving patients of eye diseases. But since his treatment was highly effective, patients with other kinds of diseases came to see Peter Parker also. In this way, Peter Parker had to deal with surgery on other parts of patients' body and he had little time preaching the Gospel. Yet through receiving patients, Peter Parker also got to know the Chinese language and customs and he never lost the opportunity to tell the recovered patients to express their gratitude to God instead of himself as a doctor because he came to China under the call of God.

Peter Parker also invented a new procedure to see his patients in the hospital. Different numbers both in Chinese and English were written on the bamboo chips. Each patient was given one chip and went upstairs to see the doctor. Then, the patient's information regarding his name, number, reception time, address and profession were all recorded in the medical chart. Before leaving the hospital, each patient would have such a chart and use it to exchange the waiting number. The prescription and acography or treatment history (治疗记录) for each patient were put into the pigeonhole and filed. In this way, the doctor could write prescriptions for 200 people every day. The number and card registration system was extremely common in modern medical service and Peter Parker might be the inventor of such a system (吉利克, 2008).

Peter Parker was the first American who combined medical treatment with the Gospel preaching, which shortened the distance between the Chinese people and Christian missionaries. When Peter Parker went back to the United States, he made numerous public speeches regarding the urgent need that China had for missionaries and encouraged more Christians to go to China. With his enthusiasm and communicative skills, Peter Parker persuaded Martin Van Buren (范布伦), President of the United States to send diplomats to China and the latter was convinced and sent Caleb Cushing (顾盛) as American Envoy to China. Peter Parker was chosen as the interpreter to the envoy and got involved in the signing of the Treaty of Wangxia between China and America in 1844.

The second Yale graduate coming to China as a doctor was Edward H. Hume (胡美). Hume was invited by the Yale-China Association (雅礼协会) or the Yale in China and was offered an opportunity to build the first modern hospital in Hunan Province, China. This promise was so appealing that Hume immediately took the offer and went to China. Edward H. Hume earned his BA in 1897 from Yale College and his MD in 1901 from Johns Hopkins Medical School. Then, he became a practitioner in Bombay, India. The Yale in China was organized partially under the influence of the Student Volunteer Movement for Foreign Missions (SVM, 学生国外传教志愿者运动) across the United States since 1886. A great number of college students were enthusiastic about sending God's message to foreign countries. Another reason for the Yale in China was to honor a Yale alumnus called Horace Tracy Pitkin (裴德金) who in 1889 signed the SVM pledge (学生国外传教志愿者运动承诺) and went to China in 1897 as a missionary of the American Board of Commissioners for Foreign Missions. But during the Boxer Uprising, when defending two single women, Pitkin was killed in Baoding, Hebei Province. Pitkin's death led to the establishment of the Yale Mission in China and many Yale volunteers went to China in order to see that Pitkin's sacrifice could be atoned for (Anon, 2017b; Anon, 2017f). Changsha was chosen because some Yale graduates and faculty members thought it was in the center of China and could make greater impact if education became popularized. Thus in the early years of the Yale Mission in China, the focus was on medical education rather than missionary work.

In 1906, Hume opened Yali Hospital (雅礼医院) in Changsha, Hunan Province. The name of the hospital was based on the Chinese pronunciation of the English word Yale. In 1915, it was changed into Xiangya Hospital whose name was a combination of the two words, i.e. xiang and ya. Xiang was a short form for Hunan and ya still referred to Yale.

It had been almost seven decades since Peter Parker began to practice oculist in Guangzhou when Edward H. Hume opened Yali Hospital in Changsha. But compared with the two cities, people in Guangzhou seemed more open-minded than the people in Changsha because it did not take long time before Peter Parker received many patients. However in Changsha, people were more suspicious or even hostile to foreigners. It took longer time for Hume to attract patients to his clinic. The reason might be that Chinese medicine could do little to treat eye diseases especially cataract. So people had no choice but went to see Parker. In addition, Guangzhou had been a treaty port for many years and people's hostility gave way to their eagerness to treat diseases.

Edward H. Hume was quick to learn Changsha dialect and picked up the Chinese custom by using humble words, such as *biren* (鄙人), i.e. your humble servant to refer to himself. It did not take him too long time to persuade a beggar to come to his clinic. The beggar had furuncle poison (疖毒) in his head and perhaps he wanted to try his luck on this foreigner. After cutting the abscess (脓疮) and having it disinfected, his head was wrapped in gauze. The patient walked out of the clinic on his own feet. In a few days' time, the scab fell off and he became well again. People began to realize the value of Western medicine and came to Hume's clinic to receive treatment.

History recorded an anecdote about how Hume's medical skills saved him and his hospital from a local riot, i.e. the Rice Plundering Movement (抢米风潮) in Hunan. When the hungry people turned their anger to the missionaries and wanted to ransack Hume's hospital, they were stopped by an outlaw who had been cured by Hume. Also due to Hume's fame among the people, they did not attack the hospital (文热心, 2012).

Hume was able to gain support from Tan Yankai (谭延闿), Hunan Provincial Governor, due to his good skill in curing pneumonia infected by the governor's mother. Once the influential person was impressed by the effect of Western medicine, he was eager to introduce it to China. "Such advanced medical skill! Why don't we introduce it to China and train our own talents?" (文热心, 2012) Hume was extremely happy to know that Tan Yankai wanted to gain financial support from the Beiyang government (北洋政府) for building a Western hospital. Yet, he failed. But he raised money from the local gentry through the organization named Hunan Yuqun Association (湖南育群协会). The governor himself also donated 10,000 *tales*. Thus, Xiangya Medical College was set up in September 1914 and eighteen preparatory students were enrolled, among whom were Zhang Qian (张骞), a renowned medical scientist, and Tang Feifan (汤非凡), a medical microbiologist, whose contributions included separation of chlamydia trachomatis (沙眼衣原体) from other microorganisms, production of penicillin, rabies vaccines (狂犬疫苗), diphtheria vaccines (白喉疫苗), life varicella vaccines (牛痘疫苗), Bacillus Calmette Guerin vaccines (卡介苗), gamma globulins (丙种球蛋白), and the first typhus vaccines (斑疹伤寒疫苗) in the world (文热心, 2012).

9.4 The Medical Education—The Rockefeller Foundation 医学教育——洛氏基金会

Although Edward H. Hume intended to build Xiangya Medical College according to the Johns Hopkins's model, he did not reach his goal due to various restraints. The only one that succeeded being built based on Johns Hopkins's model was the Beijing Union Medical College (北京协和医学院), which was financed by John D. Rockefeller (约翰·D. 洛克菲勒), the American philanthropist (讴歌, 2016).

Fig. 9–4 洛克菲勒

Rockefeller decided to invest in China's medical cause for three reasons. One was the American Foreign Missionary Movement which boomed in the late 19th century and the early 20th century. During that period of time, America had gained political and economic power in the world and the missionaries believed it was due to their Protestant belief. Thus, the foreign missionaries wanted to reach out to the Asian countries, such as China to disseminate God message together with their national spirit, advanced culture to the heathen world so as to demonstrate American power (讴歌, 2016).

In addition, New York, Rockefeller's birthplace, was the site of the Second Great Awakening. In his early life, Rockefeller was influenced by his mother who was a pious Baptist and he went to church regularly and formed the habit of donating money to the church, to the group of "unhealthy, opium-smoking, poor, and weak" people and later to universities. He truly believed what the Gospel stated, "Give, and it will be given to you. A good measure, pressed down, shaken together and running over, will be poured into your lap. For with the measure you use, it will be measured to you." (Anon, 2017c)

The third reason was the encouragement of his advisor Frederick Gates, who in 1900 suggested a university be built in this backward country, i.e. China that had many illiterates.

Influenced by the Flexner's Survey Report in 1910 which stated that there were only six good medical schools in America among a pool of 155 medical schools, Rockefeller decided to investigate in medicine, nursing, and public hygiene to raise the standard of those schools. Within ten years between 1913 and 1923, Rockefeller Foundation (洛克菲勒基金会) spent nearly 80 million US dollars on public health and medical education, among which 10 million US dollars went to Beijing Union Medical College and the total amount of money spent on establishing this college reached 48 million US dollars (讴歌, 2016).

Rockefeller's decision to invest in China's medical cause was based on three investigations carried out in 1909, 1914, and 1915 by a delegation of experts. The 1914 delegation produced a report after surveying medical schools in more than ten cities and eighty-eight hospitals. The report was named Chinese Medicine (中国医学) regarding the current health status, Chinese medicine and surgery, Western medicine in China, the criteria of medical education conducted by missionaries, the media of instruction, anatomy and autopsy (解剖与尸检), the government's attitude to Western medicine, the Chinese people's attitude to Western medicine, and relevant suggestions.

Even though the level of medical education in China was low and the situation of facilities and equipment was poor, the foundation still set a high goal for Beijing Union Medical College in consideration of long-term interest and advanced talents who could take up high positions in future so as to make a more significant impact. The newly established China Medical Board (洛氏驻华医社) was in charge of the logistics and other related things.

The standards set for the candidates were excellency in character and learning, with sympathetic missionary spirit and dynamics, professional competency and determination to develop China's medical service. Similarly, faculty members needed to have the spirit of exploring science, capability in teaching and stimulating students' interest in doing research so as to exert influence on his/her students and colleagues. The two things that were put emphasis on were medical ethics and professionalism as represented by Hippocrates Oath (希波克拉底誓言):

> I will remember that there is art to medicine as well as science, and that warmth,

sympathy, and understanding may outweigh the surgeon's knife or the chemist's drug.

I will not be ashamed to say "I know not", nor will I fail to call in my colleagues when the skills of another are needed for a patient's recovery.

I will remember that I remain a member of society, with special obligations to all my fellow human beings, those sound of mind and body as well as the infirm. (Anon, 2018a)

Hippocrates was the ancient Greek physician and developed the Humoral Theory (体液理论). In his opinion, there were four bodily fluids in humans, i.e. black bile, blood, phlegm, and yellow bile and the balance of the four fluids in our body was essential to human health (Gill, 2018). Another outstanding contribution made by Hippocrates was the ethical and professional aspects required of a doctor, i.e. the Hippocrates Oath. Today, medical students in the US medical schools are all required to take the oath so as to meet the criteria. The spiritual legacy from the ancient Greeks was inherited and passed down from generation to generation. The spirit was also reflected through the setting up of Oriental Johns Hopkins, i.e. Beijing Union Medical College. A tiny group of elite, small class, English as the media of instruction, one-on-one individualized teaching—that was the blueprint of the school. The curriculum included three parts: the preparatory stage, formal medical training, and internship starting in the third year. Thus, a medical school involved concerted efforts from different sections: a comprehensive university that offered the first two year courses among physics, chemistry, and biology. In the third year, professional subjects related to medicine were offered. Also from the third year, the students were required to practice physician work and do experiments in a hospital.

The above curriculum was borrowed from Johns Hopkins University of Medicine, which again obtained its experience from the model of German medical schools because the president of Johns Hopkins Abraham Flexner was a graduate from one of those schools. In the 19th century, medical education in Germany was much more advanced than that of America. The Germans invented the system for medical education, i.e. preparatory study at a comprehensive university, professional study at a medical school, and internship at a hospital attached to the medical school. A combination between the pathology and the clinic, the resident physicians and general resident system, and the integration among clinics, teaching, and research were all practiced in Germany in the late 19th century. Flexner brought the state-of-the-art experience back to America and transplanted it into American medical education (讴歌, 2016).

In September 1917, eight students were enrolled for preparatory studies. In October 1919, Beijing Union Medical College formally opened. Those who studied at the preparatory school needed to take an exam to enter the medical school. In June 1921, Beijing Union Hospital began to take patients. Up till then, China had its own medical school adhering to Western standards and using English as the media of instruction.

To summarize, in this chapter we discussed the process of importing general and medical education from the West. Robert Morrison devoted his life to the general education in China. Peter Parker, Edward H. Hume, and John D. Rockefeller contributed to the medical education in China. There were three different forms of medical causes carried out by American missionaries and educators. Peter Parker pioneered the medical missionary method in Guangzhou, China and he gained respect and trust of the Chinese people. Edward H. Hume opened Yali Hospital in Changsha, Hunan Province which was gradually turned into Xiangya Hospital in 1915. Xiangya Medical College was established in 1914, which produced two distinct figures for Chinese medical cause: Zhang Qian and Tang Feifan. Finally, Beijing Union Medical College was successfully established and lived up to the standard of the modern medical school. Even today, both Beijing Union Medical College and Beijing Union Hospital are ranked at the top of medical schools and hospitals in China.

◆ Topics for Discussion

1. Do you think the Yale-in-China Mission or the Yale-China Association reflected a kind of cosmopolitanism?
2. Why didn't John D. Rockefeller donate all of his money to his own country given that many schools in the United States also needed his help?
3. How do you understand the word "philanthropy" (慈善事业)? Is it equivalent to "altruism" (利他主义)?
4. A comparison and contrast between the late Qing Chinese and Western education.
5. The role played by rote learning and independent thinking.

6. The function of critical thinking in human civilization.

7. Charity in China.

Reading Assignment

Smith, C. T. 2005. The Morrison Education Society and the Moulding of Its Students. In C. T. Smith, *Chinese Christians: Elites, Middlemen, and the Church in Hong Kong*. Hong Kong: Hong Kong University Press.

Bibliography

Anon. 2000. Holy Bible, Chinese/English (Union·NIV). Hong Kong: International Bible Society (H.K.), Ltd.

Anon. 2014. Robert Morrison. 12–28. From Wikipedia website.

Anon. 2016. Diane Severance. 11–21. From Evangelical Revival in England website.

Anon. 2017a. Edward H. Hume. 04–14. From Wikipedia website.

Anon. 2017b. Horace Tracy Pitkin. 04–14. From Wikipedia website.

Anon. 2017c. John D. Rockefeller. 02–17. From Wikipedia website.

Anon. 2017d. Medicine in China. 04–14. From The Rockefeller Foundation website.

Anon. 2017e. Peter Parker: 1804–1888. 04–14. From Biographical Dictionary of Chinese Christianity website.

Anon. 2017f. Yale-China Association. 04–14. From Wikipedia website.

Anon. 2018a. Hippocratic Oath. 07–26. From Britannica website.

Anon. 2018b. Second Great Awakening. 07–23. From Wikipedia website.

Daily, C. A. 2013. *Robert Morrison and the Protestant Plan for China*. Hong Kong: Hong Kong University Press.

Gill, N. S. 2018. Hippocratic Method and the Four Humors in Medicine. 06–29. From ThoughtCo website.

Morrison, R. 2015. Encyclopedia Britannica 2006 Ultimate Reference Suit DVD. 05–05.

Smith, C. T. 2005. The Morrison Education Society and the Moulding of Its Students.

In Smith, C. T., *Chinese Christians: Elites, Middlemen, and the Church in Hong Kong*. Hong Kong: Hong Kong University Press.

爱德华 · V. 吉利克. 2008. 伯驾与中国的开放. 董少新，译. 桂林：广西师范大学出版社.

龚鹏程. 2018. 宗教与大学. 07–24. 爱思想.

黄小凡. 2017. 雅礼医院与中医的“败走”. 02–27. 看历史.

柳向春. 2018. 西方传教士如何颠覆中国传统雕版印刷. 03–19. 澎湃新闻.

讴歌. 2016. 协和医事. 北京：生活 · 读书 · 新知三联书店.

文热心. 2012. 湖南第一家西医医院:“雅礼”是“湘雅”的前身?. 06–19. 湖南日报.

张伟保. 2012. 中国第一所新式学堂：马礼逊学堂. 北京：中国社会科学出版社.

张西平. 2010. 亚洲，我们的家园. 06–16. 中华读书报.

郑诗亮. 2018. 苏精谈西方传教士与中国近代印刷变革. 07–01. 澎湃新闻.

Chapter Ten

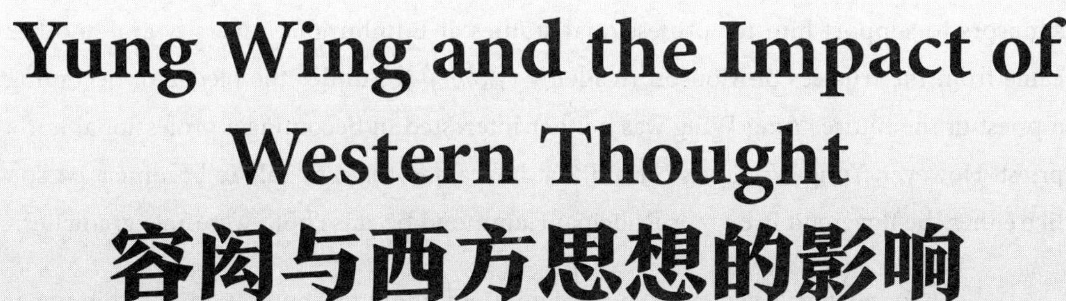

Yung Wing and the Impact of Western Thought
容闳与西方思想的影响

本章讨论容闳如何成为马礼逊学校及耶鲁大学成功培养的第一位中国学生，他在接受人文教育的过程中受到了哪些经典的影响，以至毕业后立志回国效力。接着讨论留美幼童计划的设计和实施以及提前终止的原因。最后讨论留美幼童计划对晚清外交方面所起的作用。

10.1 Yung Wing 容闳

In Chapter Nine, we have seen how Western general and medical education was introduced by Protestant missionaries and philanthropists to China. In this chapter, we will see one of the fruits produced by the importation, i.e. Yung Wing, the student at Morrison School, Macao and Hong Kong, and the first overseas Chinese who received education at Yale College and came back to serve his motherland. Yung Wing was determined to go to Yale College and refused two prior offers from the sponsors. One was from the Hong Kong sponsors to support him for professional studies at Edinburgh University and another came from the trustees of Monson Academy (孟松学校) under the pledge of becoming a priest in the future. Yung Wing was neither interested in becoming a professional nor a priest. However, Yung Wing was certain that he wanted to go to Yale to become a person like either the Reverend Brown or Principal Hammond because both were Yale graduates.

> ...To be sure, I was poor, but I would not allow my poverty to gain the upper hand and compel me to barter away (带走) my inward convictions of duty for a temporary mess of pottage (眼前利益)...I gave the trustees to understand that I would never give such a pledge for the following reasons: First, it would handicap (妨碍) and circumscribe (限制) my usefulness. I wanted the utmost freedom of action to avail myself of every opportunity to do the greatest good in China...In the second place, the calling of a missionary is not the only sphere in life where one can do the most good in China or elsewhere...In the third place, a pledge of that character would prevent me from taking advantage of any circumstance of event that might arise in the life of a nation like China, to do her a great service. (Yung, 1909: 13)

Freedom became the most important thing for Yung Wing to make his own decision and serve the country in various ways. He was aware of the situation in China which was entirely different from where he was studying and anticipated mounting difficulties to realize his dream, i.e. to send Chinese youths abroad to study the advanced Western civilization. As he wrote in his autobiography:

> I was determined that the rising generation of China should enjoy the same educational advantages that I had enjoyed; that through Western education China might be regenerated (再生), become enlightened and powerful. To accomplish that object became the guiding star of my ambition. Towards such a goal, I directed all my mental resources and energy. Through thick and thin, and the vicissitudes of a checkered life from 1854 to 1872, I labored and waited for its consummation. (Yung, 1909: 15)

Yung Wing fully understood the differences between Chinese and Western education and he could see this through the two heads of the schools. When studying at Morrison School, Macao (1841–1847), he was impressed by School Master, the Reverend Samuel Brown's character: his warm approach to teaching, his thorough understanding of his students' needs, his explicit explanations and straightforward methodology. Most of all Yung Wing very much appreciated Brown's sympathetic and considerate temperament. It was Brown who took Yung Wing and other two boys to the United States. It was Brown who actively looked for funds for Yung Wing. It was still Brown who provided accommodation for Yung Wing in his mother's house.

When he was taken to Monson Academy, a high school in Connecticut, Yung Wing benefited a great deal from the Reverend Charles Hammond, the principal of the academy. Hammond was an erudite person and had passion to guide his students to the labyrinth of Western literature both classical and modern. His instruction put emphasis on the beauty of literature. He introduced English men of letters and *Edinburgh Review* (《爱丁堡评论》) to his students and in this way, Yung Wing absorbed the essence of English literature and tried to relate what he had read to the reality back in China. By reading Oliver Goldsmith and Charles Dickens, Yung Wing realized the life of the down-trodden was all the same and he decided to use his knowledge to help with the people once he went back to China. The chivalry spirit described in Sir Walter Scott's historical novels equipped him with the qualities, such as courage, integrity, justice, and sympathy. Yung Wing was especially attracted to *Edinburgh Review*, which carried articles and essays written by historians, philosophers and sociologists. Edward Gibbon, Jeremy Bentham

(边沁), Francis Hutcheson, David Hume, Adam Smith and Sir Walter Scott formed a school of thought called the Scottish Enlightenment School around Edinburgh and published articles and essays in *Edinburgh Review*. Yung Wing had cultivated independent thinking by reading the magazine commentaries and became critical of the society he lived in (雷颐, 2015). It was not strange when Yung Wing set a high goal for Yale College and knew nothing about how he could realize his dream.

Fig. 10–1 容闳

In one of his letters from Monson Academy, Yung Wing expressed his wish to continue his study in the West because he knew how important liberal education was in dispersing one's superstitious mind and cultivating one's intellect.

> ...you know ful (full) well that the prejudice of the Chinese, how they misrepresent things, and that they are not able to see as you or any enlightened mind do, the object, the advantage, and the value of being educated. Ignorance and superstition have sealed the noble faculties of their minds, how can they appreciate things of such worth. (Worthy, 1965: 273)

Although he had no idea where to get the funds for his college life, Yung Wing was still persistent in his goal of receiving college education in America. In this way, he could help enlighten the Chinese people's minds and get rid of the Westerners' prejudice of his countrymen's narrow-mindedness. It was the Reverend Samuel Brown who came to Yung Wing's help for the second time and persuaded the Ladies Association in Savannah, Georgia to provide some financial help for Yung Wing. Eventually, Yung Wing reached his goal in 1850 of receiving secular education at Yale College. Because Greek and Latin classics were prerequisites for admission to Yale College, Yung Wing began to teach himself these two subjects in the last year of Monson Academy (Wan, 1997). In the college, Yung Wing spent one and a half year to study classics and that made great impact on him in terms of initiating a project in China to send the youths to receive Western education.

The curriculum at Yale was a four-year program. The first two years included Greek, Latin, mathematics (algebra, geometry, and trigonometry), and rhetoric. The last two years had English, German, physics, chemistry, zoology, astronomy, geology, logic and philosophy, history and social science, international and constitutional law, natural theology and evidences of Christianity (Rhoads, 2011). Since Yung Wing chose the subject for the Liberal Arts, Greek and Latin classics were extremely important in shaping his character. We need to examine closely a few important pieces of Western classics in order to see in what way those great books forged a person who made contributions to his own country.

10.2 The Impact of Greek Thought 希腊思想的影响

Three pieces of Greek classics were chosen for a close examination that might have exerted influence on Yung Wing due to their recognized value and prestige—*Pericles' Funeral Oration* (《伯利克里葬礼演说》) which was taken from Thucydides, *The Peloponnesian War* (修昔底德的《伯罗奔尼撒战争史》) (Thucydides, 2018), Plato's *The Apology* (柏拉图的《申辩论》) and Aristotle's *Politics* (亚里士多德的《政治学》). Those pieces demonstrated what the ancient Greeks treasured most: democracy, justice, equality, and freedom. Thucydides was a contemporary of Pericles and he was with the Athenian army when the Peloponnesian War took place between Athenians and Spartans at Peloponnese. He witnessed when Pericles was making this funeral oration, which was written down from his memory.

> ...Our constitution is called a democracy because power is in the hands not of a minority but of the whole people. When it is a question of settling private disputes, everyone is equal before the law; when it is a question of putting one person before another in positions of public responsibility, what counts is not membership of a particular class, but the actual ability which the man possesses. No one, so long as he has it in him to be of service to the state, is kept in political obscurity (政治默默无闻) because of poverty. (孙有中, 2008: 5)

In the above paragraph, Pericles explained what democracy meant, how it was implemented in Athens, and what benefits it possessed. In a democratic state, the power was not in the hands of the monarch, but the people. It was always the majority of the people whose opinions were accepted and put into practice. The leader was chosen not because of his family background, but because of his ability to lead. Everyone was equal before the law. Perhaps it was by reading the great pieces at Yale that stimulated Yung Wing's "intellectual excitement" (Worthy, 1965: 269). Imagine how Yung Wing would think when reading this paragraph. He might want to make a comparison between the democratic state and the political system in the Qing Dynasty where the decision was always made by the emperor himself. The Qing Dynasty was adopting a hierarchical system under which people in the lower position needed to obey the people who were in the senior position no matter whether the latter were right or wrong. The law seldom punished those who occupied important positions (刑不上大夫), but spared no efforts to punish those who had no power at all, and sometimes wrongly. That explained why Yung Wing wanted so much to send Chinese youths to America, as what he said as follows:

> All through my college course, especially in the closing year, the lamentable condition (可悲的状况) of China was before my mind constantly and weight on my spirits. In my despondency (当我消沉之际), I often wished I had never been educated, as education had unmistakable enlarged my mental and moral horizon, and revealed to me responsibilities which the sealed eye of ignorance can never see, and sufferings and wrongs of humanity to which an uncultivated (不文明的) and callous (麻木的) nature can never be made sensitive. The more one knows, the more he suffers and is consequently less happy; the less one knows, the less he suffers and hence is more happy. (Yung, 1909: 15)

Yung Wing felt pity for his own country because people there were suffering from various social ills and he felt helpless to lend a hand sometimes. However, this also served as an impetus for Yung Wing to return to China and make a change. That was the purpose of receiving Western education at a secular college and Yung Wing wanted to try his best to fulfill his dream. Now we understand why Yung Wing rejected the two scholarship offers previously granted.

Coming back from the United States, Yung Wing found a well-paid job at a salary of 75 *taels* a month in the Imperial Customs Translating Department in Shanghai. But soon he wanted to leave because taking bribes was common practice for the interpreters. Yung Wing wanted to keep a clean record as a Yale graduate because probity and integrity were his principles to be a man. As what Aristotle stated in *Politics*:

> ...(W)e must lay it down that the political association which we call a state exists not simply for the purpose of living together but for the sake of noble actions. Those who do noble deeds are therefore contributing to the quality of the political association, and those who contribute most are entitled to a larger share (of political power) than those who, though they may be equal or even superior in free birth and

> family, are inferior in noble deeds and so in the essential goodness that belongs to the polis. Similarly, they are entitled to a larger share than those who are superior in riches but inferior in goodness. (孙有中, 2008: 18)

Horatio Nelson Lay, the Chief Commissioner, tried to keep Yung Wing by offering him a higher salary to 200 *taels* per month as he thought perhaps Yung desired higher pay but used resignation as an excuse. However, Yung Wing declined such an offer and became quite indignant about what Lay thought of him. Here was what Yung Wing recalled in his autobiography:

> It did not occur to him that there was at least one Chinaman who valued a clean reputation and an honest character more than money; that being an educated man, I saw no reason why I should not be given the same chances to rise in the service of the Chinese government as an Englishman, nor why my individuality should not be recognized and respected in every walk of life. (Yung, 1909: 23)

Obviously, Yung Wing was dissatisfied with the treatment of Chinese employees by the Westerners, who regarded the former as inferior in moral standards. Besides, he was eager to demonstrate in front of a foreigner that he was an exception. Yung Wing treasured his reputation more than any other material things and he would like Lay to know about this. On other occasions, Yung Wing did not hesitate to act as "a gadfly (牛虻)" to the social ills. For instance, when analyzing the reasons for the Taiping Movement to take place, he summarized three severe problems existing with the official organization, i.e. graft, exploitation, and the system of fraud and falsehood (Yung, 1909: 41). In fact, he was sympathetic with the Taiping group but refused to identify with them due to their absence of a clear objective, a lack of discipline, and cruelty to common people.

As a government official, an expectant subprefect (准副行政长官), Yung Wing never forgot to take his responsibility and seek benefits for the country. Once he was instructed to interview a Peruvian official discussing sending the Chinese labor to Peru. During the conversation, the Peruvian Commissioner described to Yung Wing how well the Chinese were treated in Peru and how they were prospering and doing well and he persuaded China to send more Chinese of the lower class to better their lives in Peru. Yung Wing corrected the Commissioner's statement by pointing out how rampant the "coolie" traffic was in Macao and he knew exactly what happened to those Chinese who were captured and forced to sign labor contracts either for Cuba or Peru. In the designated countries, Chinese labor were treated as slaves, who could barely endure the cruelty but rose to rebellion. Yung Wing told the Commissioner that he would persuade the Chinese government not to make a deal with "coolie" labor; instead China should call off such a deal and protect its own citizens (Yung, 1909).

Having listened to Yung Wing's report of the interview with the Peruvian Commissioner, the Viceroy immediately instructed Yung Wing to go back to Harford, Connecticut and investigate the condition of the Chinese labor in Peru. Three months later, Yung Wing sent his report back to Li Hongzhang, which included a detailed investigation and some photos of the Chinese labor being lacerated and tortured. Since then, the "coolie" traffic was stopped. What Yung Wing had fulfilled reminds us of what Plato wrote about his tutor Socrates in *The Apology* who never faltered to criticize the dark side of the society for the purpose of making the state better.

> The God has sent me to attack the city, if I may use a ludicrous simile (可笑的比喻), just as if it were a great and noble horse, which was rather sluggish (懒惰的) from its size and needed a gadfly to rouse (唤起) it, and I think that I am the gadfly that the God has set upon the city: for I never cease settling on you (对付你们) as it was at every point, and rousing, and exhorting (劝说), and reproaching (责备 / 申斥) each man of you all day long. (孙有中, 2008: 15)

Besides functioning as a public intellectual, Yung Wing also made efforts in boosting Chinese people's intellectual characteristics, such as courage, confidence, self-esteem, and knowledge of one's rights. Once in an auction market which was located in the foreign settlement, Yung Wing had a fight with an American sailor who was stronger and taller. The reason was that the sailor was making fun of his queue by attaching a bunch of cotton balls to it. Since the polite remarks could not stop the sailor, Yung Wing began to fight back, leading to the sailor's blood in his lip and nose. This fight created great sensation and won him respect from the Chinese people. Previously, no Chinese was bold enough to claim his own rights and reason with the bully. By doing this, Yung Wing wanted to change the Chinese "meek and mild disposition that allowed personal insults and affronts to pass unresented and unchallenged, which naturally had the tendency to encourage arrogance and insolence on the part of ignorant foreigners" (Yung, 1909: 25).

Such kind of public spirit, together with the spirit of seeking truth, morality, open-mindedness, freedom, equality, justice, and democracy, all could be found in Greek and

Roman classics. As commented by Zhong Shuhe (钟叔河) on Yung Wing's transformation of mind:

> Experiments in Chemistry opened a door to a new world. Calculus promoted rational thinking, and Democratic Politics in ancient Greece made him realize the anti-humanity of the autocratic system. (容闳, 2011: 7)
>
> 化学实验在玻璃仪器内显示的是一个全新的世界，微积分可以启发对合理化的思考和追求，古代雅典民主政治史也足以使他痛切地感觉到专制制度的违反人性和缺乏道德基础。（容闳，2011：7）

As we can see, Yung Wing deeply realized the defects of the autocratic institution practiced by the Qing government and he was determined to stage a reform by sending youngsters abroad equipping themselves with the liberal arts and cultivating a humanistic attitude to life. When they came back to China, the returnees would certainly wish to change the current institution using the knowledge obtained from the West. Yung Wing was conscious of the fact that the advancement in Western technology was much related to their secular education and the values they held dear, such as individualism, optimism on human progress, being critical of authorities and traditional values (比勒, 2010). The importation of their manufacturing technology was insufficient to turn China into a wealthy and strong country, but the ideas behind the technology would do. In 1859, when he visited the Taiping group in Nanjing, Yung Wing made a proposal for their leader Kan Wong (干王)[1] to model after the Westerners in terms of their education. Specifically, his seven-item proposal was as follows:

> 1. To organize an army on scientific principles.
>
> 2. To establish a military school for the training of competent military officers.
>
> 3. To establish a naval school for a navy.
>
> 4. To organize a civil government with able and experienced men to act as advisers in the different departments of administration.
>
> 5. To establish a banking system, and to determine on a standard of weight and measure.
>
> 6. To establish an educational system of graded schools for the people, making the Bible one of the text books.

1 干王指洪仁玕。

7. To organize a system of industrial schools. (Yung, 1909: 37)

Although Yung Wing did not reach his expected goal, we could still see among the seven items, such as military, administration, banking, and education, he put education at the top. He hoped that a military school, a navy school, industrial schools and ordinary schools should be established in order to produce urgently needed talents. He planned to make contributions to China's prosperity and power. Disappointed by the Taiping group, Yung Wing turned his attention to the One Hundred Days Reform and later the 1911 Revolution. He showed generosity and enthusiasm to the reformists and offered his place for them to have meetings. When the reform failed, Yung Wing tried to help Kang Youwei and Liang Qichao to find shelter abroad. He wrote to Timothy Richard, an English missionary and asked him for help. During the Boxer Uprising, when the Qing government declared war against the Western powers, Yung Wing urged Zhang Zhidong to set up a new government in regions south of the Yangtze River. Receiving no response, Yung Wing planned a Red Dragon-China (红龙计划) in 1909 and began to support the revolutionaries to overthrow the Qing rulers via violence (雷颐, 2015).

Yung Wing intended to reform China after the American model. He advocated a new type of government, i.e. constitutional monarchy (君主立宪制) and introduced American science and technology in the areas of railroad, banking, shipping company, etc. (李喜所, 2006). Many of his attempts failed, but sending Chinese youths to study abroad was actualized, though not completely successful. Because he always kept education in his mind and it was also his ambition to enrich and strengthen China. When he was invited by Zeng Guofan, Yung Wing seized the opportunity of making this dream come true. After he gained trust from the Viceroy by having purchased machinery in the United States and served as interpreter for resolving the Tianjin Massacre (天津教案) issue with the French consulate, Yung Wing was appointed the Chinese Educational Mission Commissioner and looked after logistic issues in the United States.

10.3 The Chinese Educational Mission 留美幼童计划

The Chinese Educational Mission based on Yung Wing's proposal was launched in 1872 and planned to send a hundred and twenty Chinese boys who were 12 to 16 years old to study in America for 15 years and they were sent in annual four detachments. The length of the study corresponded to what Yung Wing himself had experienced when he was young and it would enable the students to finish their college education. In Yung

Wing's opinion, a college graduate would play an important role in China's economic and military development. As a part of the Self-Strengthening Movement, this program was highly expected and the government spent a large sum of money to finance it. Unfortunately, this program was not completed as expected. It terminated in 1881.

Fig. 10–2 留美幼童

The fact that the United States was chosen for the program was out of three reasons. First, the Burlingame Treaty accorded China "most-favored nation" treatment. It was stated in Article Ⅶ: "Citizens of the United States shall enjoy all the privileges of the public educational institutions under the control of the government of China, and reciprocally, Chinese subjects shall enjoy all the privileges of the public educational institutions under the control of the government of the United States, which are enjoyed in the respective countries by the citizens or subjects of the most favored nation..." (Rhoads, 2011: 10; LaFargue, 1941: 62) That article reflected that Chinese students wishing to study in the US military and naval academies, such as West Point or Annapolis would enjoy equal status as other foreigners did.

The second reason was that Yung Wing had a close contact with American educational institutions and it would be easier for the boys to study there instead of other European countries.

The third reason was due to the fact that Japan had begun a similar project and by 1868 the number of the Japanese studying in Western countries had reached at least 153, including 33 studying in the United States (Rhoads, 2011).

The budget was made by Zeng Guofan with annual cost of sixty thousand *liang* or *taels* (approximately $82,000) and the total cost for 20 years was 1.2 million *taels* (approximately $1,644,000). The expenditure would come from the Imperial Maritime Customs, and the payment would be made by the Shanghai Customs House (Rhoads, 2011). The suggestion was adopted by the court.

As a part of the self-strengthening initiative, Zeng Guofan and Li Hongzhang wrote in their memorial on September 3, 1871 expecting the boys abroad could learn "military and naval affairs, astronomy, mathematics, and engineering" to acquire the technological and military skills of the West (Rhoads, 2011: 121; LaFargue, 1941: 61). Yung Wing also thought that chemistry, natural philosophy, geology, and astronomy were important scientific subjects that the students should grasp and Li Hongzhang added mining engineering to the students' major.

The young boys were put into the local families to adapt themselves to the new environment and finish their primary schooling because many of them had passed the age of going to elementary schools. Each American family was responsible for two or three kids and preparing them for grammar schools and high schools. That was in 1872, almost two decades after Yung Wing graduated and came back from there. Things had changed a great deal including the curriculum of grammar schools which became more sophisticated compared with the period when Yung was there.

There were two different curriculums at a grammar school: classical and English. For the classical curriculum in Holyoke (霍利约克), twelve of the thirty-six courses were on Latin literature. Students were required to study Latin literature, such as Caesar (恺撒), Virgil's *Aeneid* (维吉尔的《阿涅阿斯》), Cicero (西塞罗), and Roman history (罗马史); Greek literature, such as Xenophon's *Anabasis* (色诺芬的《长征记》), Homer's *Iliad* (荷马的《伊利亚特》) and Greek history; and one on "antiquities" (古代史). Even for the scientific curriculum in the same school, seven among twenty-seven courses were devoted to Latin or French in which learners studied medieval history, geography, and English grammar, in addition to mathematics (arithmetic, algebra, geometry, and trigonometry), natural philosophy (geology, botany, and chemistry), etc. (Rhoads, 2011).

Although the majority of the students chose science and engineering as their major when entering colleges, two fifths of the total number and three fifths of those who entered Yale selected liberal arts as their major. In the meantime, the students began to hate going to the classical Chinese courses back in the legation and many of them changed their Chinese robes into the Western style suit and had their hair cut, too. On top of that some were converted to Christianity. It aroused the attention of Wu Zideng (吴子登), one of the education commissioners and he sent secret reports back to Beijing. Thus, the Censor Li Shibin was sent to America to make investigations and wrote a memorial to Emperor Guangxu on December 17, 1881 stating the following two things: "Many students had, in defiance of official policy, converted to Christianity" and "Chinese Educational Commission officials had been extraordinarily lax in controlling the students; Commissioner Ou Eliang smoked opium daily and was so infatuated with his concubine that he seldom showed up for work" (Rhoads, 2011: 167). Then, another three officials, i.e. Li Hongzhang, Liu Kunyi (刘坤一), and Chen Lanbin (陈兰彬) made further investigations to the CEM officials and students and finally Emperor Guangxu ordered the immediate termination of the CEM on June 8, 1881. Rhodes summarized four reasons for the recall of the overseas students: the students' disrespect for their Chinese studies, the unexpected rise in tuition fees and other expenditures, the American government's refusal of allowing the students to enrol at West Point or Annapolis, and finally the American anti-Chinese sentiment (2011).

10.4 The Impact of the Chinese Educational Mission 留美幼童计划的影响

Though the Chinese Educational Mission was aborted after nine years, it was undeniable that it had influenced Chinese international diplomacy and produced personnel who fit into engineering, foreign relations, and education. In the following section, a discussion of the program's influence will be made.

According to Desnoyers (1992), the byproduct of the Chinese Educational Mission was to have produced diplomats like Chen Lanbin and Yung Wing because in America they carried out many tasks other than supervising the boys. For instance, Chen Lanbin reported back to Beijing when he knew that the Japanese were purchasing "8,000–10,000 Remington breech-loading rifles (雷明顿后膛式步枪) and had loaded them aboard two warships in New York" (Desnoyers, 1992: 249) to deal with Democratic People's Republic of Korea. In the meantime, the commissioners also helped assess and purchase advanced weapons for the Qing government. A new type of American made guns called "Gatling" (格林机关枪) was reported back to Zongli Yamen and Yung Wing made an order for $100,000 worth of such guns in 1874. Zuo Zongtang took advantage of using those guns in repressing the Muslim rebels in northwest of China (Desnoyers, 1992).

The most important thing was that the mission enabled Chinese officials to have an opportunity to make contacts with foreigners and resolve international disputes. A case in point was the Chinese "coolie" traffic. Both Chen Lanbin and Yung Wing used America as a base to negotiate with Peruvian and Spanish commissioners and eventually enhanced the Chinese government's consciousness of protecting its citizens. As suggested by Chen Lanbin to Li Hongzhang concerning resolving the "coolie" issue:

> The best policy would be to wipe out the ringleaders (元凶) of the smugglers. The next best would be to induce England and America to interfere with the trade. The least advantageous policy would be to wage war against it. Although Peru is a small country, and Spain is suffering domestic turbulence (in Cuba), I fear that they can make trouble for our country in spite of their having insufficient forces to rule their own countries peacefully. (Desnoyers, 1992: 254)

As a matter of fact, the Chinese Educational Mission offered an experimental ground for the officials to deal with international affairs and confronting thorny issues, which they previously refused to do. The excuses for their refusal to send officials abroad included a lack of competent personnel, a shortage in travel expense and funding for building legations abroad, which were solved by the Chinese Educational Mission.

In addition, the ninety-two students who were recalled to China also displayed their capability in China's industrial, economic, and diplomatic development. Though most of them did not finish college education, people like Zhan Tianyou (詹天佑), Liang Cheng (梁诚), Tang Shaoyi (唐绍仪), and Tang Guo'an (唐国安) did make important achievements.

Zhan Tianyou was chosen by the Chinese Educational Commission to study in the United States in 1872. He finished his elementary and secondary schooling at New Haven. In 1878, Zhan Tianyou was admitted to Sheffield Scientific School of Yale University and majored in Civil Engineering. He was the top student at Yale and won the first prize in mathematics. Three years later in 1881, he graduated and was recalled to China. It was lucky for Zhan Tianyou and Ouyang Geng (欧阳庚) who were the only two among the 120 and finished college education.

Fig. 10–3 詹天佑

In 1888, seven years after Zhan Tianyou came back to China he began to be engaged in his major-related work, i.e. railway construction. One of the distinguished achievements made by Zhan Tianyou was the Beijing-Zhangjiakou railway

(京张铁路) which was built without foreign assistance. As the chief engineer, Zhan Tianyou was in charge of its construction and he managed to finish it two years ahead of the schedule (1905–1909). Zhan Tianyou was able to overcome the steep gradient near the Qinglongqiao (青龙桥) railway station by using a zig-zag section. He speeded the construction of the Badaling (八达岭) tunnel by drilling a vertical shaft (立井) into the path of the tunnel. He was exhausted by his hard work and died at the age of 59. Zhan Tianyou was remembered by the Chinese as the "Father of Chinese Railroads" (Anon, 2018).

Liang Cheng, the second boy, was sent to America by the Chinese Educational Mission in 1875 as the last cohort of the 120 boys. Yet Liang Cheng did not finish his college study when coming back to China in 1881. During 1903–1908, Liang Cheng served as China's Minister to the United States and he tried hard to refund the surplus indemnity paid by the Qing government to the United States after the Boxer Uprising. One of the clauses in the Peace Protocol of 1901 (《辛丑条约》) stipulated that China needed to pay an indemnity of 450 million *taels* ($333 million) to all powers incurring losses as a result of the uprising, among which the United States shared $24,440,778.81. But quickly both the Americans and the Chinese found that the amount of the losses on the part of America was no more than half of the sum (Pappas, 1987). Liang Cheng began to lobby among the dignitaries of the United States. In 1905, he began to talk to John Hay, US Secretary of State and pressed President Theodore Roosevelt. Eventually, Roosevelt announced that the surplus funds would be returned to China from January 1, 1909 to 1940 and each year 50–100 Chinese youths could study in America (佚名, 2018a; 比勒, 2010). Because of the level of Chinese students, they needed to be trained first before going to study in the United States. Therefore in 1909, the Qing government used Tsinghua Garden of the Xianfeng era as the preparatory school for the overseas students, which was located in the western suburb of Beijing. In February 1911, the preparatory school was renamed as Tsing Hua College (清华学堂) and in 1928, it became Tsinghua University.

Fig. 10–4 梁诚

Fig. 10–5 唐国安

In late 1909, Tang Guo'an escorted the first group of 47 Boxer Indemnity scholars to the United States and helped place them in five New England schools. Later when Tsing Hua College was established in Beijing in April 1911 for the purpose of preparing future Boxer Indemnity scholars to go to the United States, Tang Guo'an was its founding president.

In this chapter, we discussed how Yung Wing, the first Chinese who obtained the BA degree in Yale College, the United States, brewed the idea of educating Chinese youths abroad in the same way he had experienced and that plan was actualized 16 years after he graduated and came back to China. We also examined the reason why Yung Wing could do that and the impact of the Western education on him. Finally, we looked into the impact of the Chinese Educational Mission on the diplomatic policy of the Qing government and producing competent personnel like Zhan Tianyou, Liang Cheng and Tang Guo'an.

◆ Topics for Discussion

1. Your comment on Yung Wing's determination to go back to China after graduation.
2. In what way do Chinese traditional ideas differ from Western ideas?
3. The differences between the Chinese and Western pedagogy.
4. What is the essential driver/motivator for social/economic development?
5. To what extent do ideas influence action?
6. The role played by the Chinese Educational Mission in dealing with foreign countries.
7. Your comment on Zhan Tianyou's contribution to China's railway construction.

◆ Reading Assignment

LaFargue, T. E. 1941. Chinese Educational Commission to the United States: A Government Experiment in Western Education. *The Far Eastern Quarterly*, *1*(1): 59-70.

Bibliography

Anon. 2018. Zhan Tianyou. 08–03. From Wikipedia website.

Desnoyers, C. 1992. "The Thin Edge of the Wedge": The Chinese Educational Mission and Diplomatic Representation in the Americas, 1872–1875. *Pacific Historical Review*, *61*(2): 241-263.

LaFargue, T. E. 1941. Chinese Educational Commission to the United States: A Government Experiment in Western Education. *The Far Eastern Quarterly*, *1*(1): 59-70.

Pappas, T. D. 1987. Arthur Henderson Smith and the American Mission in China. *The Washington Magazine of History*, *70*(3): 162-186.

Rhoads, E. J. M. 2011. *Stepping Forth into The World: The Chinese Educational Mission to the United States, 1872–1881*. Hong Kong: Hong Kong University Press.

Thucydides. 2018. History of the Peloponnesian War/Book 1. R. Crawley (trans.). 07–29. From Classics Archive website.

Wan, P. P. 1997. Yung Wing, 1828–1912: A Critical Portrait (Unpublished Dissertation). Cambridge: Harvard University.

Worthy, E. H. Jr. 1965. Yung Wing in America. *Pacific Historical Review*, *34*(3): 265-287.

Yung, W. 1909. *My Life in China and America*. New York: Henry Holt Company.

雷颐. 2015. 孤寂百年：中国现代知识分子十二论. 桂林：广西师范大学出版社.

李喜所. 2006. 近代留学生与中外文化. 天津：天津教育出版社.

毛子水. 2011. 论语今注今译. 重庆：重庆出版社.

容闳. 2011. 钟叔河导读. 西学东渐记. 徐凤石，恽铁樵，等译. 北京：生活·读书·新知三联书店.

史黛西·比勒. 2010. 中国留美学生史. 张艳，译. 北京：生活·读书·新知三联书店.

孙有中. 2008. 西方思想经典导读. 北京：外语教学与研究出版社.

佚名. 2018a. 梁诚. 08–03. 360 百科.

佚名. 2018b. 詹天佑. 08–03. 百度百科.

Chapter Eleven

Yan Fu—The Chinese Enlightenment Thinker

严复——中国启蒙思想家

中日甲午战争如一声巨雷震醒了沉睡的中国人。如果说鸦片战争之后中国历经的屈辱、战败和赔款都无法唤醒大众，甲午战争却振聋发聩地使中国人立刻从睡梦中醒来。被中国人眼中的“蕞尔小国”打败可谓奇耻大辱。只有这时，中国人才开始真正思考变革的可能性。严复成为这个时期的启蒙思想家。为了救国保种，他翻译了英国 18 世纪的进化论、社会学、经济学和哲学方面的重要论著，启发并警醒了国人。本章介绍严复的思想历程以及他翻译的西方名著所针对的具体问题。

11.1 The Background 背景介绍

The thirty-year Self-Strengthening Movement (1860s–1890s) had witnessed the establishment of Jiangnan Arsenal, the Fuzhou Shipyard and the Fuzhou Navy School, and the Beiyang Fleet. The Chinese were eager to learn from the West their technological and military prowess by equipping themselves with armories and navy. However, both the Fuzhou Shipyard and the Beiyang Fleet were destroyed respectively in the Sino-French War of 1883 and the Sino-Japanese War of 1895. If the failure of the Sino-French War was expected by the Chinese, the one with the Japanese was beyond imagination. After the signing of the Shimonoseki Treaty (《马关条约》), the whole country seemed extremely shocked and disappointed, and the feeling of the literati or scholar officials was even more acute. They were forced to reflect upon the reasons and set on the painful path of truth-seeking. One of them was Yan Fu (严复), who began to write newspaper articles and translate Western works on social Darwinism, sociology, political science, and economics, trying to awaken the Chinese people to the fact that China was meeting its doom if it did not reinvigorate its people.

Yan Fu enrolled in the first batch of the students at the Fuzhou Navy School and had studied there for five years (1867–1872). The reason Yan Fu chose the navy school was that it provided stipend for its students and his family was in urgent need of money due to his father's recent death. Most parents at the times wanted to send their children to study Confucian classics because it promised a glorious prospect of officialdom once they passed the Imperial Civil Service Examination.

The Fuzhou Navy School offered courses of two major areas, i.e. shipbuilding and navigation. The former was taught in French while the latter in English. Yan Fu was studying in the English class and the subjects he learned contained English, algebra, analytic geometry, plane triangulation (平面三角法), spherical trigonometry (球面三角法), calculus, dynamic and static mechanics (动静力学), hydromechanics (流体力学), electromagnetism (电磁学), acoustics, thermology (热学), chemistry, geology, astronomy, navigation, etc. All the courses were instructed in English and Yan Fu was the top student upon graduation (永田圭介, 2014). That was the first period during which Yan Fu familiarized himself with English.

Yan Fu's English proficiency was further enhanced when he was sent to Britain to study navigation at Greenwich College (格林尼治皇家海军学院) during 1877–1879. It was planned that the six students, i.e. Yan Fu, Sa Zhenbing, Fang Boqian, Lin Yongsheng, Ye Zugui (叶祖珪) and He Xinchuan (何心川) who studied navigation at Greenwich would only stay for one year. But Yan Fu, attracted by the Western thought, would like to stay a little longer and he expressed his ideas to Guo Songtao, the Chinese ambassador to Britain. Guo Songtao agreed and managed to extend one more year for Yan Fu. The reason being through observations Guo Songtao found that Yan Fu was an ambitious and capable young man and the promising student would waste his talent on a petty job like captain after graduation because he could do something more important, for instance, a superintendent at China's navy school. Indeed Yan Fu really became the Superintendent at Tianjin Navy School (天津水师学堂教习) during 1880–1889.

Fig. 11–1 严复

In Britain, Yan Fu and other Chinese students visited Guo Songtao from time to time and they were often asked about their studies at college. Yan Fu once told Guo Songtao that Chinese students were lacking in physical strength compared with their English peers because in learning how to construct blockhouses, all the Chinese students were exhausted toward the end but not the English students. On another occasion, Yan Fu was critical of the book *The Theory of Yinghai* (《瀛海论》) written by Zhang Zimu (张自牧), an old friend of Guo Songtao. He disagreed with Zhang Zimu's opinion when the latter stated the following four points. First, it was not appropriate for China to construct railroads. Second, machines should not take the place of humans. Third, those ships and cars would be eventually replaced and no longer be useful. Finally, maritime defense for China was not urgent because other countries could help us keep the balance (孟泽, 2015; 郭嵩焘, 刘锡鸿, 薛福成, 宋育仁, 2012). Yan Fu refuted the above four points, which demonstrated that Yan Fu had independent thinking and was critical of what others said.

In addition to the engineering courses, Yan Fu also studied subjects like international law, judicatory (审判制度), civic society (公民社会), parliament (议会), and electoral system (选举制度). Here we can see how sensitive Yan Fu was. Perhaps, he realized the advantages of English society which had much to do with their legal system, administration and citizens' consciousness. He wanted to study it and bring it back to China. Since Yan Fu was appointed Candidate Instructor (候补教师) for the Qing Navy, he needed to allocate more time for studying academic theories. In addition, he also visited English courts and saw with his own eyes how the judicial decision was made. When justice was done, people on both sides, i.e. government and citizens could co-operate to make life better. While in China, no equality between ordinary people and officials existed and most people had grave complaints about the judiciary which might be one of the causes for China to remain poor. When people felt maltreated, they would not have the incentive to work for the society. So in search of wealth, the Chinese should change at least three things, he talked to Guo Songtao, exclusion of dissidents, refusal of telling the truth, and bigotry or following others blindly. Yan Fu was attracted to *The Spirit of Laws* by Montesquieu and decided to translate it into Chinese (永田圭介, 2014).

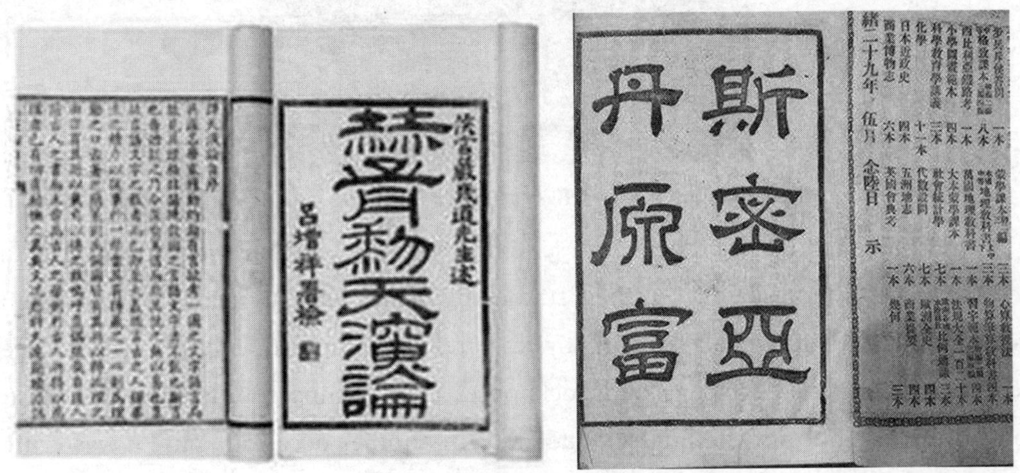

Fig. 11-2 严复译著《天演论》与《国富论》

In Britain, Yan Fu wasted no time reading extensively and seeking the recipe for China's salvation. He directed his attention to some newly published books regarding political science, sociology, economics, and science. Yan Fu believed that those renowned works could enlighten the Chinese people's mind so as to make China wealthy and strong. Adam Smith (亚当·斯密), Jeremy Bentham, Thomas Robert Malthus (马尔萨斯), John Stuart Mill (密尔), and Charles Darwin's *The Origin of Species* became what Yan Fu focused on (永田圭介, 2014). That explained why he had a wide range of knowledge on both natural and social sciences, which paved way for his future translation when he returned to China.

11.2 Translation of Thomas Huxley 翻译赫胥黎

By comparing and contrasting the economic and political situations between Britain and China, Yan Fu deeply felt the necessity to make a change to China's political institution. But his position as Superintendent was not high enough to actualize his plans and he tried a couple of times taking the Imperial Civil Service Examination in order to have personal advancement. The news that China was defeated by Japan in 1895 turned his dream into bubbles and Yan Fu saw an urgent need to reform China. He thought that Western thought could serve as a key to China's problems. The ideas of competition and survival for the fittest were something that China lacked. As such Yan Fu began to translate Thomas Huxley's *Evolution and Ethics* (《进化与伦理学》, 1893) with commentary compatible to Herbert Spencer's social Darwinian ideas represented in the latter's *A Study of Sociology* (1873). The major problem was that Chinese society had neither dynamics nor competition but remained static and conventional. People had no incentive to compete as long as they followed the Confucian doctrine of Three Cardinal Principles and Five Virtues (三纲五常) and felt content with a scanty but peaceful life. Nobody seemed to worry that such a traditional way of living implied the ruin of the state and the danger of racial preservation.

China's backwardness and debility had much to do with the Imperial Civil Service Examination, the inertia mentality, and refusal to change. In analyzing the reasons for China's failure in the Sino-Japanese War, Yan Fu found that unpreparedness and cowardice were the two major reasons. On the part of the management, it was ignorant of Li Hongzhang, the Commander-in-Chief who did not expect the Japanese intention of staging the war against China and made no arrangement for military supplies, which led to the chaos of the battlefield. On the part of the basic-level leadership, Fang Boqian, the Captain of the warship Jiyuan (济远), turned and fled at the sound of the cannon, breaking up the formation. Regarding the ground force Wei Rugui (卫汝贵), the Huai Army General whose duty was to garrison Pyongyang, Democratic People's Republic of Korea suffered a rout in the engagement with the enemy and fled back to China. Gong Zhaoyu (龚照玙), Battalion Commander of Lvshun Marine and Land Service (旅顺水陆营务处大队长), fled also to Tianjin through Lvshun and Yantai when hearing of the fall of Jinzhou (金州), a district of Dalian (永田圭介, 2014).

The two problems had much to do with the talent selection system. Those who were chosen to important positions normally had passed the Imperial Civil Service Examination. However, the person who passed the exam could only recite articles from the Confucian classics and write essays that did not solve real problems. Once put in an important post, the official was incompetent in dealing with practical issues because the knowledge of the Four Books and the Five Classics were no longer suitable for solving real problems in modern times (永田圭介, 2014). Yan Fu thought it was imperative to reform the exam system.

Thomas Huxley described in the prolegomena of *Evolution and Ethics* how plants could struggle for survival in the scanty resources, which could extend to other animals which needed to compete for limited food, habitat, etc. Only those strong could keep living while the weak would be weeded out.

> The native grasses and weeds, the scattered patches of gorse (金雀花), contended with one another (彼此竞争) for the possession of the scanty surface soil; they fought against the droughts of summer, the frosts (冰霜) of winter, and the furious gales which swept, with unbroken force, now from the Atlantic, and now from the North Sea, at all times of the year; they filled up, as they best might, the gaps made in their ranks by all sorts of underground and over-ground animal ravagers (劫掠者). One year with another, an average population, the floating balance of the unceasing struggle for existence among the indigenous plants, maintained itself.
>
> 怒生之草，交加之藤，势如争长相雄，各据一抔壤土，夏与畏日争，冬与严霜争，四时之内，飘风怒吹，或西发西洋，或东起北海，旁午交扇，无时而息。上有鸟兽之践啄，下有蚁蝝之啮伤，憔悴孤虚，旋生旋灭，菀枯顷刻，莫可究详。是离离者亦各尽天能，以自存种族而已。数亩之内，战事炽然，强者后亡，弱者先绝……长此互相吞并，混逐蔓延而已……（赫胥黎，2011：1–2）

Yan Fu translated Huxley because it was easy to read compared with Spenser's *A Study of Sociology*, which was too complicated to be rendered into Chinese. But he advocated Herbert Spenser more in that the law of nature was applicable to human society where man were craving for survival by fierce competitions. And it so happened that Huxley wrote a passage in his book describing the competition among various plants for life and it was appropriate for Yan Fu to borrow it to illustrate Spenser's idea. In order to awaken his people, Yan Fu chose the piece describing the competition in the natural world to suggest that the same thing existed in human society.

> And in the living world, one of the most characteristic features of this cosmic process is the struggle for existence, the competition of each with all, the result of which is the selection, that is to say, the survival of those forms which, on the whole, are best adapted, to the conditions which at any period obtain; and which are, therefore, in that respect, and only in that respect, the fittest. (Huxley, 1894: 3)
>
> 以天演为体，而其用有二：曰物竞，曰天择。此万物莫不然，而于有生之类为尤者。物竞者，物争自存也，以一物以与物物争，或存或亡，而其效则归于天择。天择者，物争焉而独存，则其存也，必有其所以存，必其所得于天之分，自致一己之能，与其所遭值之时与地，及凡周身以外之物力，有其相谋相剂者焉。（赫胥黎，2011：2–3）

The key words for the above translation are "natural selection" and "survival of the fittest". Whether you can continue living in the world depends on nature, which selects the strong instead of the weak and lets them keep alive. Once you are selected by nature, you belong to the fittest and you are most likely to survive.

Fig. 11-3 严复主要译著

Being competitive in human society suggests you have an edge to occupy more resources, develop more quickly, and live a better life. If you refuse to catch up and stick to the convention, you are bound to be left behind. The buying and dismantling of the Wusong railway was a case in point. In 1876, Dickson, an English merchant, bought a piece of land and built a railroad between Shanghai and Wusong in the name of constructing an ordinary road. That caused trouble with the Chinese government and a year later Shen Baozhen, the Viceroy, bought the railway and dismantled it because in the Chinese people's eyes a railroad facilitated foreigners' invasion, occupied arable land, destroyed *fengshui*, and caused unemployment. But the Self-Strengthening Movement meant to learn from the West and the railroad was just something that China lacked and needed. If the Chinese could learn how to use the railway and build locomotives through the buyout, it would certainly benefit the people.

During the 1880 debate concerning the construction of railways in China, Liu Xihong (刘锡鸿), the first Envoy to Germany, was against it and there were two reasons he wrote in his memorial. It disturbed our ancestors buried in the tomb, leading to possible natural disasters like drought and flood and the tourism brought about by such easy transportation was not something that we Chinese should imitate because it encouraged laziness. Weng Tonghe, Minister of Revenue (户部尚书), could not agree more after reading Liu Xihong's memorial and he highly praised Liu Xihong for his relevance and consideration when he read it again in 1888 (姜鸣, 2016).

Another example was the recall of the overseas students from America because the government was afraid that the overseas students would be contaminated by American culture and forgot their own tradition. Wearing a queue and being dressed in a robe were the symbol of Chinese custom and if you changed it into short hair and Western style suit, you were no longer Chinese. This was again a short-sighted action and not worth the candle. The two examples showed that some educated Chinese refused to keep up with the time and modernize the country, but persevered in the old custom and tradition.

11.3 Translation of Adam Smith's *The Wealth of Nations*
翻译亚当·斯密《国富论》

Yan Fu noticed the distinctive attitudes between Britain and China to wealth and money and he wanted urgently to turn China into a wealthy country. The book he intended to translate this time was Adam Smith's *The Wealth of Nations* (1776) because it was Smith's idea illustrated in the book that changed Britain and made it a wealthy country. As we know, social wealth is closely related to trade and exchange of goods. In the process of exchange, the two sides benefited from each other's privileged products and became easily prosperous. This kind of mutual compensation stimulated the increase of economy.

But for two thousand years in China, the policy practiced by the rulers of different dynasties was called stressing agriculture and restraining commerce (重农抑商) and this policy was first put forward by Shang Yang (商鞅), the minister of the Qin State during the Warring States Period. Merchants were not allowed to engage in grain trade in case of speculation and they were charged higher taxation. This policy was followed by Qin, Han, Tang, Song, Yuan, Ming, and Qing dynasties. Liu Bang (刘邦), the first emperor of the Han Dynasty even instructed that merchants were not allowed to wear silk clothes, take arms and ride horses, or be engaged in politics. Otherwise they would be forced to pay higher taxes as a punishment. Similarly, merchants in the Tang Dynasty were not permitted to ride horses, but they needed to help the state in time of fiscal difficulties. No merchants in the Song and Yuan dynasties were permitted to engage in the trade of salt, iron, tea, alum (明矾), coal, wine, spice and precious objects because those commodities were monopolized by the state (龚昌菊, 庞昌伟, 2014). Regarding the policy of stressing agriculture and restraining commerce practiced in both the Ming and Qing dynasties we have discussed in Chapter One, Zhu Yuanzhang's ban on maritime trade, Kangxi's order of relocating people along the coastal provinces of Fujian, Guangdong, Jiangsu, and Zhejiang 30–50 *li* to the inland areas.

According to Li Xitang (李西堂, 2016b), there were several reasons for Chinese feudal rulers to implement the policy of emphasizing agriculture and suppressing commerce. First, merchants' engagement in commerce would influence government's tax revenue, corvee (徭役), military service (兵役), and its control of the people. Second, merchants' mobility, shrewdness, and wealth might lead to the destruction of the feudal society. Third, merchants' pursuit of equality and freewill would challenge the hierarchical system. However, it would be much easier for the rulers to fool the peasants and bound them to the land through the household registration system and *Bao-jia* system (保甲制). If they refused to be ruled, the peasants' land would be withdrawn. Therefore, the policy was beneficial to the rulers rather than the ruled. And it was this policy that made the Chinese people extremely needy.

Even in the late Qing Dynasty, merchants were still ill-treated by the government officials who levied harsh duties, such as *lijin*. The famous merchant Zhang Jian (张謇) was annoyed by the repeatedly charged *lijin*, suggesting that merchants were not encouraged and protected as expected (朱英, 2017). When merchants like Zhao Licheng (赵立诚), and Wu Nanji (吴南记), and the official Yung Wing recommended founding modern steamship companies, Zeng Guofan, the Viceroy disagreed out of his distrust in Chinese merchants. Other reasons that the government did not support it included that they wanted modern steamships to be used in military service and also they were afraid that the steamships would cause a decline of traditional large junk industry and an increase in unemployment. Another example was China Merchants Steamship Company (轮船招商局), where the relationship between government and merchants was not equal and the merchants had to rely on Li Hongzhang for the prerogative of canal grain transportation, tax exemption, government loan, etc. (狄金华, 黄伟民, 2018). Once Li Hongzhang lost power, the merchants could not protect themselves alone.

However, in the 18th century Britain things were entirely different. Merchants were respected and free to choose their trade. Most British patricians believed that "commerce, especially foreign commerce, was the engine that drove a state's power and wealth, just as they took it for granted that the world's supply of raw materials and markets was strictly finite, that competition to win access to them was bound to be intense, and that if British traders were to succeed in the struggle, they must be vigorously supported abroad and protected at home" (Coley, 2012: 64). The relation between government and merchants was reciprocally dependent. The trading companies, such as British East India Company and Levant Company loaned large amount of money to the government in time of war. During the war against Americans, for instance, 40% of the cost came from merchants, even shop keepers and traders. The Royal Navy also relied on merchants' investment for expanding in size and firepower and raising navy soldiers. Linda Coley described in her book *Britons: Forging the Nation* how a merchant called Thomas Coram donated his money to a foundling hospital and won his respect from the society. Merchants like Coram not only brought wealth to the nation but also exhibited high moral character, which combined commerce and patriotism together (Coley, 2012).

Adam Smith in his book *The Wealth of Nations* called upon the British government to further free the market by not intervening in the foreign trade. In other words, the mercantile mentality was unhealthy because that helped monopolize just a few overseas companies while repressing many domestic companies. In order to enrich the country, the government should take a laissez-fair attitude and avoid any interference in the market. Market has its own mechanism to mediate between need and supply and competition and self-interest can be regarded as such mechanism, which is labelled an invisible hand. Ever since the "free trade" suggested by Smith was adopted by the British government, the country released much potential energy and people became increasingly richer.

That was the scene that attracted Yan Fu's eyes when he was studying at Greenwich College during 1877–1879 although it was a hundred years after the publication of *The Wealth of Nations*. Yan Fu's intention was to borrow ideas from Smith and apply it to China so that the Chinese could become rich. In Yan Fu's opinion, "Unless we make every effort to change our habit of shunning all talk of interest (*li*) (羞于谈利), unless we resolutely break our attitude of emphasizing agriculture and suppressing commerce, our wealth will remain undeveloped...If interest is taboo (*hui*) there can be no science of economics." (Schwartz, 1983: 123)

11.4 Translation of John Stuart Mill's *On Liberty* and Montesquieu's *The Spirit of Laws* 翻译密尔《论自由》及孟德斯鸠《论法的精神》

Before the publication of the Chinese version of *On Liberty* by John Stuart Mill (1859) in 1903, Yan Fu made penetrating critiques of China's absence of individual liberty. He thought that all the Chinese sages in ancient times were very much afraid of talking about liberty in their writings. Yet in the West, it was a common belief that all men were born with liberty and all countries were endowed with liberty so no countries could infringe other countries' liberty. The infringement of one's liberty was equivalent to do harm to other people, steal things from other people, or kill other people. Thus, liberty was so sacred that no one, including the king could trespass upon the liberty of others.

> 夫自由一言，真中国历古圣贤之所深畏，而从未尝立以为教者也。彼西人之言曰：唯天生民，各具赋畀，得自由者乃为全受。故人人各得自由，国国各得自由，第务令毋相侵损而已。侵人自由者，斯为逆天理，贼人道。其杀人伤人及盗蚀人财物，皆侵人自由之极致也。故侵人自由，虽国君不能，而其刑禁章条，要皆为此设耳。（胡伟希，1994：3）

It was quite natural for Yan Fu to choose Mill's *On Liberty* for translation. Yan Fu lived in an age when most literati had no courage to make suggestions or critiques of government and the reason could be traced back to Kangxi, Yongzheng and Qianlong. A special term was used to describe such a situation, i.e. Literary Inquisition (文字狱). The

Manchu people were hostile to Han people who expressed their disdain and anger over the oppression of the savage people by writing. If this was found out by the government, the people involved in the case would all be punished. In Kangxi's reign, for instance, the case of Zhuang Tinglong (庄廷鑨案) led to the death of 70 people who helped edit, print and sell the book titled *History of the Ming Dynasty*. The Manchu rulers did not want to see the appellations used by the people in the Ming Dynasty and they were angry about the contempt words used in the book, too.

Another case called the False Memorial of Sun Jiagan (孙嘉淦伪奏稿) caused arrest of more than a thousand people. In this memorial, the writer listed ten accusations of Emperor Qianlong and made severe criticism of the emperor. The False Memorial had been spread all over the country for more than ten years, which made the emperor extremely angry and he spent two years chasing the criminal and eventually focused on a lower-order official in Jiangxi Province named Lu Lusheng (卢鲁生) who was sentenced to death.

Such coercion policy made enormous impact on literati and officials who simply kept their mouth shut and dropped their pen. A writer called Wang Huizu (汪辉祖) advised people not to keep journals or write notes for self-protection. Gong Zizhen, another man of letters and a friend of Wei Yuan, described in his poem how scared people were of the Literary Inquisition and they wrote only for making a living (避席畏闻文字狱，著书都为稻粱谋). Similarly, Zeng Guofan complained about the fact that for more than ten years few people wanted to make critiques concerning the policy or politics concerning local interests (王汎森, 2016).

Mill in his book *On Liberty* published in 1859 defined the concept liberty as political liberties or rights and individuality. There existed a struggle between liberty and authority and liberty, according to Mill, meant "protection against the tyranny of the political rulers" by setting limits to the power that the ruler exercised over the community. If the ruler infringed liberty, people should rise to resist, or establish constitutional checks to prevent such things from happening (Mill, 2008). By individuality, Mill meant protection against the tyranny of the majority, i.e. "the prevailing opinion and feeling" "the tendency of society to impose", etc. (2008: 8). Mill advocated freedom of thought and freedom of speech as long as such an activity did not interfere others.

Yan Fu fully understood how important liberty was to the Chinese people. In the late Qing Dynasty, people still could not speak the truth if it was likely to hurt some officials' feelings. Guo Songtao was a case in point. As the first Envoy to Britain, Guo Songtao kept journal along the journey of more than 50 days and recorded what he had seen and how he thought of it. In the book, Guo Songtao made some frank remarks concerning the advancement of Britain while criticizing Chinese officials' narrow-mindedness because they still refused to admit the fact that British people were no longer barbarians but civilized people. The truth was that China was still far left behind Britain. When his journal was compiled into a book titled *The First Chinese Embassy to the West* (《使西纪程》) and was published in 1877, it caused immediate censure from the court. The officials were angry about Guo Songtao's positive comments on foreign countries and critiques of China. Li Ciming (李慈铭) said he did not understand why Guo Songtao wrote things like that. He Jinshou (何金寿) even considered Guo Songtao as a traitor because he liked Britain so much. The result was that the edition was destroyed (钟叔河, 2010).

Yan Fu felt deeply about what had happened to Guo Songtao and he really believed that people should enjoy "freedom of speech". Yan Fu's understanding of free speech was to tell the truth and seek the truth in order neither to be cheated by ancient people nor to be oppressed by power. Even if someone who was your enemy spoke truth, you should not dismiss it but accept it. If your father or an emperor confounded right and wrong, you should not take it as truth only because he was either your father or the emperor. This was what was meant by liberty. Aristotle said, "I love my tutor, but I love truth more." That was the meaning of it (马勇, 2015: 188-189).

> 须知言论自繇，只是平实地说实话求真理，一不为古人所欺，二不为权势所屈而已。使理真事实，虽出之仇敌，不可废也。使理谬事诬，虽以君父，不可从也。此之谓自繇。亚里斯多德尝言："吾爱吾师柏拉图，胜于余物，然吾爱真理，胜于吾师。"即此意耳。（马勇，2015：188–189）

The next classic Yan Fu translated was Montesquieu's *The Spirit of Laws* published in 1748 and translated into English in 1752. Although published more than a hundred years earlier than *On Liberty*, this book laid the foundation for the liberal ideology compared with Machiavelli (马基雅维利) and Locke and its recommendation of division of powers made tremendous impact on American constitution (刘小枫, 2018). Written in a narrative style, Montesquieu invoked a large number of examples from different countries including ancient Greece, Rome, and China to argue the point that "every man invested with power is apt to abuse it, and to carry his authority as far as it will go" and "To prevent this abuse, it is necessary from the very nature of things that power should be a check to power"

(Montesquieu, secoundat, 2001: 172). The solution was the division of powers into the legislative, the executive, and the judiciary. The formulation of the three independent departments ensured checks and balances among the powers. Montesquieu highly recommended the model of England because their country had the mechanism of power checks.

Indeed, England practiced power separation centuries ago. The Great Charter of 1215 forced King John to obey the law and give up levying taxes at will. The Provisions of Oxford of 1258 stipulated the principle of regular convening of Parliament, which required the king's attendance. The birth of Lords and Commons institution in 1332 promoted mutual supervision among the nobles, the commoners, and the king. The passage of the Bill of Rights in 1689 put the limit to king's power. The Two-Party System of 1679 formed the mechanism of supervision between the two parties. The Cabinet put an end to the one-party administration (李西堂, 2016a).

Two other important elements were also discussed in *The Spirit of Laws*, i.e. the commerce and moderate morals because they helped protect human liberty. In Montesquieu's opinion, commercial activities created peace, mutual respect, fair play and equality. "Peace is the natural effect of trade. Two nations who traffic with each other become reciprocally dependent; for if one has an interest in buying, the other has an interest in selling: and thus their union is founded on their mutual necessities." (Montesquieu, Secondat, 2001: 346) In addition, business was conducive to shaping people's behavior and cultivating gentle manners. As stated by Montesquieu, "Commerce is a cure for the most destructive prejudices; for it is almost a general rule that wherever we find agreeable manners, there commerce flourishes; and that wherever there is commerce, there we meet with agreeable manners." (Montesquieu, Secondat, 2001: 346)

As can be inferred, the division of powers, a moderate moral society, and commercial activities are three important components for a liberal country and an essential prerequisite for wealth and power. For thirty years, the Self-Strengthening Movement produced various manufacturers, technical schools, and the Beiyang Fleet with modern equipment, yet China had been defeated by a small country like Japan which was not respected by most Chinese people. The reason was that the Chinese people did not enjoy political rights and personal liberty. Their private properties could not be fully protected and the market was not free (袁伟时, 2016). But it was exactly the property rights and free market that indicated a modern society, where people can discuss, negotiate and even bargain with each other rather than fight and rob each other.

The fact that Yan Fu had chosen those classical works for translation that guided the Western world to the modern society showed that he fully understood what for China was in urgent need and to what extent those works could impact the society. Unlike other Western works which Yan Fu translated in an interpretative way, while translating *The Spirit of Laws*, he was faithful to the original version and did not change the meaning of the author. The Western thought was something that China needed to learn from and that was the basic principles underpinning the wealth and power of Western countries.

The contribution made by Yan Fu in introducing Western learning was far more important than buying machines and weapons without understanding the ideas underlined. From then on, Chinese literati and scholar officials began to read and understand the great thoughts embedded in those translated works and set on the path of reforming China. Kang Youwei, Liang Qichao, and Huang Zunxian (黄遵宪) were those who played an important role in turning China into a modern state.

In this chapter, we discussed Yan Fu's contribution to China's modernity. By translating the great works written by Western thinkers, Yan Fu enlightened Chinese intellectuals in terms of liberty, rights, and the separation of powers. For the first time, the Chinese people were able to read Western books and benefit from them.

◆ Topics for Discussion

1. The impact of Herbert Spenser's social Darwinism on the Chinese people.
2. Do you agree with Yan Fu when he said there was a close link between patriarchy society & anti-foreignism (宗法社会与排外), and despotism & conformism (专制与守旧)?
3. Freedom, equality, and fairness are out of human nature (自由、平等、公平乃人类天性).
4. Creativity and free thinking.
5. The significance of freedom, human rights and commerce in making a country strong and wealthy.
6. Why was Yan Fu against the patriarchy system?
7. Your comment on the translated works written by Western thinkers.

Reading Assignments

1. 严复 . 1994. 论事变之亟 . 沈阳：辽宁人民出版社 .
2. Day, J. H. 2014. Searching for the Roots of Western Wealth and Power: Guo Songtao and Education in Victorian England. *Late Imperial China, 35*(1): 1-37.

Bibliography

Chen, J. 1997. Western Learning and Social Transmutation. In F. Wakeman Jr., and X. Wang (eds.), *China's Quest for Modernization: A Historical Perspective* (pp.150-174). Berkeley: The Regents of the University of California.

Coley, L. 2012. *Britons: Forging the Nation 1707–1837*. New Haven: Yale University Press.

Day, J. H. 2014. Searching for the Roots of Western Wealth and Power: Guo Songtao and Education in Victorian England. *Late Imperial China*, *35*(1): 1-37.

Mill, J. S. 2008. *On Liberty and Utilitarianism*. New York: Random House, Inc.

Montesquieu, C. de, and Secondat, B. de. 2001. *The Spirit of Laws*. Ontario: Batoche Books.

Schwartz, B. 1983. *In Search of Wealth and Power: Yen Fu and the West*. Cambridge: Harvard University Press.

Wong, O. H.-H. 1987. *A New Profile in Sino-Western Diplomacy: The First Chinese Minister to Great Britain*. Hong Kong: Chung Hwa Book Co., Ltd.

狄金华，黄伟民. 2018. 组织依附、双边预算约束软化与清末轮船招商局的发展. 01–25. 爱思想.

丁守和. 1999. 中国近代启蒙思潮：上中下. 北京：社会科学文献出版社.

龚昌菊，庞昌伟. 2014. 中国古代“重农抑商”政策表现、成因及启示. 商业文化，(27):1–13.

郭嵩焘，刘锡鸿，薛福成，宋育仁. 2012. 郭嵩焘等使西记六种. 王立诚，编校. 上海：中西书局 .

赫胥黎. 2011. 天演论. 严复，译. 北京：中国青年出版社.

胡伟希. 1994. 论事变之亟——严复集. 沈阳：辽宁人民出版社.

姜鸣. 2016. 天公不语对枯棋:晚清的政局和人物. 北京:生活·读书·新知三联书店.

李西堂. 2016a. 残酷的专制统治. 02–06. 共识网.

李西堂. 2016b. 重农抑商政策. 03–14. 共识网.

琳达·科利. 2017. 英国人：国家的形成，1707–1837. 周玉鹏，刘耀辉，译. 北京：商务印书馆.

刘小枫. 2018. 孟德斯鸠与普遍历史. 06–18. 爱思想.

马勇. 2015. 盗火者：严复传. 北京：东方出版社.

孟泽. 2015. 首任驻外公使郭嵩焘为何视留学生严复为国士. 11–27. 凤凰网综合.

王汎森. 2016. 权力的毛细管作用：清代的思想、学术与心态. 北京：北京大学出版社.

永田圭介. 2014. 严复：中国近代探寻富国强兵的启蒙思想家. 王众一，译. 苏州：苏州大学出版社.

袁伟时. 2016. 国家盛衰的关键. 07–25. 思想酷.

钟叔河. 2010. 走向世界：中国人考察西方的历史. 北京：中华书局.

朱英. 2017. 近代中国商人与社会变革. 07–30. 爱思想.

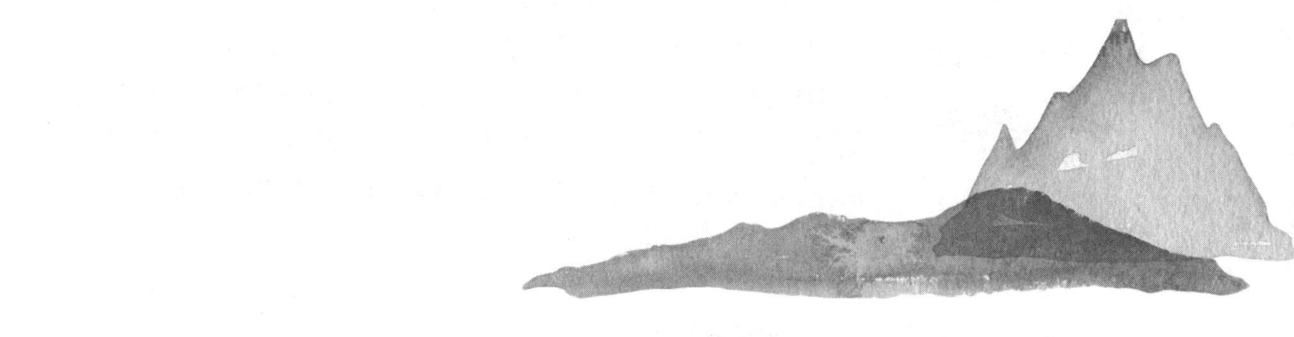

Chapter Twelve

A Comparison of Two *Quanxue Pian*

比较两部《劝学篇》

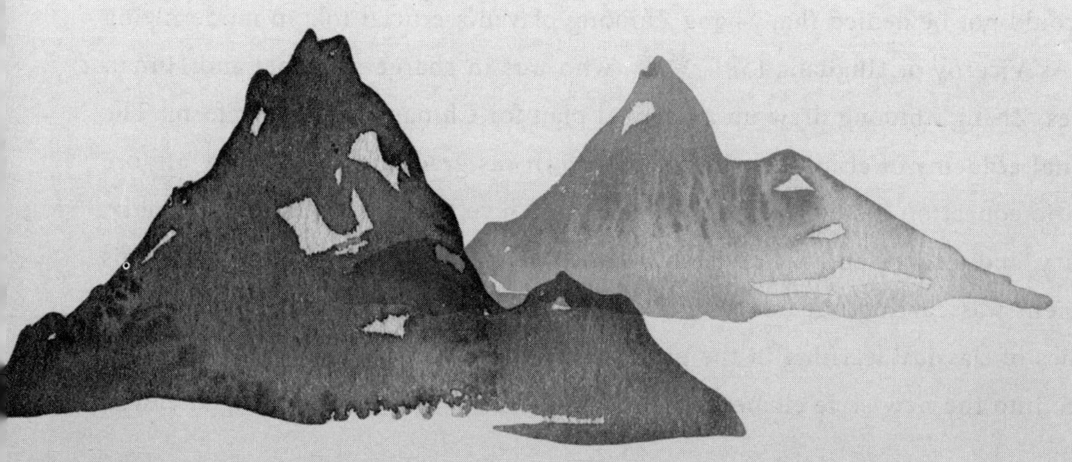

本章讨论和对比中日两部影响比较深远、题名同为《劝学篇》的著作，作者分别是张之洞和福泽谕吉。作为洋务运动的推动者，张之洞给后人留下了许多值得称道的业绩，如汉阳兵器厂、新式学堂、废除科举和参与新政。但通过分析他的作品，也可以看出他是一个复杂矛盾的人物。福泽谕吉则是推动日本明治维新的思想家。他的作品改变了日本人的思维方式和行为标准，为推动日本的近代化做出了贡献。

12.1 The Background 背景介绍

In this chapter, two renowned books are discussed and analyzed and they have the same Chinese title *Quanxue Pian*. While the English version for Zhang Zhidong's work is *Exhortation to Study* (1898), the one written by Fukuzawa Yukichi is *An Encouragement of Learning* (1872–1876). Both books had been translated into English and were well received. But the process of modernity in China and in Japan was not the same. By absorbing the essence of Western learning, Fukuzawa and other Japanese reformists entirely changed the Japanese people's mentality and made Japan wealthy and powerful. In China, Zhang Zhidong made great efforts in reforming the Chinese education system, yet China's progress to modernity was still slow. That had much to do with what Zhang Zhidong advocated in the book: "Chinese tradition as the mainstay and Western learning as application" (中体西用). In addition to the impact of the books on society, the two authors had different social status. Zhang Zhidong was a high-ranking scholar official while Fukuzawa was just an ordinary citizen and intellectual, who refused to participate in politics even under the invitation of the victorious reformers during the Meiji era.

It could not be denied that Zhang Zhidong played a crucial role in modernizing China. As Viceroy of Huguang (湖广总督) who was in charge of Hubei and Hunan provinces, Zhang Zhidong drew up a detailed plan for China's education reform. The traditional academy of classical learning (书院制) was gradually replaced by a more systematic education system in terms of the three-level school system, i.e. primary, secondary, and tertiary and the division between general and special education. This experiment was carried out in Hubei Province and Zhang Zhidong turned 60–70 academies of classical learning in the prefectures (州) and counties (县) of the whole province into the new-style elementary schools (新式小学学堂); he changed eleven

Chinese style schools in the prefectural cities (府) into the same number of modern secondary schools (李细珠, 2015). The subjects of Western learning were added to the traditional curriculum and a number of modern schools, which only offered subjects of Western learning were also established. This reform was based on the investigations into Japanese schools. Zhang Zhidong sent people to examine Japanese schools and asked them to focus on the schools specializing in political science, law, military, navigation, agriculture, engineering, forestry, medicine, mineralogy, electricity, railroad engineering, physical and chemical engineering, surveying, business, etc. and learn about their learning materials, teaching approaches and purchase their textbooks (李细珠, 2015). Together with Duanfang (端方), Zhang Zhidong's colleague, they presented their plan in a memorial of 1902 regarding the Hubei education system.

In addition, Zhang Zhidong made great efforts to facilitate the abolition of the Imperial Civil Service Examination in 1905. He shared the similar opinion with Kang Youwei and Liang Qichao in abolishing the exam because the existence of such an exam would hinder the development of new-style schools. People would still choose classical learning rather than modern learning if the Imperial Civil Service Examination still existed for it promised officialdom. Owing to his position in the court, Zhang Zhidong tried to lobby among those who had the power but were uncertain about or even disagreed to abolish such an exam and persuaded the ministers like Yikuang, Kungang (崑冈), Sun Jianai (孙家鼐), and Wang Wenshao (王文韶). Except for the last one Wang Wenshao, the rest of the ministers agreed to the abolition (李细珠, 2015). The first thing they did was to replace the eight-legged essay with commentary on current affairs (策论) and change the exam components into something more practical, such as economics. Thanks to Zhang Zhidong, the Western style schools flourished in China and the criteria for choosing capable personnel had also been changed.

Yet when reformists like Kang Youwei and Liang Qichao wanted to change the current political institution into the democratic one, Zhang Zhidong rejected it and began to turn against political reform initiated by Kang Youwei and Liang Qichao. This might have something to do with his position as Viceroy in the court. It was natural that the change in institution would certainly affect the officials' vested interests. But the question was why the Japanese reformers cared less about it.

Unlike Zhang Zhidong who studied Confucian classics in order to get promoted in his career, Fukuzawa Yukichi obtained knowledge in order to understand the world and seek truth. When Matthew Perry forced Japan to open its ports in 1853, Fukuzawa was eager to know the outside world and began to travel around his country studying foreign culture. He came out of his hometown Kyushu (九州) to Nagasaki (长崎) and Osaka (大阪) to study Dutch language because Dutch studies were popular in some areas of Japan, which brought new ideas to Japan. In 1858 when traveling to Edo (江户), he found the importance of understanding English and decided to learn English (马国川, 2018). Afterwards, Fukuzawa made three official voyages in 1860, 1862, and 1871 to the United States and European countries, sponsored by the Japanese government. The second one was the most important, according to Shunsaku, because having visited France, the United Kingdom, the Netherlands, Germany, Russia, and Portugal, Fukuzawa realized that prosperity depended on technical progress and Japan needed a revolution in people's knowledge and thinking. He told one of his friends in a letter that "the most urgent thing to do was to educate talented young people in things Western rather than to purchase machinery and armaments" (Fukuzawa, 2012: xix). Chinese officials failed to realize the important role played by Western thought in the process of modernization due to their ignorance and their attention was directed to purchasing machines and weapons.

When he came back from the second journey, Fukuzawa Yukichi set up a school called Keio-gijuku (庆应义塾) and began to transmit Western knowledge to the Japanese young people. In the meantime, he also translated Western books, such as *Political Economy* by John Hill Burton and wrote pamphlets and textbooks on topics like physics, geography, military arts, the British parliament and international relations. Among his writings, *An Encouragement of Learning* was a collection of 17 pamphlets written and published during 1872–1876. Aiming at ordinary audience, Fukuzawa used a simple and clear style to make himself understood. In this way, he initiated a colloquial style which was intended for the less educated. Yan Fu was considered as China's Fukuzawa Yukichi because his translated works of Western thought for the first time called attention to Chinese literati. Yet the language style Yan Fu adopted was classical and elegant for his target audience was the small number of educated people. Since many ordinary people had no access to the new ideas transmitted by Yan Fu, it resulted in the slow pace of development in China. That was the limitation of Chinese literati.

Fig. 12–1 福泽谕吉

Fukuzawa Yukichi was greatly impressed by Western civilization and was determined to turn Japan into a civilized nation and stand on its own feet in the world. *An Outline of a Theory of Civilization* (《文明论概略》) was another important book he wrote and published in 1875. In it he defined the word civilization as a combination of a materially comfortable life, "the refining of knowledge, and the cultivation of virtue so as to elevate human life to a higher plane...(Thus) it refers to the attainment of *both* material well-being *and* the elevation of the human spirit..." (Fukuzawa, 2012: xxiii) In other words, it was not civilized behavior when a samurai shouted to commoners for road directions. Neither was it civilized when some samurais would murder the people who held different opinions from them. The Neo-Confucianism exerted a great influence in Japan, but it did not encourage innovation; instead it made people blindly follow the instructions given by the rulers. Ordinary people did not use their brain to distinguish between right and wrong. The whole society was in need of self-reliance and independent thinking.

The private virtue (私德) and benevolent rule (仁治) as stated by the Chinese classics were advocated by traditional Japanese teaching, but the only concern of the classics was how to fool and rule people. The Japanese people relied on their hereditary positions and were not concerned with public matters. This, according to Fukuzawa Yukichi, was the dark side of the Japanese civilization (2012).

Masao Maruyama (丸山真男) further elaborated the meaning of knowledge and virtue. Here Fukuzawa meant mathematical learning (数理学) and independent spirit (独立精神). He put great emphasis on mathematical learning because Newton's mechanical system was the foundation of all the learning. The question needed to ask was what kind of spirit scientists normally possessed and the spirit referred to morals. The two things were closely connected and that was the reason why physics was taught in Keio University established by Fukuzawa Yukichi. Independence and self-esteem were the defining characteristics of those scientists. But the Japanese people lacked the two things. In order to become a civilized nation, the Japanese needed to cultivate the mathematical learning, independence and self-esteem. The combination of science and ethics was the goal that Japan aimed at (丸山真男, 2018).

Fukuzawa's analysis was based on his comparison and contrast between Neo-Confucianism and Western learning. In his opinion, the Neo-Confucianism mixed nature and morality and that was wrong logic. The so-called Unity of Heaven and Man (天人合一) did not distinguish between nature and man. When it used the heaven and ground as reason to argue that man should obey the emperor because the emperor represented the heaven as his position was given by heaven, it was completely illogical. The reason was that nature and man were governed by different laws and it was unreasonable to confuse the two (丸山真男, 2018).

While Fukuzawa Yukichi made an in-depth analysis of the weaknesses of the Neo-Confucianism believed by the Japanese and pointed out its faulty aspects, Zhang Zhidong did not have the intention to do the same because his scholarly training in the Old Text School made him believe in the hierarchical system and firmly defend it because the emperor thought it right. Since he gained favor from Empress Dowager Cixi when taking the Imperial Civil Service Examination, who moved him from the lower ranking to the top one, Zhang Zhidong felt it his obligations to be loyal to the top leader and decided to return the favor one day. That might explain why Zhang Zhidong acted in such a contradictory manner. Next, we will analyze *Exhortation to Study* written or compiled by Zhang Zhidong and see whether we can find the reason.

12.2 An Analysis of *Exhortation to Study* by Zhang Zhidong 张之洞《劝学篇》分析

The book *Exhortation to Study* was published in 1898, a few months before the One Hundred Days Reform staged by Kang Youwei and Liang Qichao and Zhang Zhidong's intention was to refute the radical opinion advocated by Kang Youwei and Liang Qichao, who wanted to abolish the current despotic institution and establish Parliament modeling after Britain and empower ordinary people with liberty. In Zhang Zhidong's opinion, if China wanted to learn from the West, the first thing to do was to understand our own culture thoroughly. It was the Chinese tradition and customs rather than the Western learning that underpinned China's future development. The argument could be summarized as one sentence, i.e. Chinese classics as the mainstay and Western learning as application. The book gained approval of Emperor Guangxu and was printed for two million copies. It was also praised by Western missionaries and translated into English by Samuel Woodbridge two years after its publication. The title Woodbridge used was *China's Only Hope* (1900). The fact that people of different political stances unanimously praised the work demonstrated how politically experienced and shrewd Zhang Zhidong was. Due to his sophistication, Zhang Zhidong avoided being punished by Cixi after the One Hundred Days Reform.

Fig. 12–2 张之洞《劝学篇》

The book comprised two parts: the Inner Part or the Moral Part (nine chapters) and the Exterior Part or the Practical Part (fifteen chapters), which included altogether twenty four chapters. Let us look at the Moral Part first. In Chapter Three of the Moral Part, Zhang Zhidong discussed three moral obligations and expressed his own opinion about it:

> The Sovereign is the head of the Subject, the Father is the head of the Son, and the Husband is the head of the Wife. These tenets have been handed down from the sages, and as Heaven does not change, so they never change. (Zhang, 1900: 43)
>
> "君为臣纲，父为子纲，夫为妻纲"……五伦之要，百行之原，相传数千年，更无异议。（张之洞，2008：24）

At the beginning of this chapter, Zhang Zhidong quoted from the Confucian canon and expressed his stand that the Three Cardinal Principles should be strictly followed and not be changed. Traditionally, one's political position, moral principle and academic tendency were mutually inclusive. Different from Wei Yuan, Gong Zizhen and Kang Youwei, who belonged to the New Text School and wanted to explore implied meanings of the Confucian classics for the sake of reform, Zhang Zhidong belonged to the Old Text School, devoting to exegesis and textual interpretations. As such, he continued:

> Know then, that the obligation of subject to sovereign is incompatible with republicanism; that the duties a son owes to a father conflict with the talk about the father and son being amenable to the same punishment and the abolition of mourning for, and sacrificing to, one's parents; and that the true relation which exists between man and wife is utterly at variance with the prattle about a man and woman having equal power. (Zhang, 1900: 44)
>
> 故知君臣之纲，则民权之说不可行也；知父子之纲，则父子同罪免丧废祀之说不可行也；知夫妇之纲，则男女平权之说不可行也。（张之洞，2008：25）

Although Zhang Zhidong agreed with the reformists like Kang Youwei in terms of concerns about China, urgency to reform, and change of conventions, he disliked immensely the reform theory developed by Kang Youwei in the book *An Examination of the Forged Classics of the Xin Dynasty* (《新学伪经考》) which was based on *Gongyang Zhuan*. He discussed the issue with Kang Youwei and asked him to give it up but Kang Youwei abruptly refused (冯天瑜, 何晓明, 2010). Thus, Zhang Zhidong called the reformers "stupid and ignorant whippersnappers" as they knew little about Western administration, but exalted it above that of China (1900: 47).

But in the following chapter, i.e. Chapter Four, having praised the European countries for their competition, determination, and strength, Zhang Zhidong began to criticize Chinese scholar officials for their pride, inertia, and inaction. Worse still, some officials took the opportunity to abuse their powers and feather their own nests (中饱私囊).

> Many of the officials and people are proud and indolent. They contentedly rest in the belief that the old order of things will suffice for these dangerous times, and in the end become the easy prey of outsiders...they take advantage of the crisis to fill their own pockets, in order to form partnerships with foreigners when the crash comes, be "Western merchants" themselves, or be naturalized abroad. (Zhang, 1900: 51-52)
>
> 独我中国士夫庶民懵然罔觉，五十年来，屡鉴不悛，守其傲惰，安其偷苟，情见势绌，而外侮亟矣……昏墨之人，则视国家之休戚漠然无动于其心，意谓此非发捻之比，中华虽沦，富贵自在，方且乘此阽危，恣为贪黩，以待合西伙，为西商，徙西地，入西籍。（张之洞，2008：29–30）

Obviously, Zhang Zhidong had realized how serious the situation was and it was extremely necessary to make a change. But since he did not share the same opinion regarding the path of reform, Zhang Zhidong was unlikely to co-operate with Kang Youwei or Liang Qichao in spite of the fact that he showed great respect for Liang Qichao's scholarship and talent. Indeed, Zhang Zhidong had invited Kang Youwei to his place for talks every other day before his split with Kang Youwei. The reason was private because Zhang Zhidong wanted to dispel his sorrow for losing his son and needed to talk to someone.

Fig. 12–3 张之洞

In Chapter Six, Zhang Zhidong clearly expressed his rejection to constructing the parliament when the scholar reformers strongly advocated it. His reason was that the Chinese were ignorant of the Western institution and not ready for the reform. The mass were uneducated and even the reformers themselves knew little about what a parliament really meant.

> There is a class of Chinese in the country just now who have become impatient and vexed with the present order of things. They chafe at the insults offered to us by foreigners, the impotency of the mandarins in war, and the unwillingness of the high

officials to reform our mercantile and educational methods: and they would lead any movement to assemble the people together for the discussion of a republic...There is not a particle of good to be derived from it. On the contrary, such a system is fraught with a hundred evils...The first thing necessary in a republic is a Parliament, and it is said that China ought to establish a House. Against such a proceeding we say that the Chinese officials and people are obstructive as well as stupid. They understand nothing about the affairs of the world at the present time, are utterly ignorant of the details and intricacies of civil government. They have never heard of the demand for foreign schools, government, military tactics, and machinery... (Zhang, 1900: 55-56)

今日愤世嫉俗之士，恨外人之欺凌也，将士之不能战也，大臣之不变法也，官师之不兴学也，百司之不讲求工商也，于是倡为民权之议，以求合群而自振……民权之说，无一益而有百害。

将立议院欤？中国士民至今安于固陋者尚多，环球之大势不知，国家之经制不晓，外国兴学、立政、练兵、制器之要不闻，即聚胶胶扰扰之人于一室，明者一，暗者百，游谈呓语，将焉用之？（张之洞，2008：37–38）

On the whole, the impossibility of setting up the parliament in China, according to Zhang Zhidong, was that the Chinese had no knowledge of it and were unprepared for a civil government. It seemed that now Zhang Zhidong forgot what he had written previously when he made sharp criticism of officials and people. He exhibited a conflict of character for the second time. As a matter of fact, Zhang Zhidong himself did not understand what a parliament really was, neither did he comprehend the word "liberty".

In Zhang Zhidong's opinion, if China adopted the republic institution, there would be no officials who could levy supplies and there would be no one who could guarantee the security of the country. This misunderstanding of the parliament might be caused by his confusion about another concept, i.e. liberty. Zhang Zhidong was under the impression that if people were given liberty, there would be social chaos or anarchy in China. Nobody would listen to the government or obey laws and the society would be in a complete mess.

In fact, a parliament is composed of two houses, i.e. the House of Lords and the House of Commons. While the Members of Parliament in the Upper House mostly inherited their position from their forebears, the MPs in the Lower House were selected by people. In Britain, all people above the age of twenty-one were eligible for voting except for criminal acts, foreigners, etc. And people who campaigned for the MP position did not need to have a large sum of money or property, as Zhang Zhidong imagined they did. The meaning of liberty refers to life rights, property rights, and human rights. Once people enjoy all those liberties at the same time, they should also take responsibilities of obeying laws, such as paying taxes and conforming to the social code of conduct. It does not necessarily mean that people will be no longer restrained by law and can do whatever they want.

Next, we will move onto the second part, i.e. the Practical Part. In Chapter Two "Travel", the writer extolled the benefits of overseas studies and used Japan as an example. The main point was that it was better to send Chinese youths to Japan to study rather than to European countries or America because it not only saved money but also was a shortcut to obtain the Western technology.

> The diminutive country of Japan has suddenly sprung into prominence. Ito, Yamagata, Yanomoto, Mutsui and others visited foreign countries twenty years ago and learned a method by which to escape the coercion of Europe. Under their leadership more than one hundred Japanese students were sent to Germany, France, and England, to learn foreign systems of conducting government, commerce, war, etc. After these had completed their course, they were recalled and employed by the Japanese Government as generals and ministers. When the government was once changed they developed into the Heroes of the Orient. (Zhang, 1900: 91-92).
>
> 日本，小国耳，何兴之暴也？伊藤、山县、夏本、陆奥诸人，皆二十年前出洋之学生也，愤其国为西洋所胁，率其徒百馀人分诣德、法、英诸国，或学政治工商，或学水陆兵法，学成而归，用为将相，政事一变，雄视东方。（张之洞，2008：72）

From the comment above, we see clearly that Zhang Zhidong had no problem understanding the value of foreign systems of government, commerce and war, and he encouraged Chinese youths to do the same by learning from the Japanese and to make China powerful. But as we have seen, the institutional change was not advocated by Zhang Zhidong and he did not support Kang Youwei in his reform. In fact, this piece of writing was intended at refuting Kang Youwei's radical ideas. In many places, Zhang Zhidong demonstrated conflicting opinions. The same was true with his attitude to the media. In Chapter Six "Reading Newspaper", Zhang Zhidong thought highly of the functions of the public media and he made no attempt to avoid this method in China. Instead he believed criticism helped the Chinese correct their mistakes and move forward faster.

We do not perceive our own faults, and if we did, would not dare to speak unreservedly about them. Every way seems just in our own eyes, but our strong neighbors come and search us out. If the Emperor and officials of our country, who read the newspapers and are exercised thereby, should fear the consequences of inaction and reform, would this not make for China's welfare? Readers of foreign newspapers perceive at once that the Chinese are unmercifully abused. We are compared with drunkards and rotten stuff. The partition of our country by foreigners, and the question of who can seize the largest portion, are freely discussed. This discussion arouses the ire of every patriotic Chinese...Is it wise to be angry? Ought we not to court the acquaintance of those who frankly tell us our faults as Chu Ko did; and following the example of Chow Tsz, bewail the diseases that are eating away the life of China?..."The wise country holds on to its critical neighbors." (Zhang, 1900: 118-119)

大抵一国之利害安危，本国之人蔽于习俗，必不能尽知之。即知之，亦不敢尽言之。惟出之邻国，又出之至强之国，故昌言而无忌。我国君臣上下，果能览之而动心，怵之而改作，非中国之福哉？近人阅洋报者，见其抵訾中国，不留馀地，比之醉人，比之朽物，议分裂，议争先，类无不拂然怒者。吾谓此何足怒耶！勤攻吾阙者，诸葛之所求；讳疾灭身者，周子之所痛。古云"士有诤友"，今虽云"国有诤邻"，不亦可乎？（张之洞，2008：89）

The above remark was well versed and rather reasonable and it was not easy for Zhang Zhidong to speak it out. He impressed us as an open-minded person and did not care about foreigners' criticism. But in Chapter Seven "Reform of Methods", Zhang Zhidong came back to his original theme: Chinese learning as the basis of education, and Western knowledge as utilities because he thought that Chinese institutions should be preserved and that was the basis to make China powerful (Zhang, 1900).

But there are certain principles in China that are immutable. We cannot change the Obligations and the Records, but we can change the administration of laws; we cannot change the Holy Religion, but we can change our implements and weapons of war; we cannot change the sense of right, but we can change the *modus agendi* of the workmen and artificers. (Zhang, 1900: 122)

夫不可变者，伦纪也，非法制也；圣道也，非器械也；心术也，非工艺也。（张之洞，2008：91）

The controversial character shown in Zhang Zhidong in terms of a mover of Self-Strengthening Movement and an opportunist had much to do with his belonging to the "Qingliu Group" and stuck to Confucian principles of restoring former norms of excellence (复古) and imitating ancient models (效古). That explained why he first helped Kang Youwei and Liang Qichao with financial aid in publishing newspapers, but became a murderer of the One Hundred Days reformers (戊戌改革者) later. The character of Qing elites was extremely complicated. In order to understand it, we need to make an in-depth analysis of what they wrote and further explore the elements that determined their strange behavior.

12.3 Fukuzawa Yukichi and His *An Encouragement of Learning* 福泽谕吉与《劝学篇》

Fig. 12-4 福泽谕吉《劝学篇》

In *An Encouragement of Learning*, Fukuzawa Yukichi wanted to convince the Japanese about the important relationship between liberty, independence, equality, and the strength of the country. At the beginning of the first section, he stated, "Heaven, it is said, does not create one person above or below another. This signifies that when we are born from Heaven we all are equal and there is no innate distinction between high and low." (Fukuzawa, 2012: 3) The fact that people enjoy different social status or live on different means is attributed to whether they possess knowledge or not. Knowledge refers to the modern subjects of natural and social sciences, such as geography, physics, history, economics, and ethics, but not the impractical learning in Confucian classics, such as study of incomprehensible Chinese characters, reading difficult-to-understand ancient texts, or enjoying or writing poetry, because those who are learned in Chinese classics are not capable of carrying out practical work, such as business management. Once you have the knowledge, you will understand what personal freedom is and how it comes about. Fukuzawa Yukichi defined freedom as follows:

> We are born unrestricted and unbounded, and full-fledged men and women are free to act as they wish. Nevertheless, many will become selfish and fall into dissipation if they assert only their own freedom and do not know their place. "Place" or capacity means to achieve one's own personal freedom without infringing upon that of others, based on natural principle and in harmony with human feeling. The borderline between freedom and selfishness lies at the point where one does or does not infringe upon the freedom of others. (2012: 5)

Unlike Zhang Zhidong who interpreted freedom as something similar to anarchy, Fukuzawa had an accurate understanding of freedom or liberty defined by John Locke, an English philosopher of the 17th century. In his opinion, personal freedom did not mean you could do whatever you liked, but it meant while making your own decision you did not harm other people's freedom. Once the meaning of personal freedom was made clear, Fukuzawa continued to discuss an associated concept, i.e. equality and equality among different nations.

> Japan and the nations of the West are peoples who live between the same heaven and earth, feel the warmth of the same sun, look up at the same moon, share the same oceans and air, and possess the same human feelings. Therefore, nations which have should share with those which have not. We should mutually teach and learn from each other, without shame or pride. We should promote each other's interests and pray for each other's happiness. We should associate with one another following the laws of Heaven and humanity. (Fukuzawa, 2012: 6)

His argument was that since people of different nations lived under the same sun, on the same earth, shared the same oceans and air, and shared the same human feelings, they should show respect for each other, live in harmony, and benefit each other.

> By contrast, nations such as China has behaved as if there were no other countries in the world but their own. Whenever they see foreigners, they call them barbarians, and revile and scorn them as animals. Without calculating the power of

> their own country, they have recklessly attempted to banish the foreigners, only to be rebuked by the foreigners in return. Such a situation can be said to have come about because they did not truly understand the "place" of a single nation. If their case be compared to that of an individual person, they have been like someone who has fallen into selfish and dissolute habits because he has not attained natural freedom. (Fukuzawa, 2012: 6)

Fukuzawa's criticism was penetrating and persuasive. His intention was to teach the Japanese people who shared the similar attitude to change their ideas and respect other nations because only when they respected others, could others respect them. Chinese arrogance suggested that they did not understand the fact that all humans share similarities and no one is superior to any other people. Then, he moved on to discuss the issue of how the ordinary Japanese avoided treating the government as their superior but regarded it as their equals. The benefits were as follows:

> ...while it is natural that we show deference to a government official, this is not because of the dignity of that person's status. He is accorded that respect only because he performs that important role through his talent and virtues, and because he deals with weighty laws for the sake of the people. It is the laws which have dignity, not the man. (Fukuzawa, 2012: 7)

Fukuzawa explained what should be a reasonable relationship between ordinary people and the government. It was the law, not the man that endowed power with the government, whose responsibility was to serve the people. Thus, people should not feel humble in front of government officials but should have courage to think differently and behave differently.

> Therefore people should be relieved and if ever they harbor any feeling of injustice against the government, they will not have to swallow their resentment and hate the government in silence. They can seek out the office or authorities concerned, quietly lodge their complaints, and discuss them openly. If their case is in accord with natural principle and human feeling, they should not hesitate to fight for it even at the risk of their lives. These are now the "responsibility" of the citizens of the nation. (Fukuzawa, 2012: 7)

Since people and the government are on the same footing, people should air their views when the government does something wrong or improper. It is people's obligation to make suggestions and help government correct its mistakes. Equality between people and the government empowers people to criticize the government so as to improve its administration and satisfy people's needs. In Section Two "The Equality of Men", Fukuzawa explicitly stated that the meaning of equality referred to equality in human rights, i.e. the rights of life, property, and political participation. It did not mean equality in material possessions, physical strength and intellect. Take a look at the following:

> Equality means equality in essential human rights, even though in external conditions there may be extreme differences between rich and poor, strong and weak, intelligent and stupid persons.
>
> In other terms, human rights are the great moral obligations that give dignity to an individual human life, protect a man's fortune and possessions, and dignify his honor and reputation. When Heaven gives birth to man, it gives him faculties of body and mind and the powers to realize his rights in practice. Therefore under no circumstances should a man be deprived of his rights. (Fukuzawa, 2012: 13)

Fukuzawa made use of logical reasons and common sense to drive his point home. Having read the piece, the Japanese people must have been convinced what Fukuzawa had said was absolutely correct. Reasoning has its power to convince people and it is a good way to use in arguing a point. In Section Three "Equality of Nations", Fukuzawa explained what independence stood for, the benefits of being independent of others, and why the Japanese people were in need of it.

> Independence means to manage one's own personal affairs and not to have a mind to depend upon others. The person who can himself discern the right and wrong of things, and who does not err in the measures he takes, is independent of the wisdom of others. The person who makes his own livelihood through his own physical or mental labors is independent of the financial support of others. If people do not have these independent qualities of mind and are merely reliant on the power of others, the entire nation will be dependents and there will be no one to support them. (Fukuzawa, 2012: 21)

Influenced by Confucianism, the Japanese people, according to Fukuzawa, lacked in independent thinking. Here he wanted to illustrate what independence stood for and why it was essential to human beings. Then, he went on to make critiques of one of the Chinese classics *The Analects*. In fact, education in ancient China was not popular and it was only a handful of elites or scholars who had knowledge of reading and writing. In Confucius's opinion, the little people knew, the better for government to take control of them. But Fukuzawa had different opinions.

> Some may say that "the people should be kept in a state of dependence and left uninformed" (*Analects*) (民可使由之，不可使知之); or that for every thousand blind men there are equally a thousand with sight. Thus, they say, let the wise control the masses from above; let the masses obey the will of their superiors from below. This argument is in fact from the school of Confucius. But it is a great error in actual fact. And in fact there is only one in a thousand who possesses sufficient talent and virtue to be able to govern others in the nation. (Fukuzawa, 2012: 21)

According to Fukuzawa, a clear distinction between the ruler and the people made the ordinary Chinese show no concern over their own country. When the country was in danger, it was natural that the indifferent people became onlookers, let alone being patriotic. When the war really broke out, the fact that some Chinese villagers even helped the foreign invaders was not strange indeed. Many soldiers did not want to sacrifice their lives for defending the country because they did not see any value of doing so. When the country really needed protection, what was left in the army was only a few people. As could be imagined, it was difficult for a country like China to achieve independence (福泽谕吉, 2014: 17).

Fukuzawa intended to achieve national independence through personal independence and his plan was fulfilled as the majority of the Japanese people were educated since the Meiji Restoration and Japan as a country became increasingly powerful and wealthy. Fukuzawa's ideas gained recognition of the government and his portrait appeared on every 10,000-yen note, in memory of his dedication to the cause of introducing Western institutions and thought into Japan (Fukuzawa, 2012: xiii).

In this chapter, we discussed two *Quanxue Pian* written by Zhang Zhidong and Fukuzawa Yukichi. By analyzing the two authors' different attitudes to the concepts of equality and freedom, we came to the conclusion that Japan developed much faster because it was guided by great thinkers like Fukuzawa and its people's willingness to make a change. In China, Zhang Zhidong made great contributions to China's education reform and brought an end to the Imperial Civil Service Examination and to some extent promoted China's modernization, although it was comparatively slow.

Topics for Discussion

1. Why do you think Zhang Zhidong was contradictory when making comment in *Quanxue Pian*?
2. Chinese learning as core value while Western learning as application.
3. The role played by Chinese students who studied in Japan.
4. Western ideas translated by the Japanese.
5. Which was more important in changing the Japanese national character: independence, patriotism, public spirit, or confidence according to Fukuzawa Yukichi?
6. Fukuzawa Yukichi's reflections on Chinese traditional culture.
7. The reason for the Japanese people to be attracted to Fukuzawa Yukichi's ideas.
8. The impact of Fukuzawa Yukichi's ideas on the Meiji Restoration.

Reading Assignments

1. 张之洞 . 2008. 劝学篇 . 桂林：广西师范大学出版社 .
2. 福泽谕吉 . 2014. 劝学篇 . 北京：商务印书馆 .

Bibliography

Ayers, W. 1971. *Chang Chih-Tung and Educational Reform in China.* Cambridge: Harvard University Press.

Fukuzawa, Y. 2012. *An Encouragement of Learning*. Tokyo: Keio University Press.

Zhang, Z. D. 1900. *China's Only Hope*. S. I. Woodbridge (trans.). New York: Fleming H. Revell Company.

范福潮. 2014. 清末新政的设计师张之洞. 08-08. 南方周末.

冯天瑜. 2006. 张之洞及其《劝学篇》. 05-29. 光明日报.

冯天瑜，何晓明. 2010. 张之洞传. 南京：南京大学出版社.

福泽谕吉. 2012. 福泽谕吉自传. 杨永良，译. 上海：文汇出版社.
福泽谕吉. 2014. 劝学篇. 北京：商务印书馆.
福泽谕吉. 2016. 文明论概略. 北京：商务印书馆.
李细珠. 2015. 张之洞与清末新政研究（增订版）. 北京：中国社会科学出版社.
李喜所. 2006. 近代留学生与中外文化. 天津：天津教育出版社.
马国川. 2018. 国家的启蒙：日本帝国崛起之源. 北京：中信出版集团股份有限公司.
丸山真男. 2018. 福泽谕吉与日本近代化. 区建英，译. 北京：北京师范大学出版社.
张之洞. 2008. 劝学篇. 桂林：广西师范大学出版社.

Chapter Thirteen

Kang Youwei—The First Reformer in China

康有为——中国第一位改革家

本章讨论《万国公报》如何从西方的制度、思想、教育、人格等方面影响了康有为，使其在甲午战争中国战败之际，发动了震惊中外的公车上书运动。同时探讨在百日维新中，为了说服光绪皇帝及广大知识分子，康有为撰写的两部著作《新学伪经考》和《孔子改制考》所起的作用。

13.1 Kang Youwei's Ideas 康有为思想

Kang Youwei's reform ideas were heavily influenced by the publications by Western missionaries and the transition of his ideas from belief in Chinese classics to the Western learning had much to do with his two trips from Guangdong to Hong Kong and Shanghai. The third reason for him to become a reformist was related to his character: curiosity, love of learning, and a desire to explore.

Kang Youwei was born in the year when China was defeated during the Second Opium War and the signing of the Treaty of Tianjin. That was 1858. When he was 19 years old, he failed in the Imperial Civil Service Examination at the provincial level because he could not write the eight-legged essay well. Then, he decided to study Chinese classics under the guidance of Zhu Ciqi (朱次琦), a family friend. For three years, Kang Youwei deeply immersed himself in works of pre-Qin thinkers (先秦思想家), i.e. Zhuangzi (庄子), Xunzi (荀子), Guanzi (管子), and Hanfeizi (韩非子). Among the Neo-Confucians (理学家), unlike his tutor who was fond of Cheng-Zhu School or Neo-Confucianism, Kang Youwei enjoyed instead reading Lu Jiuyuan (陆九渊) and Wang Shouren (王守仁). He did not want to blindly follow what his tutor had said. In fact, Kang Youwei had a fierce debate with his tutor Zhu Ciqi about Han Yu (韩愈), whose writing tended to be flowery and superficial (黄晶, 2013). Kang Youwei's three-year study with Zhu Ciqi laid the foundation for his classical learning, which helped Kang Youwei decide to use the knowledge to save the country. However, Kang Youwei quickly realized his knowledge of Chinese learning would not offer the recipe to save China from its poverty and weakness, having witnessed the Russian occupation of Yili (伊犁), Xinjiang in 1871, Japan's invasion of Taiwan, China in 1874, and the Sino-French War from 1883 to 1885. Kang Youwei was eager to find a path of salvaging the country and the nation.

Fig. 13-1 康有为

The chance came before long. Inspired by the book *A New Record of Traveling Around the World* (《环游地球新录》) written by Li Gui (李圭) in 1877, Kang Youwei was enthusiastic about seeing the outside world. In 1879, when he made a trip to Hong Kong, which was close to his hometown Nanhai County, Guangdong Province, Kang Youwei was shocked to see the good social order and modern facilities Hong Kong people enjoyed: the water supply system, gas lighting, and the telegraph system. There were also a sugar refinery, banking and insurance services, and Hong Kong and Shanghai Banking Corporation (HSBC, 汇丰银行) opened by the British. The roads in Hong Kong were neat and clean and the police were on duty. Kang Youwei began to wonder why such great changes could have taken place in more than thirty years. To this he realized that the Western capitalist system was much more superior to that of the ancient feudal system and he bought a great deal of Western books back home and began to study them (黄晶, 2013).

Three years later in 1882, Kang Youwei visited Shanghai on his way home after taking the exam. Again he saw the fast developments of the city: new roads were built; a dockyard and some Western style architectures could be seen. One could see the foreign settlement tall buildings with large windows, wide streets and avenues crisscrossed at regular, one-block intervals. There was no mud in the gravel roads. What he had seen about Shanghai reaffirmed his belief that the Westerners had better administrative methods in keeping social order and governing a city. Kang Youwei decided to learn from the West and bought more than 3,000 copies of the newly printed books of Western learning translated by the Translation Department of Jiangnan Arsenal. The quantity of the books he bought occupied one fourth of the total number of the books translated and published since 1867, covering all aspects of Western learning, i.e. subjects of natural sciences like acoustics, optics, chemistry, and electricity. There was also a book titled *A Compilation of Recent Events in the West* (《西国近事汇编》) introducing current international affairs, one hundred and eight volumes of which had been published (黄晶, 2013).

Kang Youwei's idea of making a change to Chinese society came from the scientific knowledge published in *Globe Magazine*. Though not fully understanding it, Kang Youwei was attracted to and influenced by astronomy, celestial mechanics, physics, and mathematics because the knowledge contained in those subjects indicated that the world kept changing all the time and nothing remained unchanged in the globe. The solar system was not born in its present form, but evolved to be so through a long period of time. The view held by Dong Zhongshu (董仲舒), a Confucian scholar, that "Nature does not change neither does the way" (天不变，道亦不变) was not true and refuted by Kang Youwei. That laid the foundation for Kang Youwei's reform ideas (郑大湖, 1993).

Young John Allen opened a column in *Globe Magazine* named "Relations Between China and the West" ("中西关系论略"), which contained three articles written separately by Allen, Robert Hart and Thomas Wade, aiming at political reform. Allen in his article "On the Measure of Becoming Rich" (《论谋富之法》) criticized the Chinese who stuck to their ancestors' way to govern the country without considering whether the way was suitable or not as modern society was entirely different from that of ancient times. The Chinese studied Confucian classics for years but many of them still had no idea of what it was about. What they could only do was to write the eight-legged essays for passing the Imperial Civil Service Examination and climbing up in the social ladder (李天纲, 2012). In his opinion, Chinese learning had little use and it only encouraged people to load their writing with hackneyed phrases without originality. However, Britain produced a great figure called Francis Bacon who was actually skeptical about what ancient scholars had said and used new methods to replace the old ones followed by the British people for 300 years and found the secret of prosperity.

Allen thought highly of Peter the Great, the Russian emperor, who traveled to the Netherlands and Britain to investigate their administration and studied their technology. Russia at the beginning of Peter's reign was rather weak and poor. The emperor wanted to find the key to wealth and power by learning from wealthy countries. He invited back two foreigners to teach people technology and sent envoys to make investigation tours to different countries. Peter the Great also attracted foreign experts to Russia as advisors. In this way, Peter made great changes to Russia and was remembered by his people ever since (李天纲, 2012).

Being influenced by the articles he read from *Globe Magazine*, Kang Youwei first recommended strongly to Emperor Guangxu that China have a reform in his second memorial (上清帝第二书). This memorial was in response to China's signing of the Shimonoseki Treaty with Japan (佚名, 2019), i.e. the so-called Gongche Shangshu Movement. In the memorial, Kang Youwei vehemently objected to the cession of China's territories like Taiwan and the adjacent Penghu Islands, the Liaodong Peninsula, and the payment of 200 million *taels* of the indemnity. The cession was the government's betrayal of its people and the indemnity could be used for education purposes. Then, Kang Youwei pointed out the fact that that China was in such a treacherous situation was due to the problems existing with the government and the necessity to stage a reform in three aspects: education, Chinese religion, and personnel.

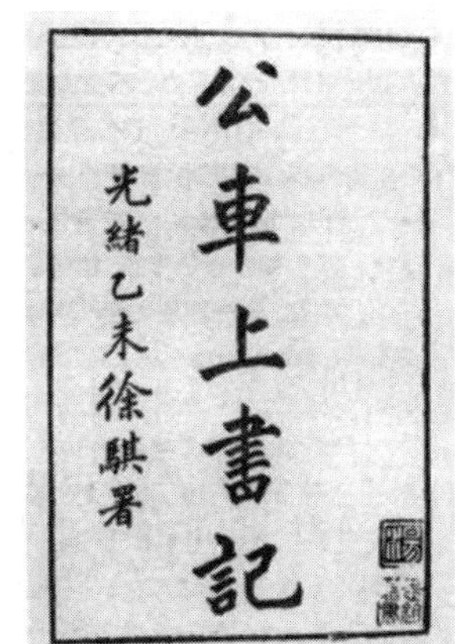

Fig. 13-2 《公车上书记》

上清帝第二书：窃以为弃台民之事小，散天下民之事大，割地之事小，亡国之事大，社稷安危，在此一举。

何以谓弃台民即散天下也？天下以为吾戴朝廷，而朝廷可弃台民，即可弃我；一旦有事，次第割弃，终难保为大清国之民矣。民心先离，将有土崩瓦解之患……日本之于台湾，未加一矢，大言恫喝，全岛已割。诸夷以中国之易欺也，法人将问滇、桂，英人将问藏、粤，俄人将问新疆，德、奥、意、日、葡、荷皆狡焉思启。有一不与，皆日本也，都畿必惊。若皆应所求，则自啖其肉，手足腹心，应时尽矣，仅存元首，岂能生存！（丁守和，1999：183）

Fig. 13-3 杨椒山祠（戊戌变法时举人聚会处）

Regarding education, Kang Youwei considered it an urgent task to popularize education because more than 80% of the Chinese people were illiterate. The fund used for education in China was a few dozen times less than that for military. Few Chinese literati had the knowledge of both China and foreign countries. In contrast, 70% of the people in the West could read and write. America, for instance, allocated 80 million dollars to school education. In England, there were more than 10,000 university students. Every year, America produced more than 10,000 various books and they had more than one million copies of books in England stored in the libraries of counties and provinces. The key to their wealth and power did not lie in their machines, cannons, or military strength, but in their grasp of knowledge (丁守和, 1999: 186).

> 尝考泰西之所以富强，不在炮械军兵，而在穷理劝学。彼自七八岁皆入学，有不学者责其父母，故乡塾甚多。其各国读书识字者，百人中率有七十人。其学塾经费，美国乃至八千万，其大学生徒，英国乃至一万余。其每岁著书，美国乃至万余种。其属郡县，各有藏书，英国乃至百万余册。所以开民之智者亦广矣。而我中国文物之邦，读书识字仅百之二十，学塾经费少于兵饷数十倍，士人能通古今达中外者，郡县乃或无人焉。（丁守和，1999：186）

In the memorial, Kang Youwei supported Shen Baozhen and Pan Yantong (潘衍桐) in abolishing the Imperial Civil Service Examination and adding subjects of modern science to the school curriculum. In fact, Robert Hart in his "A Bystander's View" had already criticized the outmodedness and the impracticality of the subjects learned for the exam. The Chinese who passed the exam were incapable of the jobs required of them in the modern times. They had little knowledge of international relations, the customs and culture of other countries, natural sciences and social sciences. In addition, the rote learning method and the writing of the eight-legged essays hindered creative thinking and rendered people rigid and inflexible facing different situations. Kang Youwei suggested calligraphy not be taken into consideration, but straightforward critiques be given high scores. The candidate should possess knowledge of both liberal arts and science and his academic works with original ideas should be highly evaluated. Apart from the reform in the examination methods, modern subjects of Western learning should be included in the curriculum, such as agriculture, business, astronomy, geology, religion, law, politics, physics, and military (丁守和, 1999: 187).

> 殿试策问，不论楷法，但取直言极谏、条对剀切者入翰林。其文科、艺科愿互应者听。其有创著一书，发明新义，确实有用者，皆入翰林，进士授以检讨，举人授以庶吉士，诸生授以待诏。
>
> ……外国农业、商学、天文、地质、教会、政律、格致、武备各有专门，以为新报，尤足以开拓心思，发越聪明，与铁路开通，实相表里。（丁守和，1999：187）

Kang Youwei submitted a memorial to ask for abolition of the eight-legged essays (请废八股以育人才折) (丁守和, 1999). In his opinion, the reason for China to be backward and be defeated by far smaller countries was that the Chinese people only focused on how to write the eight-legged essays, which stifled the mind and closed the eyes of people who saw nothing else except the essay. He quoted Otto von Bismarck (俾斯麦) as saying that the key to Prussian victory lay not in strong weapons but in the students. Similarly, Japan could win over China because they established hundreds of modern schools, teaching students different disciplines and modern ideas, which equipped the Japanese with knowledge and power. In another memorial (请开学校折) (丁守和, 1999), Kang Youwei asked to open modern schools and he believed China was not short of talents in ancient times because we had so many schools. But the Imperial Civil Service Examination did not require schools and that explained why China was short of qualified personnel while Western countries were more powerful.

Fig. 13–4 万木草堂

As to Chinese religion, Kang Youwei proposed that Confucianism should be deified as Chinese religion so that people with faith or belief had a clear goal of striving for wealth and power. According to Feng Youlan (冯友兰), the Chinese philosopher, facing the pressure of the Westerners, Chinese elites began to wonder if their wealth and power were derived from their religious belief, i.e. Christianity, which defined their advanced civilization. If China wanted to catch up, they also needed to have a religion and make a change in every aspects of the society (冯友兰, 2001). That explained why Kang Youwei regarded it necessary for the Chinese to have a religion and he chose Confucianism as one.

According to Liao Ping (廖平) (冯友兰, 2001), a New Text School scholar (今文学家), Confucius in his early years decided to follow the rites of Zhou (周礼), i.e. the institution of Zhou for social norms which emphasized the hierarchical society because he expected a peaceful and stable state. Yet in his later years, Confucius changed his mind and began to advocate reform by writing the book named *The Wang Institution* (《王制》). Another

Qing scholar Pi Xirui also thought that Confucius himself wrote the book, thus starting the debate between the Old Text School and the New Text School. The details regarding the two schools will be discussed later. The intention of making changes held by the New Text School corresponded to what *The Book of Changes* stated: "Poverty entails a change, changes lead to a conducive state, and a conducive state holds a good momentum for a long time." (穷则变，变则通，通则久。) That became the theoretical basis for Kang Youwei to reform the Qing institution and the reason for him to choose Confucianism as China's religion. We will take a look at Kang Youwei's work *Confucius as an Institutional Reformer* (《孔子改制考》) in 1897 in the following section.

The fact that Kang Youwei intended to use Confucianism as China's religion did not mean he was not critical of it. In 1882, when passing Shanghai, he came across *From West to East* (《自西徂东》) by Ernst Faber (花之安), a German Christian and critic of Confucianism. Kang Youwei was actually influenced by that book. He formed the idea of human equality and said that all men were born to be equal. The equality was "not only confined to friends, men and women, parents and children, commoners and sages, but it also means equality between the emperor and his subordinates, the emperor and his people. People of equal rights enjoy autonomy and any discount is inhumane and should be discarded" (董士伟, 2015: 13).

> "天地生人，本来平等。"不但朋友平等、男女平等、子女与父母平等、凡人与圣贤平等，甚至君臣、君民间也平等。平等之人"有自主之权"，丝毫的折扣（"人不尽有自主之权"）都不合人道而应摒弃。（董士伟，2015：13）

He pointed out the insufficiency of Confucian classics in that *The Analects* neither included mathematics nor touched upon practical knowledge, such as agriculture, medicine, astronomy, and geography. It was full of ostentatious and empty stuff. The method of understanding the outside world was nothing but exegesis or explanation of the classic texts, which tried to discover the sages' view, but rejected new knowledge (董士伟, 2015). Chinese traditional culture was characteristic of conservatism and introversion, in contrast to the progressive and pioneering culture of the West.

With regard to political reform, Kang Youwei stated four major adjustments: staff reducing, communication between the emperor and his subordinates, abolition of using money to buy official positions, and election of the township officer (乡长选举). Kang Youwei stated that the Qing administration had more personnel than work available and the staff's salaries were too low, easily causing corruption. Robert Hart in his "A Bystander's View", a memorial presented to Zongli Yamen on November 6, 1865 also criticized the nepotism, corruption and self-interest at all levels of government (Smith, Fairbank, Bruner, 1991). For instance, some officials were only concerned with the benefits obtained through occupying the position while ignoring their responsibilities. Other greedy officials tried to obtain interests for their relatives and hate those who did not take any advantage of the position to make money. Those who gained their official position by money were not doing anything for their post, pointed out by Kang Youwei. The soldiers were lack of adequate pay and many of them were too old to fight in the battlefield. The rosters were padded and the military training was in severe shortage (李天纲, 2012).

The corruption at the lower level was not known to the upper level and officials tried to hide their wrongdoings from the emperor. Two things caused the lack of communication between the emperor and his subordinates. One was the corrupted officials' fear of revealing their deal to the emperor. The other was the emperor's dislike of hearing of ill reports about the Qing government. The soldiers in the front line seldom reported failures to the upper class, leading to the top leaders' ignorance of what was happening in the battlefields. This also left some room to the ruler, in dealing with international affairs, to change his mind though China had signed a treaty with foreign countries. During the First Opium War, Lin Zexu failed to report to Emperor Daoguang about China's failure in some battles. When the truth was made known to him, Emperor Daoguang immediately dismissed Lin Zexu and exiled him to Xinjiang. Before leaving, Lin Zexu seriously advised the emperor that if China wished to win over the foreigners, we must build shipyard, and import machinery and technology from the West. But Daoguang simply replied, "Nonsense!" China's Self-Strengthening Movement was delayed for 20 years probably because the emperor neither trusted nor wanted to listen to Lin Zexu. When Wenxiang and Huashana signed the Treaty of Tianjin with Britain, following Emperor Xianfeng's instruction, the latter changed his mind and denied the clauses about foreign consuls residing in Beijing. The emperor even wanted to allow foreign merchants tax exemption as long as they agreed not to send anyone to Beijing, China.

Concerning the solution to the government or administration reform, Kang Youwei, in his sixth memorial to the emperor (上清帝第六书), gave clear delineation, i.e. to follow the democratic institution practiced by Western countries (丁守和, 1999). Specifically, Kang Youwei proposed China adopt the Japanese political system and learn from Peter the Great because China and Japan were neighbors and had many similarities in culture and customs while it was far away from Western countries like America, France, Britain and Germany and shared few characteristics with them. During the Meiji Restoration, the Japanese mainly did three things. First, they gathered the officials to discuss the national policy and select among many the best government practiced by other countries so as to trigger a complete change for the whole country. Second, they provided a channel for communication between the talents from all over the country and the top leaders in the government to exchange information. Third, they passed the constitution and relevant laws for everyone including the emperor to abide by. Kang Youwei also introduced the separation of powers practiced by Western countries, i.e. the separation among legislation, administration, and the judiciary.

> ……臣故请皇上以俄大彼得之心为心法，以日本明治之政为政法也。
>
> ……考其维新之始，百度甚多，惟要义有三：一曰大誓群臣以定国是，二曰立对策所以征贤才，三曰开制度局而定宪法。（丁守和，1999：208–209）

Kang Youwei made three proposals for the emperor to follow. First, the emperor should convene a conference declaring the reform and ask all the officials to sign a pledge undertaking to correct their past mistakes and become upright. Otherwise, they would be dismissed from office. Second, the emperor should announce that he would attract talented people all over the country to serve in the government and allow them to make suggestions and critiques to the administration. Third, the emperor should select a dozen polymaths to form a System Board (制度局) in the government and treat them equally with other high-ranking officials. The emperor should attend the meeting every day to approve what was justified and dismiss what was not.

> 皇上若决定变法，请先举三者……令群臣具名上表，咸革旧习，黾（min）勉维新；否则自陈免官，以激励众志。一定舆论，设上书处于午门，日轮派御史二人监收，许天下士民皆得上书……设制度局于内廷，选天下通才十数人，入直其中，王公卿士，仪皆平等……皇上每日亲临商榷，何者宜增，何者宜改……重定章程，然后敷布施行，乃不缪紊。（丁守和，1999：209）

Kang Youwei's idea of political reform and the separation of powers obviously came from reading the translated works and the newspaper articles. As we know, Yan Fu translated eight works of Western philosophy, sociology, political economics and social Darwinism. In addition, *Globe Magazine* published articles regarding Western politics.

Young John Allen and Ren Baoluo (任保罗) in their *Globe Magazine* article (《欧美十八周进化纪略》) (李天纲, 2012) introduced the enlightenment thinkers and philosophers, such as Voltaire, Rousseau, Montesquieu, Diderot, and Kant. The ideas of natural rights, equality, and independence were highly recommended in the essay, too. They interpreted the term law as human conscience first, and then it became rules and regulations observed by people. In the West, everyone in the society must obey law. Even the king would be punished as commoners if he broke the law. It exhibited equality among people. In addition to equality, freedom and property rights were also the consensus of the whole society. The government's job was to ensure individuals' rights in life, freedom, and property, and government officials should be elected by the majority of the people.

Kang Youwei's objective, according to Hsiao (1965), was to transform China politically, economically and intellectually following the modern West's example. And he planned to eliminate autocracy in two steps: "constitutional monarchy" and "full-fledged democracy" (成熟的民主). Kang Youwei had long prepared for his reform by writing two renowned books: *An Examination of the Forged Classics of the Xin Dynasty* in 1891 and *Confucius as an Institutional Reformer* in 1897. Next, we will discuss the two books separately.

13.2 Kang Youwei's Theoretical Framework 康有为理论框架

13.2.1 *An Examination of the Forged Classics of the Xin Dynasty*《新学伪经考》

In order to achieve his political goal of reform, Kang Youwei had to build a theoretical framework to convince the literati and scholar officials so that he could gain more support. The chance came soon when he met with Liao Ping in 1889 (光绪十五年), a well-known Confucian scholar, who was familiar with the New Text Confucianism. Liao Ping held the view that the Confucian classics after the Western Han Dynasty were all fabricated by Liu Xin (刘歆) and it could be used by Kang Youwei for his reform purpose. Liu Xin, a scholar in the Han Dynasty, switched his interest from the New Text Confucianism to the Old Text Confucianism when Liu Yu (刘余), the son of Emperor Jing of the Han Dynasty (汉景帝) discovered in the old mansion of Confucius the ancient texts of *Book of History* (《古文尚书》) or *Shangshu* and *Rites of Zhou*, *Yili* (《逸礼》) or *Rituals*, *The Analects* and *Classic of Filial Piety* (《孝经》). By digging into the ancient texts, Liu Xin believed the Old Text Confucianism was much more valuable than the New Text Confucianism and he made it known to the officials and began to promote the ancient classics ever since. It so happened that Wang Mang (王莽), Prince Regent usurped the power from Minor Emperor Liu Kan (刘衎) and established the Xin Dynasty (新朝, AD 9–23). Wang Mang wanted to nationalize the land and adopt the Well Field System (井田制), the "nine squares" system of land ownership in China's slave society described in *Rites of Zhou* (Anon, 2017b; 黄朴民, 2015). Liu Xin, Wang Mang's friend, was the right person to help with his policy by finding theoretical support from the ancient classics.

The common consensus was that the Old Text Confucianism or the Han Learning as named during the Qianlong and Jiaqing eras was bent on recovering the original version of Confucian classics or verifying its truthfulness while the New Text Confucianism was actively engaged in social critiques by applying the implied messages of the classics. In the book *An Examination of the Forged Classics of the Xin Dynasty* published in 1891, Kang Youwei stated that the ancient classics, such as *Rites of Zhou*, *Rituals*, *Book of History*, *Zuo Zhuan* and *Mao Poetry* (《毛诗》) were all forgeries by Liu Xin of the Western Han Dynasty and his purpose was to help the usurpation of power by Wang Mang. Thus, all the ancient classics were fake. However, *Gongyang Zhuan*, especially He Xiu's (何休) *Commentary on* Gongyang Zhuan (《春秋公羊解诂》) was given high esteem because the text revealed the true wisdom of Confucius (Anon, 2017a). Compared with other New Text School scholars, such as Wei Yuan, Gong Zizhen, and Feng Guifen, Kang Youwei went to extremes by regarding all the classics prior to the Western Han Dynasty as fabricated by Liu Xin. His purpose was to push a reform of the Qing Dynasty though his claim was neither historically true nor academically grounded.

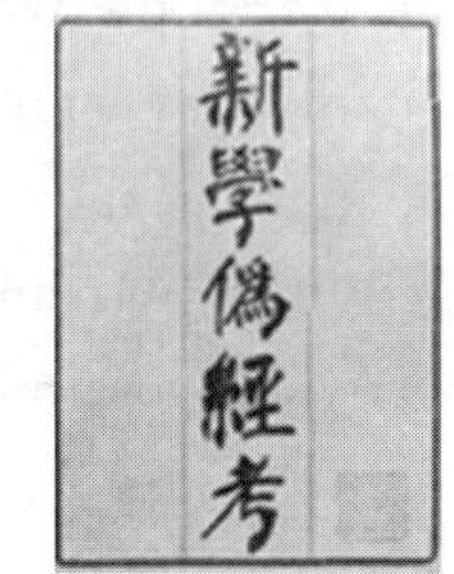

Fig. 13–5 《新学伪经考》

According to Liang Qichao, Kang Youwei was imitating Martin Luther of Germany who initiated the Reformation in the West by going back to the original version of the Bible. Luther challenged the authority of the church in determining whether a layman was sinful or not. Luther believed whether a person was sinful or not was dependent upon whether he had faith in God or not, the so-called "Justification by Faith", but not by the judgment of the church. In this way, Luther staged a movement that changed hundreds and thousands of people's mind. Kang Youwei wanted to do the same and he did achieve his goal. After its publication, *An Examination of the Forged Classics of the Xin Dynasty* was twice banned because it frightened the Qing authority. But it stirred up a huge shock in the academic arena and made a hard attack on those who preferred to stick to our ancestors' system rather than to reform.

The sad truth was that Kang Youwei had to stage a reform by using one Confucius against another Confucius and he could not reveal his real purpose to others. Perhaps that was the only way for a reformer like Kang Youwei to do because Chinese philosophy had only experienced two stages, i.e. the classical and the medieval periods, using the standard of Western criteria (冯友兰, 2001). Chinese literati could only make use of the theories available to convey their modern ideas. Having read so many newspaper articles printed by Western missionaries, Kang Youwei had already picked up the new concepts, such as liberty, equality, and parliament and he was determined to do something for China. However, the Qing scholars in general buried themselves in Confucian classics and they could only understand Kang Youwei's message by reading the book like *An Examination of the Forged Classics of the Xin Dynasty*. That was the situation of the Qing Dynasty.

13.2.2 *Confucius as an Institutional Reformer*《孔子改制考》

The controversy between the Old Text School of Confucianism and the New Text School of Confucianism lay in their different attitudes to the ownership and the function of the Confucian classics. The Old Text School believed that Confucius only transmitted but did not write the classics, which simply served as historical records. But the New Text School believed that Confucius was the writer of the classics including *Book of Poetry* (《诗》), *Book of History* (《书》), *Book of Rites* (《礼》), *Book of Music* (《乐》), and *Book of Changes* (《易》) and he expressed hidden meanings in the classics which served the guidance for social reform (茅海建, 2018). And those classics were written down from memory by the Confucian Scholars in the Han Dynasty using the new script called clerical script (隶书). It was said that those Confucian scholars survived the Burning of the Books by Qin Shi Huang, the first emperor of the Qin Dynasty. On the other hand, the Confucian classics advocated by the Old Text School were written in the archaic style, i.e. Pre-Qin script.

Having claimed that all the Confucian classics written in Pre-Qin script were forgeries by Liu Xin with the purpose of political usurpation for Wang Mang, Kang Youwei finished another book *Confucius as an Institutional Reformer* in 1897 and demonstrated his faith in progress. Kang Youwei depicted Confucius as a great reformist like Meiji Emperor, and an "uncrowned king" (素王), who made the blueprint for future reform. Kang Youwei used *Gongyang Zhuan* as his theoretical basis of reform. As the canon of the New Text School of

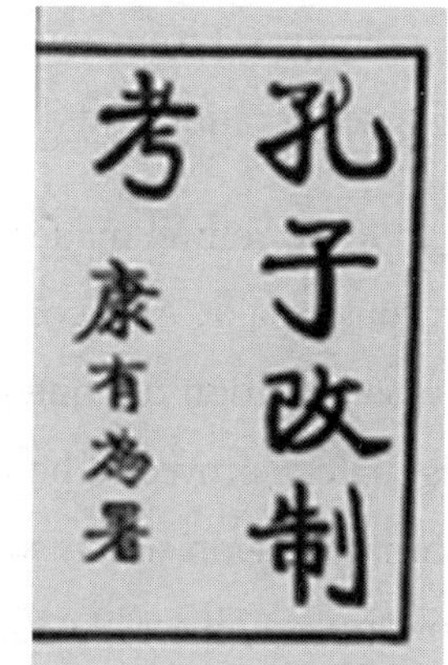

Fig. 13-6 《孔子改制考》

Confucianism, *Gongyang Zhuan* emphasized institutional changes and the Three Ages (三世说), i.e. the Ages of Disorder (据乱世), Emerging Peace (升平世), and Great Peace (太平世), which was followed by human history, exhibiting a pattern of changes. This theory served as a rationale for Kang Youwei's progressive view and social reform. Another notion borrowed by Kang Youwei was the "three unities" (三统) recommended by Dong Zhongshu, the first New Text School scholar of Confucianism. "The 'three unities' linked cosmological forces with historical institutions as well as powerful symbols with their appropriate age and dynasty. All followed the workings of Heaven, and so each dynasty had its own appropriate set of institutions." (Zarrow, 2012: 49)

By drawing on the theories of "three unities" and Three Ages, Kang Youwei argued that China needed to change its political institution by respecting popular sovereignty (民权). That change was dependent upon China's contemporary situation in which we had seen frequent failures China experienced when confronting Western civilizations. China's inability to deal with Western powers showed that the traditional values were no longer suitable for China to survive in the modern era. The reason that Western countries were more powerful and wealthier was that they practiced constitutional monarchy by which people enjoyed the rights of life, liberty, and equality. If China wanted to catch up with Western countries, it needed to build a parliament and take everyone's valuable suggestions and critiques into consideration. As shown in Kang Youwei's proposal in 1898 to the emperor, five months before the One Hundred Days Reform:

> I humbly beg Your Majesty...to summon talented men for consultation with a view to broadening Your Majesty's understanding, to encourage men of the empire to voice their sentiments so that they may be brought to (Your Majesty's) attention, and to announce formally a policy of reform, thereby inaugurating a new era for the empire. From now on all affairs of the state are to be turned over to parliament for deliberation and decision. (Hsiao, 1965: 14)

Kang Youwei made use of Confucius for his political reform and that was the only choice he could make. As a common man of letters, Kang Youwei could find no more resources to attract attention of contemporary literati and scholar officials in the late Qing Dynasty and his strategy proved to be very effective. Kang Youwei's intention of turning Confucianism into China's religion was inspired by Christianity, the religion of Western countries. Facing the powerful countries like Britain and France, Kang Youwei called upon people to defend Chinese religion, China as a country, and the Chinese as a race (保教、保国、保种).

In *Exhortation to Study*, Zhang Zhidong evaluated Kang Youwei's idea but with different interpretations. Although Zhang Zhidong somewhat supported Kang Youwei's idea of reform, he disagreed with Kang Youwei in human equality. In Zhang Zhidong's opinion, the three cardinal principles upheld by Confucius was China's religion and should not be abandoned. As to China as a country, Zhang Zhidong understood it as the Qing government. But in Kang Youwei's opinion, the Three Ages theory put forward by Confucius was the basis of China's religion and China as modern sovereignty was what he meant by the country to be defended (陈壁生, 2018).

Kang Youwei made extensive preparations for his political reform. First, by reading newspaper articles published by the Westerners, Kang Youwei began to form an idea of reform. Second, Kang Youwei taught young people in 1891 new ideas in Wanmu Caotang (万木草堂), Guangzhou—a place of the One Hundred Days Reform. Third, Kang Youwei established the Qiangxue Hui (强学会, Society for the Study of Self-Strengthening) in 1895 and attracted donations from both the Westerners and Chinese officials (Hsiao, 1965: 25). Fourth, Kang Youwei established newspapers, such as *Chinese and Foreign News* (《中外纪闻》) in 1895, *Qiangxue Bao* (《强学报》) in 1896, and *Shiwu Bao* (《时务报》) in 1896 to publicize his ideas of political reform. In 1895, Kang Youwei staged the Gongche Shangshu Movement and made a petition to Emperor Guangxu. Finally in 1898, Kang Youwei, winning the support of Guangxu, began the One Hundred Days Reform. Eventually, Kang Youwei's political reform failed. However, Kang Youwei was the first Chinese who built a systematic theory for staging reform in China. Although people like Guo Songtao, Yan Fu, Feng Guifen, and Wang Tao had all engaged themselves in one way or another in China's reform, they did not produce a theory like Kang Youwei. Kang Youwei set an example for the future social changes in China and he was remembered as a great reformer in history.

In this chapter, we mainly discussed the two works written by Kang Youwei, with which he initiated the political reform in China. Kang Youwei was the first Chinese intellectual who built a theoretical framework for his institutional reform and he did win respect and followers from progressive young people. Thanks to his efforts, China began to take a step toward constitutional monarchy and it won the support from Emperor Guangxu. Though it did not succeed, the One Hundred Days Reform was a milestone for China to move toward a civilized and democratic state.

◆ Topics for Discussion

1. In what way did the publications transmitted from the West influence Kang Youwei?
2. Kang Youwei's enlightenment approach of using Chinese traditional culture.
3. Kindness-oriented culture tends to be conservative and introverted while knowledge-oriented culture tends to be progressive and pioneering.
4. Compared with Gong Zizhen, Feng Guifen, and Wei Yuan, Kang Youwei was the first reformer who set up a systematic theory.
5. Your comment on the statement: the Chinese people were not ready for democracy during the late Qing Dynasty.
6. Emperor Guangxu was not qualified for leading the political reform in China.
7. Kang Youwei's two-stage reform—a transition from constitutional monarchy to democracy.

◆ Reading Assignment

Hsiao, K.-C. 1965. The Case for Constitutional Monarchy: K'ang Yu-Wei's Plan for the Democratization of China. *Monumenta Serica*, *24*: 1-83.

◆ Bibliography

Anon. 2017a. New Text Confucianism. 09–29. From Wikipedia website.

Anon. 2017b. Old Texts. 09–29. From Wikipedia website.

Hsiao, K.-C. 1965. The Case for Constitutional Monarchy: K'ang Yu-Wei's Plan for the Democratization of China. *Monumenta Serica*, *24*: 1-83.

Smith, R. J., Fairbank, J. K. and Bruner, K. F. 1991. *Robert Hart and China's Early Modernization: His Journals, 1863–1866.* Cambridge: Council on East Asian Studies.

Zarrow, P. 2012. *After Empire: The Conceptual Transformation of the Chinese State, 1885–1924.* Stanford: Stanford University Press.

陈壁生. 2018. 文明史上的戊戌变法：重新认识推动这场变革的那些思想家. 09–28. 澎湃新闻.

丁守和. 1999. 中国近代启蒙思潮：上. 北京：社会科学文献出版社.

董士伟. 2015. 康有为评传. 南昌：百花洲文艺出版社.

冯友兰. 2001. 中国哲学史：上下册. 上海：华东师范大学出版社.

郭延坡. 2012. 清末《万国公报》的出版及对中国社会的影响. 重庆科技学院学报（社会科学版），（18）：139–141.

黄晶. 2013. 康有为传. 北京：北京联合出版社.

黄朴民. 2015. 王莽的历史悲剧. 09–16. 中华读书报.

康有为. 2010. 孔子改制考. 姜义华，等编校. 北京：中国人民大学出版社.

康有为. 2012. 新学伪经考. 朱维铮，等编校. 上海：中西书局.

李天纲. 2012. 万国公报文选. 上海：中西书局.

茅海建. 2018. 康有为的“大同三世说”. 06–24. 爱思想.

佚名. 2018a. 古文经学. 10–05. 百度百科.

佚名. 2018b. 井田制度. 10–05. 搜狗百科.

佚名. 2018c. 廖平（清末民国初经学大师）. 10–05. 搜狗百科.

佚名. 2018d. 刘歆. 10–05. 搜狗百科.

佚名. 2018e. 周礼（儒家经典）. 10–05. 搜狗百科.

佚名. 2019. 马关条约. 09–24. 中文百科在线.

赵琳，冯荣. 2007.《万国公报》对康梁变法的影响. 河北省社会主义学院学报，（1）：74–78.

郑大湖. 1993. 康有为对《万国公报》的扬与弃. 上海师范大学学报，（2）：105–108.

Chapter Fourteen

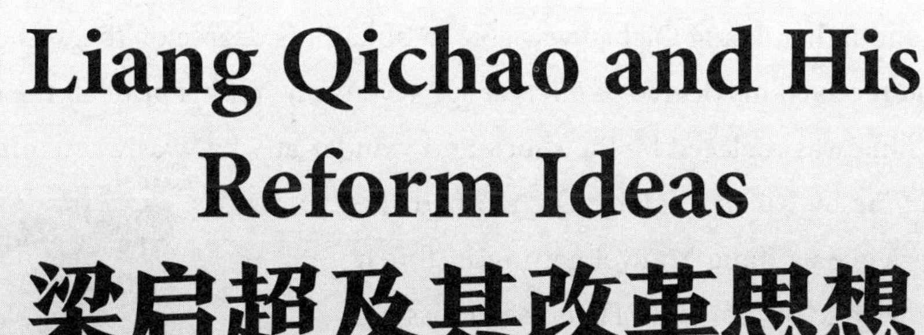

Liang Qichao and His Reform Ideas
梁启超及其改革思想

本章讨论梁启超从尊崇中国古典传统转向倡导西学的过程。首先，少年成才的梁启超通过阅读《瀛寰志略》及拜康有为为导师开阔了眼界，了解了世界。逃亡到日本后，对西学的进一步接触使他产生了仿照日本模式对中国进行改革的想法。梁启超的改革思想是在对传统文化弊病的认识上进行的。于是，产生了他对国家意识、公民权利、公权与私权的关系以及如何塑造新民形象的宏伟蓝图。

14.1 Liang Qichao's Education Experience 梁启超受教育背景

Like his tutor Kang Youwei, Liang Qichao advocated political reform in the Qing government. However, unlike Kang Youwei who built his theory on Confucianism, Liang Qichao's reform framework was based on his serious critiques of the defects and weaknesses of the Qing government and the Chinese people. Having read extensively the Western works in Japan, Liang Qichao absorbed the essential meaning delineated in those works and aimed at the institutional reform of the government. Under the guidance of his grandfather and father, Liang Qichao was able to obtain his degree of *Tongsheng* (童生) at age seven and received his degree of *Juren* at age seventeen. Yet his pride in the mastery of classical learning was replaced by the shock and wonder at what was written in the book *Yinghuan Zhilue* by Xu Jiyu. Liang Qichao had the similar experience as Kang Youwei getting in touch with the knowledge of the West. He came across Xu Jiyu's book also in Shanghai when going back home after taking the Imperial Civil Service Examination. His eyes were widely opened by the geographical knowledge of the world and later the teaching of Kang Youwei in Wanmu Caotang. The materials used by Kang Youwei were knowledge of Western science and technology translated by the Translation Department of Jiangnan Arsenal. However, Kang Youwei's knowledge of Western learning was limited and superficial because the areas he touched upon were only related to technology and military strategies and tactics, but little about political sciences.

Fig. 14–1 梁启超

Influenced by his tutor, Liang Qichao's knowledge of the West was also restrained by the translation quality of the books and the outmodedness of the knowledge. The fact was that at the beginning of the introduction of Western learning to China, the Chinese did not have the ready-made expressions and words for Western ideas and the translated works were inevitably inaccurate and sometimes the meaning was distorted. Though Liang Qichao had read some translated Western books in the areas of history, administration, education, law, commerce, military, etc., it was no better than communicating with Timothy Richard and reading his translated book *Nineteenth Century: A History* (《泰西新史览要》) by Robert Mackenzie (罗伯特·麦肯西) (张朋园, 2007). In spite of this, Liang Qichao's knowledge of the Western ideas still remained unsystematic, let alone profound.

Having stayed in Wanmu Caotang for three years, Liang Qichao studied with Kang Youwei and helped Kang Youwei with his two important works, i.e. *An Examination of the Forged Classics of the Xin Dynasty* and *Confucius as an Institutional Reformer*. He displayed strong ability in Chinese classics. After the failure of the One Hundred Days Reform in 1898, Liang Qichao was pursued by the Qing court as a rebel and he found shelter in Japan with the help of the Japanese people. During the 15-year exile in Japan, Liang Qichao read seriously and extensively the Japanese version of Western works and had an in-depth understanding of modern political and legal theories, which paved the way for his engagement in political writing and public activities, such as editing *Journal of Disinterested Discussion* (《清议报》), *New Citizen Journal* (《新民丛报》) and organizing societies like Qiangxue Hui to continue helping reform for China (梁启超, 1994).

Upon his arrival in Japan, Liang Qichao began to conscientiously study Japanese language as he understood that many Western works in social sciences and humanities had been translated into Japanese and made Japan fast develop into a modern country since the Meiji Restoration. By reading Rousseau, Montesquieu, and Bluntschli (伯伦知理), the German jurist, Liang Qichao realized that to make a country strong, the first thing to do was to liberate people's mind and awaken their consciousness of liberty and human rights because the strength of the Western countries lay in the power of their people. It was during this period that Liang Qichao's political view began to change. Before the One Hundred Days Reform, Liang Qichao followed the statecraft thought and tried to reform the institution by returning to the ancients (托古改制). But now having learned about freedom of speech, freedom of thought, and freedom of press, Liang Qichao gave up the Confucian classics and resorted to the Western thought for his reform activities (梁启超, 1994).

Fukuzawa Yukichi's *An Outline of Civilization*, Mill's *On Liberty* and Bluntschli's *A Theory of the State* (《国家论》) all enlightened Liang Qichao and guided him to publish essays and articles discussing the path of reform for China. By reading Bluntschli, Liang Qichao had a rough idea regarding the consciousness of the nation state and the distinction between the state and government (Tang, 1996).

Discourse on the New Citizen (《新民说》) was a series of articles Liang Qichao wrote between 1902 and 1906 and was published in *New Citizen Journal* when he was in Japan. His purpose was to reform the country by changing its citizens' character first. According to Liang Qichao, the Chinese people, under the two-thousand-year despotism, had no sense of rights and liberty. What they did have were servility, dependence, self-perpetuation, a lack of group concepts, indifference to state affairs and a state of disunity (一盘散沙) among the four hundred million people (梁启超, 1994). In order to change such a distorted character, Liang Qichao called for an image of the new citizen with public spirit and capacity for self-government.

14.2 The Impact of Japan on Liang Qichao 日本对梁启超的影响

The books Liang Qichao read during his exile in Japan were concerned with utilitarianism, ethics, social contract, separation of powers, and evolution, which were either translated from English into Japanese by Mutsu Munemitsu (陆奥光宗), Nakae Atsusuke (中江笃介), Yamazawa Zhichun (山边知春), or directly written by Japanese authors, such as Teng Jiro Shiyama (衫山滕次郎, *A Brief Biography of Western Political Scientists*, 《泰西政治学者略传》), Hiroichiro Kojima (纲岛荣一郎, *A History of Western Ethics*, 《西洋伦理学史》, *The Ethics of Hedonism*, 《主乐派之伦理说》), Takeuchi Kusunomi (竹内楠三, *Ethics*, 《伦理学》), Ono Azusa (小野梓, *A Survey of National Constitution*, 《国宪泛论》), Okamura Division (冈村司, *An Introduction to Law*, 《法学通论》), and Aruga Nagao (有贺长雄, *The Political Theory*, 《政体论》) (钟叔河, 2010). After the extensive reading, Liang Qichao began to realize that the causes of Western wealth and power did not lie in their extraordinry weaponry but in their ideas and civilization.

It was the social contract proposed by Thomas Hobbes, John Locke, and Rousseau that endowed people with rights of liberty, property and life. It was the concept of power division argued by Montesquieu that prevented government from corruption. It was Francis Bacon and Rene Descartes who challenged superstition and the idol of minds that equipped people with free thinking and imagination. And it was Jeremy Bentham and

John Stuart Mill who showed respect for human nature that cautioned people about the importance of humanity and ethics. Together with evolution described by Ben Jaman Ridd in his *The Principles of Western Civilization* (《泰西文明原理》), Liang Qichao introduced the modern Western ideas to the Chinese people by publishing articles and commentaries in newspapers. Compared with Yan Fu, Liang Qichao wrote in vernacular Chinese with great passion so that he enjoyed a larger readership and successfully disseminated Western ideas to China. In the meantime, Liang Qichao also pondered about the way to turn China into a modern country. The first thing he did was to point out the current problems existing in China and make a breakthrough by analyzing and critiquing the Chinese national character. Conrad Bornhak (波伦哈克), the German jurist, stated two criteria for republics, i.e. self-government and public spirit (蔡双全, 王正相, 2017). In *Discourse on the New Citizen*, Liang Qichao made an analysis of the Chinese people and commented that the Chinese people neither had public spirit nor the capacity of self-government. Instead they were conservative, lacking in courage, and ignorant of man's rights. Changing Chinese citizens' character became the starting point for Liang Qichao's reform.

14.3 *Discourse on the New Citizen* 《新民说》

In his book *Discourse on the New Citizen*, Liang Qichao pointed out several characteristic defects in the Chinese people, among which was a lack of public spirit. Liang Qichao argued that the absence of public spirit in the Chinese character was because of the emphasis of private virtues found in Confucian classics and he used several examples to illustrate his point. The five virtues were recommended in *The Analects*, which were temperate, kind, courteous, restrained, and magnanimous (温、良、恭、俭、让). *The Great Learning* proposed another four private virtues, i.e. knowing when to stop (知止), self-restraining in private (慎独), shunning deception (戒欺), and seeking satisfaction (求慊). Mencius highly recommended that one should maintain his heart and cultivate his nature (存心养性) (梁启超, 1994). What ordinary people did was to show filial obedience to their seniors at home and be friendly to relatives and friends. But no one showed concern over the society they lived in because they did not understand that the well-being of one person was closely related to any other person. If a person in a community was unfairly treated and no other people came to help, the maltreatment was likely to extend to any other person as well. Thus, it was one's obligation to be interested

Fig. 14–2 《新民说》

in public affairs and actively participate in social activities. Only when everyone showed concern over public affairs could a society function well and the well-being of people could be guaranteed.

Arthur Smith, an American missionary who stayed in China for fifty-four years, made keen observations on the Chinese people's lack of public spirit. He used roads, the public transportation means, as an example. "A man who wishes to load or to unload his cart leaves it in the middle of the roadway while the process is going on, and whoever wishes to use the road must wait until the process is completed. If a farmer has occasion to fell a tree he allows it to fall across the road, and travelers can tarry until the truck is chopped up and removed." (Smith, 2007: 106) Many roads were in need of repair and people considered it the emperor's duty to do it because the emperor was the patriarch and everything was his property. That explained why common people showed no concern over public property as long as their own was preserved.

Another quote in *The Analects* "He who is not in office is not in charge" or "Out of position, out of administration" (不在其位不谋其政) may account for the Chinese indifference to public affairs. But obligation is often related to rights. If you do not enjoy any rights, you would not be willing to care about things related to others. Rousseau, the French enlightenment thinker, stated in *The Social Contract* (1968) how public spirit originated. When man lived in a natural state, i.e. a primitive society, the strongest always had say in the obligations of the weak because force became a kind of rights. In the slave society, the slave owner had the power or right to order his slaves to do whatever he liked while the slaves could not request any right of their own. But that phenomenon took place in an unequal society. In a civilized society, it was not justified for man to enjoy rights without fulfilling his duties. In Rousseau's opinion, all men have the instinct of protecting their private property and liberty and dislike them to be violated no matter how strong the infringers are. In order to protect the rights of the weak, a contract must be agreed and signed by both the strong and the weak. It is a consent of each member of the community who is willing to give "all his rights to the whole community" or the so-called general will (公意) chosen by the people, which is to ensure the safety of the community (Rousseau, 1968: 60). At the same time, the members of the community need to fulfill their obligations to obey the rules and regulations stipulated by the government which represents the general will. The formation of such a government in a civilized society is permitted by each member of the community so as to protect people's liberty and private property from being infringed. If either the government or the person breaches the social contract, it or he would be punished by law. The government of this kind is legitimated. Thus, the equality among people is political, but not physical (Rousseau, 1968).

Because the government consented by the public represents the general will, each member in the community shows great concern over public affairs. For instance, if the government acts according to the general will or if people under the government do their parts in terms of paying tax or joining the army, the whole society will be in a good order and people will live a happy life. Thus, whether the government does a good job is closely related to everyone's wellbeing. This interest in or concern over the public affairs is called public spirit. Public spirit is shared by people living in modern society and it has much to do with one's rights and obligations. It is also related to the concept of nation.

When Liang Qichao or Arthur Smith criticized that the Chinese people in the late Qing Dynasty lacked public spirit, they meant the Chinese did not have the rights thinking yet. People obtain a sense of rights only when they are oppressed or exploited, leading to a clear sense of injustice. Therefore, people want to fight for their equal rights. Two historical events could serve as examples: the American Revolution of 1776 which eliminated the oppression imposed by the British imperialism and the French Revolution of 1789 which broke the chains bound by monarchism. According to Hunt, "the American and French revolutions stipulated that the legitimacy of governments depended on their ability to guarantee human rights" (Zarrow, 2008: 186). In other words, only when human rights are ensured, will the government be supported by its people.

People in the late Qing Dynasty were enslaved and exploited under despotism and they did not, like citizens in modern society, possess rights, responsibilities, freedom, equality and independence. As what Liang Qichao stated:

> For thousands of years Chinese emperors were traitors to its people, who took the whole country as his private property and turned people into his slaves. Not feeling a little ashamed the emperor claimed his special relationship to *Tian* or Heaven, an idea borrowed from the ancient Confucian tradition so as to aid his ferocity. Consequently, people in the country were forced to be slaves. They had no way to be patriotic although they wanted to love the country. (谢玺璋, 2015: 127-128)
>
> ……数千年之民贼，既攘国家为己之产业，挚国民为己之奴隶，曾无所于怍，反得援大义以文饰之，以助其凶焰，遂使一国之民，不得不转而自居于奴隶，性奴隶之性，行奴隶之行，虽欲爱国而有所不敢，有所不能焉。（谢玺璋，2015：127–128）

That explained why the Chinese people sold horses to the invaders when the Allied Troops of Britain and France entered China during the Second Opium War, and the officials in Tianjin and Tongzhou even surrendered to the enemies as long as the invaders would not harm their interests, which was described by Arthur Smith in his book *Chinese Characteristics* (2007).

As we can see, rights talk is related to the citizenship, government and nation. But the Chinese people, according to Liang Qichao, had no idea of what citizens, nations or countries really meant. What they knew was that they were the subjects of the empire, serving the court and living in the place called *Tianxia* (天下). (梁启超, 1994). In fact, the Chinese people had no sense of rights whatsoever. In "On Rights Consciousness", Chapter Eight of *Discourse of the New Citizen*, Liang Qichao discussed the meaning of rights. He compared rights to sovereignty and pointed out that the sense of rights was derived from being oppressed or unjustly treated by other nations. He quoted Rudolf von Jhering (鲁道夫·冯·耶林) from *The Struggle for Law* (《为权力而斗争》) that the goal of rights was to achieve peace, but you could only obtain peace through fighting against infringers (梁启超, 1994). According to Jhering, the English had the strongest sense of rights and they would fight for it no matter what price to pay. For instance, an English would refuse to pay irrational fees for hotel service and struggle for justice even if it meant the extension of his stay in the hotel. The consciousness of rights made England a strong nation.

In fact, the rights refer to equality, independence, and liberty. What Liang Qichao discussed about rights could mean political rights or independence while Jhering discussed in his example of an English man was about fairness or equality. The Chinese people did not feel miserable or ashamed when the powers ceded several Chinese ports, such as Jiaozhou Bay and Lvshun Port (旅顺港). Liang Qichao attributed the indifference to the absence of rights thinking among the Chinese people. The fact had much to do with the idea of benevolence. Confucius linked benevolence with righteousness and he thought that once you treated others with benevolence, you would be rewarded with righteousness. Liang Qichao stated that the expectation of benevolence from others blinded the Chinese people's eyes, and debased their character, causing them to tolerate the evil rulers and bear the injustice imposed on them (梁启超, 1994). Confucianism under despotism became a tool in controlling people and made them weak, timid and have no courage to fight for their rights. Since people's rights could be guaranteed by legislation, Liang Qichao highly recommended adopting constitutionalism, which could turn people into citizens who would understand their rights and responsibilities.

However, it was no easy task to claim one's rights or regain legitimate rights from the ruling class as people had to fight for it and sometimes even at the cost of their lives. When the Westerners in some European countries and the United States wanted to establish constitutional government, abolish slavery, liberate the indentured workers, or gain freedom in working and religious belief, they were fighting for them and some lost their lives. So Liang Qichao thought that the Chinese should learn from the Westerners and the Japanese in terms of military spirit. He highly praised the Japanese soldiers when they vowed and even prayed to die in the battlefield.

In *Discourse on the New Citizen*, Liang Qichao stated in greater detail what liberty referred to. He discussed four aspects of liberty, i.e. political, religious, national, and economic liberty. Here political liberty was about the relationship between people and government. Religious liberty stood for people's freedom to believe. National liberty referred to sovereignty and economic liberty stood for the mutual freedom enjoyed by both labor and capitalists. According to Liang Qichao (梁启超, 1994), the Chinese people had neither political liberty nor national liberty. In the Qing Dynasty, people from different walks of life were not treated equally but divided into a hierarchy of scholars, farmers, artisans and merchants (士、农、工、商). Merchants were at the bottom of the hierarchy and looked down upon by other classes. They were neither given due respect nor the right to manage their own business as the rulers feared that they were likely to disturb the social stability out of their mobility, being well-informed and broader vision. As a country, China's territories were not integral but partially occupied by the powers. Liang Qichao also pointed out that in a civilized society freedom was realized through law abiding while practices, such as default (欠账不还) or opium abuse were not considered as proper freedom, but infringement of law.

Rights and responsibilities are two essential components of public spirit, in which rights involve an understanding of equality, independence, and liberty. Those qualities could not be found in the Chinese people living in the Qing Dynasty, which was related to one of the problems discussed by Liang Qichao, i.e. obscurantist policy (愚民政策). To better control its people, the Qing rulers did not encourage formal education among common people and the only available schools, i.e. the old-style private schools and academies of classical learning were to train people to pass the Imperial Civil Service Examination rather than to satisfy young people's curiosity or needs for knowledge and practical jobs. What they did was to learn the Confucian classics, such as the Four Books and the Five Classics by heart and compose eight-legged essays in the exam. The strict rules set for the eight-legged essays focused on the structure and language instead of content. The candidates' sole purpose of learning was to become an official and more often than not they had no idea of what they were reciting. Thus, the knowledge learned by heart became useless. That was something the authority wished to see because if everyone was attracted to reciting the Confucian classics, there would be no fear of disturbances or even rebellion. Therefore, the Imperial Civil Service Examination was a tool for keeping people ignorant.

The situation in the West was entirely different. Francis Bacon, the English philosopher, was the first one to dispel superstition from the people. To enlighten the benighted, he made a stunning statement: We should not accept a theory to be true just because a Greek philosopher said it was. The slogan "Knowledge is power" was widely accepted and English people released their amazing power of innovation and built England into a modern state. Liang Qichao also commented as follows:

> Furthermore, it is not true that the Great West is now wealthy and powerful, stronger than all the other continents, because Heaven finds its particular favorite among people there. I once made a study of this situation and discovered that everything started with Bacon, the English gentleman. (Tang, 1996: 18)

As a result, "new laws and reason, new instruments and technology, new knowledge and institutions" (Tang, 1996: 18) all followed each other and made a daily difference.

14.4 *On Enlightened Despotism* 《开明专制论》

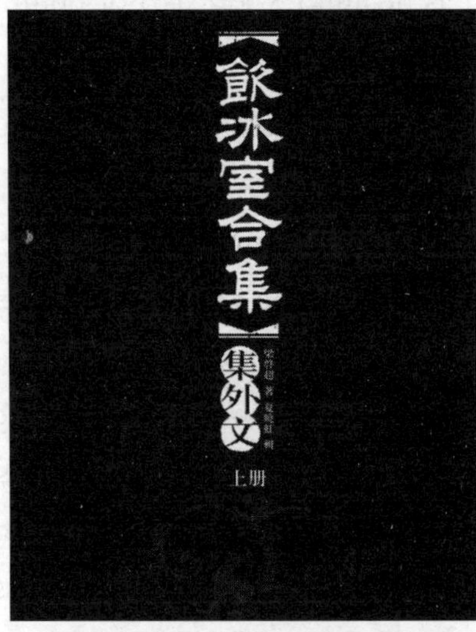

Fig. 14–3 《饮冰室合集》

The One Hundred Days Reform led by Kang Youwei was aimed at overthrowing the despotic institution of the Qing court and establishing constitutionalism in China. Liang Qichao was a staunch adherent to constitutionalism and he believed that if the emperor agreed to reform the old system, there would be no blood and casualties and the whole country could have a smooth transfer from the old order to modern society. While the reformists preferred a top-down approach for gaining human rights for the Chinese people, the radical reformers wanted to resort to violence to fulfill the job. Zou Rong (邹容), for example, urged people to put an end to the Manchu despotism and obtain independence, equality, and political rights for the Chinese people. In his well-known tract *Revolutionary Army* (《革命军》), Zou Rong stated the following:

> Everyone should know the principles of equality and freedom. At birth, there are none who are not free and equal. In the beginning there were neither rulers nor subjects...Later generations were ignorant of this principle. As soon as they achieved power, countless traitors, despots, and thieves monopolized what belonged to the common people and made it the private property of their families and clans. They called themselves rulers and emperors, so that nobody in the empire was equal and free...So today the revolution of our compatriots should drive out the foreign races ruling us and exterminate the autocratic monarchs to restore our natural rights. (Zarrow, 2008: 188)

Although Liang Qichao shared Zou Rong's attitude toward the Qing court, he disagreed to use violence and overthrow the regime. On one hand, Liang Qichao still cherished hope for the emperor to stage the reform and implement constitutionalism. On the other hand, Liang Qichao believed that the Chinese were not ready for republicanism as the two criteria suggested by Conrad Bornhak, the German philosopher were not met, i.e. public spirit and capacity of self-government.

Liang Qichao defined despotism as a type of government in which the ruler decided on everything concerning the state's activities without people's participation and the decisions made were basically arbitrary. If the arbitration turned into a negative form which served only the ruler's interest, it became brutal despotism (野蛮专制). If the arbitration was conducive to the country and people, it was called enlightened despotism (开明专制). When Louis XIV, King of France, said "I am the country" (朕即国家), he adopted brutal despotism for the purpose of self-interest. When Frederick the Great (腓特烈大帝), Prussian Emperor said, "The king is the chief civil servant of the country"

(国王者国家公仆之首长也), he practiced enlightened despotism for the interest of the state. In addition to that, Niccolò Machiavelli, the Italian diplomat and political theorist, and Thomas Hobbes, the English philosopher were also the advocates for enlightened despotism. According to Machiavelli, when a country was at the brink of collapse, the monarch was justified to use whatever he wanted to save the country even at the cost of people's lives (梁启超, 2001). In his treatise *The Prince* (《君主论》), the Italian philosopher gave advice to Lorenzo (洛伦佐) as follows:

> ...a prince may be perceived to be merciful, faithful, humane, frank, and religious, but most important is only to *seem* to have these qualities. A *prince* cannot truly have these qualities because at times it is *necessary* to act against them. In fact, he must sometimes deliberately choose evil. Although a bad reputation should be avoided, it is sometimes necessary to have one. (Anon, 2019b)

In order to keep order, the newly inaugurated prince must choose cruelty over benevolence, being feared over being loved because he is facing many pitfalls and needs to take drastic measures. He needs to be shrewd like a fox and strong like a lion (马基雅维利, 1999).

In the same manner, Thomas Hobbes was also a supporter of enlightened despotism and he stated his idea in his work *Leviathan* (2014). Living in a natural state, humans are struggling for their survival and self-defense and everyone is entitled to the right of nature which is "the liberty each man hath, to use his own power, as he will himself, for the preservation of his own nature; that is to say, of his own life; and consequently, of doing anything which in his own judgment and reason, he shall conceive to be the aptest means thereunto" (Hobbes, 2014: 100). Man lives in "a condition of war of every one against every one...every man has a right to every thing; even to one another's body. And therefore, as long as this natural right of every man to everything endureth, there can be no security to any man..." (Hobbes, 2014: 100-101). Men, out of their selfishness, fear, greed, cruelty, stage wars against each other and no one has a sense of security. In order to protect one's own life from being harmed, people come to an agreement to transfer their natural rights to a monarch, or a group of people, who will ensure their security. Once the contract is reached, no one is supposed to retrieve it and under the pact people should obey the monarch no matter what orders he issued (霍布斯, 2010).

Liang Qichao admired Frederick the Great, Napoleon Bonaparte (拿破仑), and Otto von Bismarck, the three enlightened European rulers who made great achievements for their countries. As an enlightened absolute monarch, Frederick Ⅱ considered it his duty to protect his subjects from foreign attack. During his forty-six year reign (1740–1786), the monarch effectively dealt with France, Austria, and Russia and defeated them one by one. He also gained Polish provinces and places and made a link between the Central Prussia and East Prussia. By making laws, he ensured the state's order. He also tailored to people's needs and gave them freedom of speech and freedom of religion. But "the ruler could carry out his duties effectively only if he kept the reins of government firmly in his own hands" (Anderson, 2014; Malcolm, 2015).

The second enlightened monarch that Liang Qichao appreciated was Napoleon Bonaparte. Napoleon's contributions mainly lay in three areas, i.e. a great conqueror who loved peace, a culturist who saved people from other European places from obscuration and ignorance, and a legislator who set *Napoleon Code* (《拿破仑法典》) (昭杨, 2015). He not only conquered many places in Europe but also brought an end to French Revolution. When his army swept across Europe, Napoleon brought the concepts of liberty and democracy derived from the French Revolution principles to those countries. His invasion of Spain, Italy, and Germany instilled the national consciousness to the people there and strengthened the same sentiment to the people in Britain and Russia (郑佳明, 2018). The most important of the three was *Napoleon Code* or *Civil Code* (《民法典》). By organizing people to draft *Civil Code*, Napoleon implemented the principle of equality and liberty in the code, setting up the rules of property ownership (财产所有权), freedom of contract (契约自由), and liability for damage (损害赔偿责任). According to the code, all French people enjoy the civil rights which is unrestrained by their social status and property and people's equality before the law is ensured. The law only applies after legislation and has no retroactive effect (法律只适用于立法后，不具有追溯既往的效力) (郑佳明, 2018). Under his reign, Napoleon also tolerated different religions and specifically he surprised people by giving equal status to Jewish people and their religion. Yet Napoleon grabbed all the power and became the emperor. He cracked down on intellectuals with different views, restricted freedom of speech, and made concessions to the nobles and the church.

A monarchist, Otto von Bismarck made two major contributions to Germany, i.e. the unification of Germany in 1871, and establishment of the insurance system for industrial workers. As Minister President of Prussia under King Wilhelm Ⅰ (德皇威廉一世), Bismarck won three consecutive victories over Denmark, Austria, and France. In the first battle with Denmark, Prussia managed to receive Schleswig, a part of the Danish territory. In the second battle against Austria, Bismarck successfully annexed German principalities, such as Schleswig, Holstein, Frankfurt, Hanover, Hesse-Kassel, and Nassau using his diplomatic strategies. He also coerced Austria into agreement not to intervene in German affairs. In the third battle against France, Bismarck tricked France into the war with Prussia though France was not fully ready for the war. As a result, Prussia defeated France. The second aspect of Bismarck's contribution was that Sickness Insurance Law of 1883 was passed under the supervision of Bismarck, followed by two other laws, i.e. Accident Insurance Law of 1844, and Old Age and Disability Insurance Law of 1889. By passing those laws especially the first one, the German workers became the majority representation due to their large financial contribution and their opinions began to be considered in public administration. However, for twenty-eight-year tenure, Bismarck was in actual control of making government policies and supported by Wilhelm Ⅰ. He "allowed no effective constitutional check on the power of the emperor...took steps to silence or restrain political opposition, as evidenced by laws restricting the freedom of press" (Anon, 2019a).

Having discussed the advantages of enlightened despotism, Liang Qichao continued to argue that China was not fit to implement the republic institution because of the two drawbacks the Chinese people had, i.e. lack of public spirit and capacity of self-government as suggested by Bornhak. For the first aspect, we have seen to what extent the Chinese did not possess public spirit. As to the second aspect, Liang Qichao began to use facts again to illustrate his point. First, he analyzed three republican countries, i.e. Switzerland, the United States, and France and pointed out the slight differences existing in the three institutions despite their essential similarity in constitutionalism. Then, he stated that France and England were sharing a similar institution, i.e. constitutional monarchy. Yet England could move smoothly forward following the established policies for years but France had to change their policies every two years, which meant that French people were not suitable for the political system.

When discussing why China should not adopt the republican system, Liang Qichao used two examples, i.e. Chinese Students' Boycott in Tokyo (东京罢学) against the strict rules governing students and Shanghai Strike (上海罢市). Both events took place in the year of 1905. In the first incident, Chen Tianhua (陈天华), a Chinese overseas student in Japan committed suicide because the students could not come to terms concerning the method of protest. In order to avoid overseas students' rebellion against the Qing government, the newly issued rules by the Japanese government stated that each student needed to register with the Qing Minister to Japan and the Japanese schools they were studying at. The students needed to register if they wrote letters home and they were not allowed to move around but stayed at school. The students in Japan were extremely angry about the rules which were made in collusion with the Qing government and decided to protest against it. Yet one group led by Qiu Jin (秋瑾) and Song Jiaoren (宋教仁) suggested all students boycott by returning to China while the other group headed by Wang Zhaoming (汪兆铭) and Hu Hanmin (胡汉民) advocated enduring the humiliation and continuing to study in Japan. Both parties had fierce quarrels and ended up giving up the protest (佚名, 2019). Liang Qichao used this example to illustrate that the Chinese people did not have the capacity of self-government and their public spirit was far from enough.

The second incident was about the maltreatment of Chinese women by the Joint Hearing Tribunal (公审公廨) in Shanghai Concession. A woman named Huang was passing Shanghai when sending her husband coffin to Guangdong and was falsely charged as a woman trafficker because of the fifteen young women who accompanied her. In the court, there was a dispute between two Chinese officers and an English jury regarding where to put the prisoners, leading to the fight between the two sides and the two Chinese officers were injured. Then, the concession was made by Shanghai Municipal Council (工部局) to release the mistakenly arrested women. That would not change anything and December 18, 1905 witnessed strikes of Chinese merchants and workers. Angry demonstrators broke into the sluice house (老闸捕房) and burnt it. The foreign police was ordered to open fire, leading to 18 casualties and dozens of injuries. Though justice was on the Chinese side, it was the English who won the case and obtained 50,000 *taels* of silver as compensation (马长林, 2010; 孙慧, 2019).

In the above case, Liang Qichao was criticizing the irrationality of the Chinese people. The general rule of thumb was to stop the demonstration once the opposite side made concessions and there would be no more chaos or deaths. However, what had happened further proved that it was not time for China to implement the republic institution yet. He did not want to see the violence and blood in French Revolution of 1789 were repeated in China. The so-called crowd phenomenon described by the French social psychologist Gustav Le Bon (勒庞) left a deep impression in Liang Qichao's mind (Sun, 1992: 240). Liang Qichao knew clearly that when people had no public spirit and capacity of self-government, what they were concerned with was only their own interests. No one was willing to reconcile with others. Under such circumstances, if we pushed forward the republic rashly, it would certainly cause great disruption of social order.

Thus, it was better to have a powerful government first before moving to republics. This view corresponded with what Samuel Huntington (亨廷顿) stated. Huntington, the American international political theorist, recommended "authoritarian transition" (威权过渡), "whereby a modernizing dictatorship (专制) provides political order, a rule of law, and the conditions for successful economic and social development. Once these building blocks were in place, other aspects of modernity like democracy and civic participation (公民参与) could be added" (Fukuyama, 2011).

Similarly by observing countries like Turkey, Democratic People's Republic of Korea and Indonesia, Francis Fukuyama (福山) thought it a must to follow the pattern of "authoritarian transition" and "realize economic modernity before opening up democratic competition in the political system" (蔡双全, 王正相, 2017).

Admittedly, Liang Qichao's ideas had undergone some changes. After the failure of the One Hundred Days Reform, Liang Qichao sided with Sun Zhongshan (孙中山), the representative of revolutionaries and advocated Rousseau's idea of liberty, equality and using violence to overthrow reactionary government (谢玺璋, 2015). But after coming back from America in 1903 where Liang Qichao investigated the American political system and the Chinese communities, he began to doubt about his previous view. To his disappointment, Liang Qichao found some defects in American institutions, such as mediocracy of president elect, the spoils system (政党分赃制), and preference of public applause to problem solving. Regarding the overseas Chinese, they were still dominated by familism (家族主义) which hindered them from developing public spirit. Their indifference to public affairs led to some Chinese institutions controlled arbitrarily by local people or mob government (张灏, 2016). Especially when Liang Qichao read critiques made by Bluntschli and Conrad Bornhak regarding defects of the republic, such as difficulty in reconciling the interests of different groups and the possibility of political instability or even revolution, Liang Qichao switched his idea from advocating the republic to enlightened autocracy. The examples of France and some Latin American countries taught Liang Qichao how important the cultural soil or a country's tradition was (张灏, 2016).

In this chapter, we discussed Liang Qichao's reform ideas and analyzed his two important works, i.e. *Discourse on the New Citizen* and *On Enlightened Despotism*. Through close reading of what Liang Qichao has written, we can see his profound vision and earnest hope for a better China. We understand that Liang Qichao really deserves the title of the Chinese enlightenment thinker and his ideas paved way for China's future progress though history did not follow the blueprint drawn by him.

◆ Topics for Discussion

1. The difference between "state" and "*Tianxia*", "state" and "court".
2. Your comment on the "authoritarian transition" for countries which do not have democratic tradition before.
3. The functions of propriety and music are to make people obedient and content with what they have.
4. The damaging effect caused by the Qing ruler who considered China as his/her own property.
5. Your comment on the statement that Chinese ancient rulers used obscurantism or policy of keeping the people in ignorance to rule the country.
6. Why was servility so prevalent in China during the Qing Dynasty?
7. Do you agree or disagree with Liang Qichao when he listed the causes for China's poverty and weakness?
8. The defects of changing the title of a reigning dynasty when a new ruler takes office.

◆ Reading Assignment

梁启超. 1994. 新民说 . 宋志明，选注. 沈阳：辽宁人民出版社.

◆ Bibliography

Anderson, M. S. 2014. Frederic Ⅱ. Encyclopedia Britannica 2006 Ultimate Reference Suite DVD. 07–12.

Anon. 2019a. Otto von Bismarck. 01–31. From Wikipedia website.

Anon. 2019b. The Prince. 01–28. From Wikipedia website.

Fukuyama, F. 2011. Samuel Huntington's Legacy. 01–06. *Financial Times*.

Hobbes, T. 2014. *Leviathan*. Hertfordshire: Wordsworth Editions, Ltd.

Malcolm, N. 2015. Frederick the Great by Tim Blanning, Review: "Masterly". 10–01.

The Telegraph.

Rousseau, J.-J. 1968. *The Social Contract*. London: Penguin Books, Ltd.

Smith, A. 2007. *Chinese Characteristics*. Stanford: Stanford University Press.

Sun, L.-K. 1992. Social Psychology in the Late Qing Period. *Modern China*, *18*(3): 235-262.

Tang, X. B. 1996. *Global Space and the Nationalist Discourse of Modernity: The Historical Thinking of Liang Qichao*. Stanford: Stanford University Press.

Zarrow, P. 2008. Anti-despotism and "Rights Talk": the Intellectual Origins of Modern Human Rights Thinking in the Late Qing. *Modern China*, *34*(2): 179-209.

蔡双全，王正相. 2017. 梁启超"开明专制论"之学理辨析. 08–10. 爱思想.

霍布斯. 2010. 利维坦. 黎思复，黎廷弼，译. 北京：商务印书馆.

雷颐. 2015. 孤寂百年：中国现代知识分子十二论. 桂林：广西师范大学出版社.

梁启超. 1994. 新民说. 宋志明，选注. 沈阳：辽宁人民出版社.

梁启超. 2001. 开明专制论. 饮冰室文集点校. 昆明：云南教育出版社.

卢梭. 2010. 社会契约论. 北京：商务印书馆.

马长林. 2010. 1905 年大闹会审公堂案始末. 09–01. 新民晚报.

马基雅维利. 1999. 君主论. 俞卓立，译释. 北京：中国社会出版社.

明恩浦. 2007. 中国人的气质. 刘文飞，刘晓旸，译. 上海：上海三联书店.

孙慧. 2019. 1905 年大闹会审公廨事件（附图）. 02–05. 上海档案信息网.

狭间直树. 2016. 东亚近代文明史上的梁启超. 张勇，评议. 上海：上海人民出版社.

谢玺璋. 2015. 梁启超传：上下部. 上海：上海文化出版社.

佚名. 2019. 陈天华：中国近代民主革命家. 10–02. 百度百科.

张灏. 2016. 梁启超与中国思想的过渡：1890—1907. 崔志海，葛夫平，译. 北京：中央编译出版社.

张朋园. 2007. 梁启超与清季革命. 长春：吉林出版集团有限责任公司.

昭杨. 2015."千古一帝"拿破仑：我的形象我做主. 05–03. 澎湃新闻.

郑佳明. 2018. 拿破仑争霸的意识形态背景. 01–19. 爱思想.

钟叔河. 2010. 走向世界：中国人考察西方的历史. 北京：中华书局.